Nov 13-09

To Peg—
all best to
you + your
work—

Judy

the JUDY GRAHN READER

aunt lute books SAN FRANCISCO

Aunt Lute Books
P.O. Box 410687
San Francisco, CA 94141
www.auntlute.com

Cover design: Amy Woloszyn
Text design and typesetting: dendesign
Cover Photos: Irene Young (front) and Joey Williams (back)

Senior Editor: Joan Pinkvoss
Managing Editor: Shay Brawn
Production: Noelle de la Paz, Mayka Mei, Soma Nath, Kara-Ann Young Ha Owens, Ladi Youssefi

This book was funded in part by grants from the Horizons Foundation and from the National Endowment for the Arts.

Library of Congress Cataloging-in-Publication Data

Grahn, Judy, 1940-
[Selections. 2009]
The Judy Grahn reader / edited with an Introduction by Lisa Maria Hogeland.
p. cm.
ISBN 978-1-879960-80-0
I. Hogeland, Lisa Maria. II. Title.

PS3557.R226A6 2009
818'.54--dc22

2009004439

Printed in the U.S.A. on acid-free paper

10 9 8 7 6 5 4 3 2 1

My thanks to the people of all genders and descriptions who have supported this work over the years and decades of its being. You help make it happen and keep it alive. Thanks also to Joan Pinkvoss, Lisa Hogeland, Shay Brawn and the other workers of Aunt Lute Books for this collection, and to Irene Young for a fun photo shoot. Thanks ever and always to the people who put up with me, my family Kris Brandenburger, Dianne Jenett, Ed May, and Debbi Grenn.

TABLE OF CONTENTS

FICTION

DRAMA

NONFICTION

the JUDY GRAHN READER

Introduction

Poet, feminist, lesbian feminist thinker and theorist Judy Grahn came to the San Francisco Bay Area in 1968; in 1969, she co-founded the Gay Women's Liberation Movement, and soon after, The Women's Press Collective, the second women's independent press. It is thus entirely appropriate that this new collection of her work issues from Aunt Lute Books, another independent feminist press in the Bay Area. *The Judy Grahn Reader* is the most comprehensive collection of Grahn's work ever assembled, including poetry, fiction, drama, and nonfiction. The *Reader* aims to make possible new and newly complex understandings of this important body of work.

The work assembled here dates from 1964 to the present, from Grahn's first chapbook to recent poems, and—for the first time—brings the poetry into conversation with Grahn's work in other genres. The *Reader* includes selected poems from her chapbooks, *Edward the Dyke and Other Poems, She Who,* and *A Woman Is Talking to Death,* as well as the series *Confrontations with the Devil in the Form of Love.* It also includes the full-length epic poems Grahn has published so far, in selections from *The Queen of Wands,* and the entire titular verse drama from *The Queen of Swords.* Additionally, the *Reader* samples the next epic in the series, *The Queen of Cups,* with the newer poem, "To the Mother of All Bowls." This volume also includes Grahn's work in other genres: her fiction, in the excerpt from her novel, *Mundane's World,* and the stories "Boys at the Rodeo" and "Green Toads of the High Desert," and her nonfiction in selections from the two works of cultural studies, *Another Mother Tongue: Gay Words, Gay Worlds,* and *Blood, Bread, and Roses: How Menstruation Created the World,* essays from the two works of literary studies, *The Highest Apple: Sappho and the Lesbian Poetry Tradition* and *Really Reading Gertrude Stein,* and a newly revised essay, "Ground Zero: The Rise of Lesbian Feminism."

Judy Grahn is best known as a poet and most often represented in literary anthologies for her portrait sequence, "The Common Woman," written in 1969 and included in *Edward the Dyke*. The sequence was written to mimic—more accurately, to create—a consciousness-raising group, of a sort rarely found in 1969: working-class women talking about their lives. These poems have circulated widely: they've adorned posters and websites, been quoted and misquoted in speeches by women politicians, been set to music and performed on stages and even in churches, too often omitting the central poem about Carol, who "has taken a woman lover / whatever shall we do / she has taken a woman lover / how lucky it wasn't you." Ani DiFranco read "Detroit Annie, Hitchhiking" in concert at Carnegie Hall; the poem currently adorns a sidewalk in Berkeley. These poems continue to circulate because readers and listeners love them. Their enduring popularity comes from their promise that ordinary women "will rise / and will become strong"—a promise that working-class women's and lesbian lives have power and meaning—and we share that promise with the poet when we read them aloud. The pleasure we take in the promise is a clue to the importance of Grahn's work.

It is time to read that work again, and to read it in new ways. It is time that we see aspects of feminist and queer thinking (or theorizing, as we like to say in the academy) in a larger historical context and a longer historical reach—that we see, for instance, the notion of gender performativity in the early prose poem, "The Psychoanalysis of Edward the Dyke." That poem has us notice not only costume and the various forms of gender drag we assume, but also the mandating and enforcing of gender by the state—by the police and the medical profession in common with ordinary people. The poem insists that conventional gender is coerced and coercive. "Boys at the Rodeo" also plays with this idea: "Since we are too short to be men, we must be boys. Everyone else at the rodeo are girls." More poignantly, "I split into two pieces for the rest of the evening, and have never decided if it is worse to be thirty-one years old and called a boy or to be thirty-one years old and called a girl." Grahn's characters and speakers are often positioned as outsiders to the conventional sex/gender system. "I'm not a girl / I'm a hatchet," the first poem in *Edward the Dyke* announces in its first lines, and its penultimate line is "look at me as if you had never seen a woman before."

What if we took that imperative seriously? What if we scratched out what we think we know about "woman" and started over? This is, of course, a major project of second-wave feminism and one central to Grahn's work; it continues to be a critical project of feminist and queer thinking today. What would it matter, for instance, to our understanding of what it means to be human and female if we saw menstruation rituals as foundational to evolutionary development? This is the argument of *Blood, Bread, and Roses: How Menstruation Created the World.* More than the usual tales of (male) hunters vs. (female) gatherers is at stake here, and certainly more than the cheesy insistence by masculinist evolutionary biologists that "man-spreading-his-seed" is the origin of human culture. This is more than a biological-essentialist claim about blood; instead, Grahn argues that human ritual, women's and men's activities, in the face of the specific female experience of menstruation created human culture. Feminists have been thinking about evolution for a long time, and Grahn's contribution to this thinking is original and provocative—and under-read and under-appreciated. Her arguments are concrete and pragmatic, interspersed, as much of her nonfiction is, with embedded memoir.

It is time to read this work again, and to read it in new ways. The interrogation of love—intimate, romantic, communal, familial, civic—is another critical project of feminist, lesbian, and queer thinking. Grahn furthers this project in the stories she tells in poetry, fiction, and drama, in the linguistic clues she traces in *Another Mother Tongue,* in the imagined communities in *Mundane's World,* in the lesbian poetic tradition she assembles in *The Highest Apple,* in the passages of memoir in her nonfiction—one might argue, in fact, that this interrogation is the central concern of her work. It's a grand project squarely in the tradition of Walt Whitman, and, as Grahn points out, of Sappho. How do these levels and versions and visions interrelate, and what can we know about ourselves and our world from their interrelations?

In the poem, "Helen you always were / the factory," from *The Queen of Wands,* the character Nancy watches the soldiers gather "to board the ships / to ride the tanks / around the walls," and asks this question: "And who am I // if it is me / they say / they do it // for?" What is done in our name—and by whom and to whom and toward what end? What is our responsibility? How to reconcile being the women for whom—even, in the Helen of Troy story, for *love* of whom—the war is allegedly waged? Feminists ask and have asked these questions globally and locally, politically and personally. I set it here to underline, as Grahn does in "Ground Zero," the relationship of Gay Women's Liberation to other social movements, notably anti-war and anti-racism movements, then and now. The story of Helen as Grahn develops it in *The Queen of Wands* forwards these questions of the meaning of love—as do the works of the cohort of contemporary poets she discusses in *The Highest Apple:* Pat Parker, Audre Lorde, Adrienne Rich, Paula Gunn Allen, Olga Broumas. They are profoundly feminist and queer questions.

Grahn comes at these questions differently elsewhere in her work. In "A Mock Interrogation," a section of the poem "A Woman Is Talking to Death," Grahn transforms the verb *to want* into a state of longing and hunger that links personal and political, turning the intimate inside out; she writes, "and I wanted her as a very few people have wanted me—I wanted her and me to own and control and run the city we lived in, to staff the hospital I knew would mistreat her, to drive the transportation system that had betrayed her, to patrol the streets controlling the men who would murder or disfigure or disrupt us, not accidentally with machines, but on purpose because we are not allowed out on the street alone—" Everything we *want*—love and sex, protection and power, safe passage and nurturance—are rolled up together here, as they are elsewhere in this important poem. This is the poem in which Grahn transforms the accusatory "indecent acts with women" into "acts of omission," where the indecency is "lacking courage, lacking a certain fire behind the eyes, which is the symbol, the raised fist, the sharing of resources, the resistance that tells death he will starve for the lack of the fat of us, our extra." I have often taught this poem in dialogue with Emily Dickinson's "Death is the supple suitor" and "Because I could not stop for death," part of the tradition of women's poetry that Grahn draws from and transforms. To speak aloud the energy and rhythm of this section of the poem is to commit to its vision, and to invite its interrogation of love to transform our own lives.

The question of love takes subtler forms in Grahn's work as well. Playing the game of "spot the dyke" and noticing the girl who loses the contest, Grahn's narrator in "Boys at the Rodeo" has this moment: "I wish I could give her a ribbon. Not for being a dyke, but for sitting on her horse well. For believing there ever was a contest, for not being the daughter of anyone who owns thousands and thousands of tracts of anything." The girl who takes the rodeo seriously even though no one else does, who tries, who gives it her dignified effort, ought to be rewarded. In a just world, she would be, and we feel the injustice of her un-reward acutely. It is a failure of love and a failure of justice—and they are the same thing in this moment.

Ultimately—and here is the center of the spirituality of Grahn's work, I think—an interrogated love is a discipline. It is a refusal of death, a refusal of patriarchy's depredations, a refusal to be a victim of history, a refusal to participate in furthering anything that makes us less—to ourselves and each other—than central. But this refusal is hard work and it requires difficult transformations in how we think and act. It requires that we not abandon each other "much too soon to get the real loving done," as Grahn writes in "A Woman Is Talking to Death." The interrogation of love is detailed and specific rather than abstract—even when it involves abstractions like justice, they are then made concrete in images like "our meat and potatoes"—in which we look our failures straight in the face and resolve to do better. It asks us to throw off love as an idea and ideology, and focus on love as a practice. Perhaps even as a pragmatic.

It is time to read this work again and to read it in new ways. It is time to reconsider the idea of commonality as Grahn lays it out in *The Highest Apple,* and to rethink the story we tell about the second wave of American feminism. We've become habituated in the academy—and perhaps outside of it as well—to the story that second wave feminism couldn't deal with difference, and only now, only post 1981-ish or post 1992-ish, can we see women in our multiplicity. Only a post-modernist, post-structuralist, post-second-wave feminism has ever centered difference and multiplicity. This conventional story of second-wave feminism significantly underestimates feminists' and lesbian feminists' participation in other social movements, and especially their anti-racist work. Grahn's "Ground Zero" tells a more complete and more nuanced story. The essay opens with Grahn and her girlfriend standing in a crowd outside the Black Panther Party's San Francisco office in 1969, answering a call for white radicals to protect the office from an attack by police. Gay Women's Liberation was deeply influenced by the violent destruction of the Black Panthers, she argues.

Grahn also points out that "dyke multiculturalism" was on lesbian feminism's agenda, forwarded by the readings she did with African-American poet Pat Parker and Korean-American poet Willyce Kim (both of whom were published by the Women's Press Collective). In fact, Grahn's work has always attended to racism—to its power to thwart our responsibilities to each other, to the shame and pain of its internalization, to its murderous violence. It is a misreading of her idea of commonality—circulating in feminism since the Common Woman poems and expanded in her prose—not to see its connection to difference and multiplicity.

Rather than seeing a static, two-dimensional world of center vs. margin, Grahn argues in *Really Reading Gertrude Stein* that we should perceive the world more complexly. In what she calls a "many-centered multiverse," margin and center are in motion; both center and margin shift and trade places. She writes, "exiles from one place are first class citizens of another, margins of one 'globe' are centers of another, 'marginality' itself becomes a ribbon of road, a continual and vital interaction shaping and reshaping whatever lies within borders, and 'difference' is so essentially common (and Self-centered) that it is duplication that is the oddity." "Common," she writes in *The Highest Apple,* "means many-centered, many overlapping groups of islands each of which maintains its own center and each of which is central to society for what it gives to society." The struggles for "self-determination, autonomy, and community…that preoccupy any group attempting to maintain its identity in a hostile world," are not the same struggles for each group or individual.

It's time to read this work again, and to read it in new ways. Grahn's poetry is rightly celebrated for its content—for its depictions of the complexities of intersectionality (the academic term for what Grahn calls "the criss-cross of oppressions"), for giving voice to working-class women and lesbians. But not enough critical attention has been paid to its aesthetics, to its craft, nor to its variety and intricacy. Grahn writes in many modes and forms—lyric, narrative, dramatic monologue, prose poem, portrait, epic—and uses many kinds of lines. The variety of Grahn's repetitions is astonishing, including not only alliteration and assonance, but also refrain, chant, chorus, and even the incremental repetition of traditional folk ballad. Among the many formal and technical achievements of the 2008 poem, "Mental," is a particular variant of repetition. In three sections of the poem, Grahn expands *mental* by using a series of words containing it—monumental, governmental, judgmental, developmental, experimental, departmental, elemental, incremental, ornamental, sacramental, detrimental, deploymental, sentimental, fundamental, and instrumental. We have to ask what *mental* means in all this variety, this repetition and difference. Grahn then distills these meanings back into the word *mental* and once again into the poem's final word: *craaazy*. If mental is crazy and crazy is all this—what isn't it? Who does it not name—and whom does it not police?

Moreover, because the poems have an accessible vocabulary, they can seem to hide their intricacy—and if you don't read them aloud, you'll miss their gorgeous sound play. Helen's lesson in *The Queen of Swords* is an example of a particular kind of sound play Grahn often creates; here's the passage:

> help me remember
> how to dance in place;
> when to witness,
> when to harness,
> when to charge with all my forces.

The slippage of sound from *dance* and *place* through *witness* to *harness* to *charge* to *forces*, both vowels and consonants in motion and repeating and changing, recapitulates the transformations the play enacts at the level of the language. Grahn alternates the forcefulness of single-syllable play with the lightness of the feminine almost-rhyme, much as she does in this passage from "Slowly: a plainsong from an older":

> was I not ruling
> guiding naming
> was I not brazen
> crazy chosen
>
> even the stones would do my bidding?

Again, the sounds are in motion, intricately changing in a dance of the single- and double-syllable words; the vowels seem to rest in *stones* for a moment, but then take flight again by the end of the line in *bidding*. This sound play is one of the signature delights of Grahn's work: accessible vocabulary, ordinary words, set in motion, combining repetition and surprise.

We can see this sort of sound play in part as a kind of distillation of what Grahn learned from Stein—and Grahn is one of the finest readers of Stein's work going. She rightly understands Stein as a philosopher of language, and takes seriously Stein's idea that everything is equally important—not only every word, every syllable, every punctuation mark, in a literary mode, but also every person and every other-than-human creature in modes both literary and political. The sound play of the poetry—in which every syllable is as important as every other syllable—is part of Grahn's distillation of Stein's philosophy of language. And you can see this philosophy at work, in a different way, in Grahn's novel, *Mundane's World.* There are many pleasures in the novel, including how the novel extrapolates the ideas in *Blood, Bread, and Roses,* but I suggest that its depictions of other-than-human intelligences are among its finest achievements. *Mundane's World* is a coming of age story, an eco-topia, a speculative fiction about pre-history—and it's a novel in which mice and owls get to have their say about their lives.

The novel is also terrifically funny, as is much of Grahn's work. Sometimes the humor is bitter, ironic: "I am a pervert, therefore I've learned / to keep my hands to myself in public," she writes in "A Woman Is Talking to Death." Sometimes the humor is serious in the guise of silly, as it is in the dialogue of the crow dikes in *The Queen of Swords,* who play on the word *violent* until it turns to *violet*. Always, Grahn takes seriously the *play* in sound play, word play, and her tone shifts and slides and moves just as do her vowels and consonants, just as do margin and center in a multi-centered multiverse. Play is a very serious business indeed, a central part of orality and ritual, a central part of the process of transformation and learning.

In *The Highest Apple,* Grahn names her work "mythic realism," which she suggests is a method that combines "the sacred, the political, the social, the details of everyday life." None of these are separate or separable, connected as they are in her work by the practice of an interrogated love. In *Really Reading Gertrude Stein,* she writes of Stein, "what on earth could be more exciting than to have a woman's philosophical work expand its influence and power within our culture after so many centuries of profound silence." I want here to make that claim for Grahn's own work: it is time to really read Judy Grahn, to read this work again and in new ways. Grahn's work always moves toward a vision of integrity, of wholeness, and the *Reader* aims to present a more complete vision of that work. I am delighted to introduce and re-introduce this body of work to readers.

Lisa Maria Hogeland
University of Cincinnati
January 2009

POETRY

The Common Woman

I. Helen, at 9 am, at noon, at 5:15

Her ambition is to be more shiny
and metallic, black and purple as
a thief at midday; trying to make it
in a male form, she's become as
stiff as possible. 5
Wearing trim suits and spike heels,
she says "bust" instead of breast;
somewhere underneath she
misses love and trust, but she feels
that spite and malice are the 10
prices of success. She doesn't realize
yet, that she's missed success, also,
so her smile is sometimes still
genuine. After a while she'll be a real
killer, bitter and more wily, better at 15
pitting the men against each other
and getting the other women fired.
She constantly conspires.
Her grief expresses itself in fits of fury
over details, details take the place of meaning, 20
money takes the place of life.
She believes that people are lice
who eat her, so she bites first; her
thirst increases year by year and by the time
the sheen has disappeared from her black hair, 25
and tension makes her features unmistakably
ugly, she'll go mad. No one in particular
will care. As anyone who's had her for a boss
will know
the common woman is as common 30
as the common crow.

II. Ella, in a square apron, along Highway 80

She's a copperheaded waitress,
tired and sharp-worded, she hides
her bad brown tooth behind a wicked
smile, and flicks her ass 35
out of habit, to fend off the pass
that passes for affection.
She keeps her mind the way men
keep a knife—keen to strip the game
down to her size. She has a thin spine, 40
swallows her eggs cold, and tells lies.

She slaps a wet rag at the truck drivers
if they should complain. She understands
the necessity for pain, turns away
the smaller tips, out of pride, and 45
keeps a flask under the counter. Once,
she shot a lover who misused her child.
Before she got out of jail, the courts had pounced
and given the child away. Like some isolated lake,
her flat blue eyes take care of their own stark 50
bottoms. Her hands are nervous, curled, ready
to scrape.
The common woman is as common
as a rattlesnake.

III. Nadine, resting on her neighbor's stoop
She holds things together, collects bail, 55
makes the landlord patch the largest holes.
At the Sunday social she would spike
every drink, and offer you half of what she knows,
which is plenty. She pokes at the ruins of the city
like an armored tank; but she thinks 60
of herself as a ripsaw cutting through
knots in wood. Her sentences come out
like thick pine shanks
and her big hands fill the air like smoke.
She's a mud-chinked cabin in the slums, 65
sitting on the doorstep counting
rats and raising 15 children,
half of them her own. The neighborhood
would burn itself out without her;
one of these days she'll strike the spark herself. 70
She's made of grease
and metal, with a hard head
that makes the men around her seem frail.
The common woman is as common as
a nail. 75

IV. Carol, in the park, chewing on straws
She has taken a woman lover
whatever shall we do
she has taken a woman lover
how lucky it wasnt you
And all the day through she smiles and lies 80
and grits her teeth and pretends to be shy,
or weak, or busy. Then she goes home
and pounds her own nails, makes her own

bets, and fixes her own car, with her friend.
She goes as far 85
as women can go without protection
from men.
On weekends, she dreams of becoming a tree;
a tree that dreams it is ground up
and sent to the paper factory, where it 90
lies helpless in sheets, until it dreams
of becoming a paper airplane, and rises
on its own current; where it turns into a
bird, a great coasting bird that dreams of becoming
more free, even, than that—a feather, finally, or 95
a piece of air with lightning in it.
 she has taken a woman lover
 whatever can we say
She walks around all day
quietly, but underneath it 100
she's electric;
angry energy inside a passive form.
The common woman is as common
as a thunderstorm.

V. Detroit Annie, hitchhiking

Her words pour out as if her throat were a broken 105
artery and her mind were cut-glass, carelessly handled.
You imagine her in a huge velvet hat with great
dangling black feathers,
but she shaves her head instead
and goes for three-day midnight walks. 110
Sometimes she goes down to the dock and dances
off the end of it, simply to prove her belief
that people who cannot walk on water
are phonies, or dead.
When she is cruel, she is very, very 115
cool and when she is kind she is lavish.
Fishermen think perhaps she's a fish, but they're all
fools. She figured out that the only way
to keep from being frozen was to
stay in motion, and long ago converted 120
most of her flesh into liquid. Now when she
smells danger, she spills herself all over,
like gasoline, and lights it.
She leaves the taste of salt and iron
under your tongue, but you dont mind. 125
The common woman is as common
as the reddest wine.

VI. Margaret, seen through a picture window

After she finished her first abortion
she stood for hours and watched it spinning in the
toilet, like a pale stool. 130
Some distortion of the rubber
doctors with their simple tubes and
complicated prices,
still makes her feel guilty.
White and yeasty. 135
All her broken bubbles push her down
into a shifting tide, where her own face
floats above her like the whole globe.
She lets her life go off and on
in a slow strobe. 140
At her last job she was fired for making
strikes, and talking out of turn;
now she stays home, a little blue around the edges.
Counting calories and staring at the empty
magazine pages, she hates her shape 145
and calls herself overweight.
Her husband calls her a big baboon.
Lusting for changes, she laughs through her
teeth, and wanders from room to room.
The common woman is as solemn as a monkey 150
or a new moon.

VII. Vera, from my childhood

Solemnly swearing, to swear as an oath to you
who have somehow gotten to be a pale old woman;
swearing, as if an oath could be wrapped around your shoulders
like a new coat: 155
For your 28 dollars a week and the bastard boss
you never let yourself hate;
and the work, all the work you did at home
where you never got paid;
For your mouth that got thinner and thinner 160
until it disappeared as if you had choked on it,
watching the hard liquor break your fine husband down
into a dead joke.
For the strange mole, like a third eye
right in the middle of your forehead; 165
for your religion which insisted that people
are beautiful golden birds and must be preserved;
for your persistent nerve
and plain white talk—
the common woman is as common 170

as good bread
as common as when you couldnt go on
but did.
For all the world we didnt know we held in common
all along 175
the common woman is as common as the best of bread
and will rise
and will become strong—I swear it to you
I swear it to you on my own head
I swear it to you on my common 180
woman's
head

"I'm not a girl"

I'm not a girl
    I'm a hatchet
I'm not a hole
    I'm a whole mountain
I'm not a fool   5
    I'm a survivor
I'm not a pearl
    I'm the Atlantic Ocean
I'm not a good lay
    I'm a straight razor   10
look at me as if you had never seen a woman before
I have red, red hands and much bitterness

The Psychoanalysis of Edward The Dyke

Behind the brown door which bore the gilt letters of Dr. Merlin Knox's name, Edward the Dyke was lying on the doctor's couch which was so luxurious and long that her feet did not even hang over the edge.

"Dr. Knox," Edward began, "my problem this week is chiefly concerning restrooms."

"Aahh," the good doctor sighed. Gravely he drew a quick sketch of a restroom in his notebook.

"Naturally I can't go into men's restrooms without feeling like an interloper, but on the other hand every time I try to use the ladies room I get into trouble."

"Umm," said Dr. Knox, drawing a quick sketch of a door marked 'Ladies'.

"Four days ago I went into the powder room of a department store and three middle-aged housewives came in and thought I was a man. As soon as I explained to them that I was really only a harmless dyke, the trouble began…"

"You compulsively attacked them."

"Oh heavens no, indeed not. One of them turned on the water faucet and tried to drown me with paper towels, but the other two began screaming about how well did I know Getrude Stein and what sort of underwear did I have on, and they took off my new cuff links and socks for souvenirs. They had my head in the trash can and were cutting pieces off my shirttail when luckily a policeman heard my calls for help and rushed in. He was able to divert their attention by shooting at me, thus giving me a chance to escape through the window."

Carefully Dr. Knox noted in his notebook: 'Apparent suicide attempt after accosting girls in restroom.' "My child," he murmured in featherly tones, "have no fear. You must trust us. We will cure you of this deadly affliction, and before you know it you'll be all fluffy and wonderful with dear babies and a bridge club of your very own." He drew a quick sketch of a bridge club. "Now let me see. I believe we estimated that after only four years of intensive therapy and two years of anti-intensive therapy, plus a few minor physical changes and you'll be exactly the little girl we've always wanted you to be." Rapidly Dr. Knox thumbed through an index on his desk. “Yes yes. This year the normal cup size is 56 inches. And waist 12 and ½. Nothing a few well-placed hormones can’t accomplish in these advanced times. How tall did you tell me you were?”

“Six feet, four inches,” replied Edward.

“Oh, tsk tsk.” Dr. Knox did some figuring. “Yes, I’m afraid that will definitely entail extracting approximately 8 inches from each leg, including the knee-cap… standing a lot doesn’t bother you, does it my dear?”

“Uh,” said Edward, who couldn’t decide.

“I assure you the surgeon I have in mind for you is remarkably successful.” He leaned far back in his chair. “Now tell me briefly, what the word ‘homosexuality’ means to you, in your own words.”

“Love flowers pearl, of delighted arms. Warm and water. Melting of vanilla wafer in the pants. Pink petal roses trembling overdew on the lips, soft and juicy fruit. No teeth. No nasty spit. Lips chewing oysters without grimy sand or whiskers. Pastry. Gingerbread. Warm sweet bread. Cinnamon toast poetry. Justice equality higher wages. Independent angel song. It means I can do what I want.”

“Now my dear,” Dr. Knox said, “Your disease has gotten completely out of control. We scientists know of course that it’s a highly pleasurable experience to take someone’s penis or vagina into your mouth—it’s pleasurable and enjoyable. Everyone knows that. But after you’ve taken a thousand pleasurable penises or vaginas into your mouth and had a thousand people take your pleasurable penis or vagina into their mouth, what have you accomplished? What have you got to show for it? Do you have a wife or children or a husband or a home or a trip to Europe? Do you have a bridge club to show for it? No! You have only a thousand pleasurable experiences to show for it. Do you see how you’re missing the meaning of life? How sordid and depraved are these clandestine sexual escapades in parks and restrooms? I ask you.”

“But sir but sir,” said Edward, “I’m a *woman*. I don’t have sexual escapades in parks or restrooms. I don’t have a thousand lovers—I have *one* lover.”

“Yes yes.” Dr. Knox flicked the ashes from his cigar onto the floor. “Stick to the subject, my dear.”

“We were in college then,” Edward said. “She came to me out of the silky midnight mist, her slips rustling like cow thieves, her hair blowing in the wind like Gabriel. Lying in my arms harps played soft in dry firelight, Oh Bach. Oh Brahms. Oh Buxtehude. How sweetly we got along how well we got the woods pregnant with canaries and parakeets, barefoot in the grass alas pigeons, but it only lasted ten years and she was gone, poof! like a puff of wheat.”

“You see the folly of these brief, physical embraces. But tell me the results of our experiment we arranged for you last session.”

“Oh yes. My real date. Well I bought a dress and a wig and a girdle and a squeezy bodice. I did unspeakable things to my armpits with a razor. I had my hair done and my face done and my nails done. My roast done. My bellybutton done.”

“And then you felt truly feminine.”

“I felt truly immobilized. I could no longer run, walk bend stoop move my arms or spread my feet apart.”

“Good, good.”

"Well everything went pretty well during dinner, except my date was only 5'3" and oh yes. One of my eyelashes fell into the soup—that wasn't too bad. I hardly noticed it going down. But then my other eyelash fell on my escort's sleeve and he spent five minutes trying to kill it."

Edward sighed. "But the worst part came when we stood up to go. I rocked back on my heels as I pushed my chair back under the table and my shoes—you see they were three inchers, raising me to 6'7", and with all my weight on those teeny little heels…"

"Yes yes."

"I drove the spikes all the way into the thick carpet and could no longer move. Oh, everyone was nice about it. My escort offered to get the check and to call in the morning to see how I made out and the manager found a little saw and all. But, Dr. Knox, you must understand that my underwear was terribly binding and the room was hot…"

"Yes yes."

"So I fainted. I didn't *mean* to, I just did. That's how I got my ankles broken."

Dr. Knox cleared his throat. "It's obvious to me, young lady, that you have failed to control your P.E."

"My God," said Edward, glancing quickly at her crotch, "I took a bath just before I came."

"This oral eroticism of yours is definitely rooted in Penis Envy, which showed when you deliberately castrated your date by publicly embarrassing him."

Edward moaned. "But strawberries. But lemon cream pie."

"Narcissism," Dr. Knox droned, "Masochism, Sadism. Admit you want to kill your mother."

"Marshmellow bluebird," Edward groaned, eyes softly rolling. "Looking at the stars. April in May."

"Admit you want to possess your father. Mother substitute. Breast suckle."

"Graham cracker subway," Edward writhed, slobbering. "Pussy willow summer."

"Admit you have a smegmatic personality," Dr. Knox intoned.

Edward rolled to the floor. "I am vile! I am vile!"

Dr. Knox flipped a switch at his elbow and immediately a picture of a beautiful woman appeared on a screen over Edward's head. The doctor pressed another switch and electric shocks jolted through her spine. Edward screamed. He pressed another switch, stopping the flow of electricity. Another switch and a photo of a gigantic erect male organ flashed into view, coated in powdered sugar. Dr. Knox handed Edward a lollipop.

She sat up. "I'm saved," she said, tonguing the lollipop.

"Your time is up," Dr. Knox said. "Your check please. Come back next week."

"Yes sir yes sir," Edward said as she went out the brown door. In his notebook, Dr. Knox made a quick sketch of his bank.

A History of Lesbianism

How they came into the world,
the women-loving-women
came in three by three
and four by four
the women-loving-women 5
came in ten by ten
and ten by ten again
until there were more
than you could count

    they took care of each other 10
    the best they knew how
    and of each other's children,
    if they had any.

How they lived in the world,
the women-loving-women 15
learned as much as they were allowed
and walked and wore their clothes
the way they liked
whenever they could. They did whatever
they knew to be happy or free 20
and worked and worked and worked.
The women-loving-women
in America were called dykes
and some liked it
and some did not. 25

    they made love to each other
    the best they knew how
    and for the best reasons

How they went out of the world,
the women-loving-women 30
went out one by one
having withstood greater and lesser
trials, and much hatred
from other people, they went out
one by one, each having tried 35
in her own way to overthrow
the rule of men over women,
they tried it one by one
and hundred by hundred,
until each came in her own way 40
to the end of her life
and died.

The subject of lesbianism
is very ordinary; it's the question
of male domination that makes everybody 45
angry.

"I have come to claim"

I have come to claim
Marilyn Monroe's body
for the sake of my own.
dig it up, hand it over,
cram it in this paper sack. 5
hubba. hubba. hubba.
look at those luscious
long brown bones, that wide and crusty
pelvis. ha Ha, oh she wanted so much to be serious

but she never stops smiling now. 10
Has she lost her mind?

Marilyn, be serious—they're taking
your picture, and they're taking the pictures
of eight young women in New York City
who murdered themselves for being pretty 15
by the same method as you, the very
next day, after you!
I have claimed their bodies too,
they smile up out of my paper sack
like brainless cinderellas. 20

the reporters are furious, they're asking
me questions
what right does a woman have
to Marilyn Monroe's body? and what
am I doing for lunch? They think I 25
mean to eat you. Their teeth are lurid
and they want to pose me, leaning
on the shovel, nude. Dont squint.
But when one of the reporters comes too close
I beat him, bust his camera 30
with your long, smooth thigh
and with your lovely knucklebone
I break his eye.

Long ago you wanted to write poems;
Be serious, Marilyn 35
I am going to take you in this paper sack

around the world, and
write on it:—the poems of Marilyn Monroe—
Dedicated to all princes,
the male poets who were so sorry to see you go, 40
before they had a crack at you.
They wept for you, and also
they wanted to stuff you
while you still had a little meat left
in useful places; 45
but they were too slow.

Now I shall take them my paper sack
and we shall act out a poem together:
"How would you like to see Marilyn Monroe,
in action, smiling, and without her clothes?" 50
We shall wait long enough to see them make familiar faces
and then I shall beat them with your skull.
hubba. hubba. hubba. hubba. hubba.
Marilyn, be serious
Today I have come to claim your body for my own. 55

A Woman Is Talking To Death

One

Testimony in trials that never got heard

my lovers teeth are white geese flying above me
my lovers muscles are rope ladders under my hands

we were driving home slow
my lover and I, across the long Bay Bridge, 5
one February midnight, when midway
over in the far left lane, I saw a strange scene:

one small young man standing by the rail,
and in the lane itself, parked straight across
as if it could stop anything, a large young 10
man upon a stalled motorcycle, perfectly
relaxed as if he'd stopped at a hamburger stand;
he was wearing a peacoat and levis, and
he had his head back, roaring, you
could almost hear the laugh, it 15
was so real.

"Look at that fool," I said, "in the
middle of the bridge like that," a very
womanly remark.

Then we heard the meaning of the noise 20
of metal on a concrete bridge at 50
miles an hour, and the far left lane
filled up with a big car that had a
motorcycle jammed on its front bumper, like
the whole thing would explode, the friction 25
sparks shot up bright orange for many feet
into the air, and the racket still sets
my teeth on edge.

When the car stopped we stopped parallel
and Wendy headed for the callbox while I 30
ducked across those 6 lanes like a mouse
in the bowling alley. "Are you hurt?" I said,
the middle-aged driver had the greyest black face,
"I couldn't stop, I couldn't stop, what happened?"

Then I remembered. "Somebody," I said, "was *on* 35
the motorcycle." I ran back,
one block? two blocks? the space for walking
on the bridge is maybe 18 inches, whoever

engineered this arrogance. in the dark
stiff wind it seemed I would 40
be pushed over the rail, would fall down
screaming onto the hard surface of
the bay, but I did not, I found the tall young man
who thought he owned the bridge, now lying on
his stomach, head cradled in his broken arm. 45

He had glasses on, but somewhere he had lost
most of his levis, where were they?
and his shoes. Two short cuts on his buttocks,
that was the only mark except his thin white
seminal tubes were all strung out behind; no 50
child left *in* him; and he looked asleep.

I plucked wildly at his wrist, then put it
down; there were two long haired women
holding back the traffic just behind me
with their bare hands, the machines came 55
down like mad bulls, I was scared, much
more than usual, I felt easily squished
like the earthworms crawling on a busy
sidewalk after the rain; *I wanted to*
leave. And met the driver, walking back. 60

"The guy is dead." I gripped his hand,
the wind was going to blow us off the bridge.

"Oh my God," he said, "haven't I had enough
trouble in my life?" He raised his head,
and for a second was enraged and yelling, 65
at the top of the bridge—"I was just driving
home!" His head fell down. "My God, and
now I've killed somebody."

I looked down at my own peacoat and levis,
then over at the dead man's friend, who 70
was bawling and blubbering, what they would
call hysteria in a woman. "It isn't possible"
he wailed, but it was possible, it was
indeed, accomplished and unfeeling, snoring
in its peacoat, and without its levis on. 75

He died laughing: that's a fact.

I had a woman waiting for me,
in her car and in the middle of the bridge,
I'm frightened, I said.
I'm afraid, he said, stay with me, 80

please don't go, stay with me, be
my witness—"No," I said, "I'll be your
witness—later," and I took his name
and number, "but I can't stay with you,
I'm too frightened of the bridge, besides 85
I have a woman waiting
and no license—
and no tail lights—"
So I left—
as I have left so many of my lovers. 90

we drove home
shaking, Wendy's face greyer
than any white person's I have ever seen.
maybe he beat his wife, maybe he once
drove taxi, and raped a lover 95
of mine—how to know these things?
we do each other in, that's a fact.

who will be my witness?
death wastes our time with drunkenness
and depression 100
death, who keeps us from our
lovers.
he had a woman waiting for him,
I found out when I called the number
days later 105

"Where is he" she said, "he's disappeared."
He'll be all right" I said, "*we* could
have hit the guy as easy as anybody, it
wasn't anybody's fault, they'll know that,"
women so often say dumb things like that, 110
they teach us to be sweet and reassuring,
and say ignorant things, because we dont invent
the crime, the punishment, the bridges

that same week I looked into the mirror
and nobody was there to testify, 115
how clear, an unemployed queer woman
makes no witness at all,
nobody at all was there for
those two questions: what does
she do, and who is she married to? 120

I am the woman who stopped on the bridge
and this is the man who was there
our lovers teeth are white geese flying

above us, but we ourselves are
easily squished. 125

keep the women small and weak
and off the street, and off the
bridges, that's the way, brother
one day I will leave you there,
as I have left you there before, 130
working for death.

we found out later
what we left him to.
Six big policemen answered the call,
all white, and no child *in* them. 135
they put the driver up against his car
and beat the hell out of him.
What did you kill that poor kid for?
you mutherfucking nigger.
that's a fact. 140

Death only uses violence
when there is any kind of resistance,
the rest of the time a slow
weardown will do.

They took him to 4 different hospitals 145
til they got a drunk test report to fit their
case, and held him five days in jail
without a phone call.
how many lovers have we left.

there are as many contradictions to the game, 150
as there are players.
a woman is talking to death,
though talk is cheap, and life takes a long time
to make
right. He got a cheesy lawyer 155
who had him cop a plea, 15 to 20
instead of life
Did I say life?

the arrogant young man who thought he
owned the bridge, and fell asleep on it 160
he died laughing: that's a fact.
the driver sits out his time
off the street somewhere,
does he have the most vacant of
eyes, will he die laughing? 165

Two

They don't have to lynch the women anymore

death sits on my doorstep
cleaning his revolver

death cripples my feet and sends me out
to wait for the bus alone, 170
then comes by driving a taxi.

the woman on our block with 6 young children
has the most vacant of eyes
death sits in her bedroom, loading
his revolver 175

they don't have to lynch the women
very often anymore, although
they used to—the lord and his men
went through the villages at night, beating &
killing every woman caught 180
outdoors.
the European witch trials took away
the independent people; two different villages
—after the trials were through that year—
had left in them, each— 185
one living woman:
one

What were those other women up to? had they
run over someone? stopped on the wrong bridge?
did they have teeth like 190
any kind of geese, or children
in them?

Three

This woman is a lesbian be careful

In the military hospital where I worked
as a nurse's aide, the walls of the halls 195
were lined with howling women
waiting to deliver
or to have some parts removed.
One of the big private rooms contained
the general's wife, who needed 200
a wart taken off her nose.
we were instructed to give her special attention
not because of her wart or her nose

but because of her husband, the general.
as many women as men die, and that's a fact. 205

At work there was one friendly patient, already
claimed, a young woman burnt apart with X-ray,
she had long white tubes instead of openings;
rectum, bladder, vagina—I combed her hair, it
was my job, but she took care of me as if 210
nobody's touch could spoil her.

ho ho death, ho death
have you seen the twinkle in the dead woman's eye?

when you are a nurse's aide
someone suddenly notices you 215
and yells about the patient's bed,
and tears the sheets apart so you
can do it over, and over
while the patient waits
doubled over in her pain 220
for you to make the bed *again*
and no one ever looks at you,
only at what you do not do

Here, general, hold this soldier's bed pan
for a moment, hold it for a year— 225
then we'll promote you to making his bed.
we believe you wouldn't make such messes

if you had to clean up after them.

that's a fantasy.
this woman is a lesbian, be careful. 230

When I was arrested and being thrown out
of the military, the order went out: dont anybody
speak to this woman, and for those three
long months, almost nobody did;   the dayroom, when
I entered it, fell silent til I had gone; they 235
were afraid, they knew the wind would blow
them over the rail, the cops would come,
the water would run into their lungs.
Everything I touched
was spoiled. They were my lovers, those 240
women, but nobody had taught us to swim.
I drowned, I took 3 or 4 others down
when I signed the confession of what we
had done   together.

No one will ever speak to me again. 245

I read this somewhere; I wasn't there:
in WW II the US army had invented some floating
amphibian tanks, and took them over to
the coast of Europe to unload them,
the landing ships all drawn up in a fleet, 250
and everybody watching. Each tank had a
crew of 6 and there were 25 tanks.
The first went down the landing planks
and sank, the second, the third, the
fourth, the fifth, the sixth went down 255
and sank. They weren't supposed
to sink, the engineers had
made a mistake. The crews looked around
wildly for the order to quit,
but none came, and in the sight of 260
thousands of men, each 6 crewmen
saluted his officers, battened down
his hatch in turn and drove into the
sea, and drowned, until all 25 tanks
were gone. did they have vacant 265
eyes, die laughing, or what? what
did they talk about, those men,
as the water came in?

was the general their lover?

Four
A Mock Interrogation 270

Have you ever held hands with a woman?

Yes, many times—women about to deliver, women about to have breasts removed, wombs removed, miscarriages, women having epileptic fits, having asthma, cancer, women having breast bone marrow sucked out of them by nervous or indifferent interns, women with heart condition, who were vomiting, overdosed, depressed, drunk, lonely to the point of extinction: women who had been run over, beaten up. deserted. starved. women who had been bitten by rats; and women who were happy, who were celebrating, who were dancing with me in large circles or alone, women who were climbing mountains or up and down walls, or trucks or roofs and needed a boost up, or I did; women who simply wanted to hold my hand because they liked me, some women who wanted to hold my hand because they liked me better than anyone.

These were many women?

Yes. many.

What about kissing? Have you kissed any women? 275

I have kissed many women.

When was the first woman you kissed with serious feeling?

The first woman ever I kissed was Josie, who I had loved at such a distance for months. Josie was not only beautiful, she was tough and handsome too. Josie had black hair and white teeth and strong brown muscles. Then she dropped out of school unexplained. When she came back she came back for one day only, to finish the term, and there was a child in her. She was all shame, pain, and defiance. Her eyes were dark as the water under a bridge and no one would talk to her, they laughed and threw things at her. In the afternoon I walked across the front of the class and looked deep into Josie's eyes and I picked up her chin with my hand, because I loved her, because nothing like her trouble would ever happen to me, because I hated it that she was pregnant and unhappy, and an outcast. We were thirteen.

You didn't kiss her?

How does it feel to be thirteen and having a baby? 280

You didn't actually kiss her?

Not in fact.

You have kissed other women?

Yes, many, some of the finest women I know, I have kissed. women who were lonely, women I didn't know and didn't want to, but kissed because that was a way to say yes we are still alive and loveable, though separate, women who recognized a loneliness in me, women who were hurt, I confess to kissing the top of a 55 year old woman's head in the snow in boston, who was hurt more deeply than I have ever been hurt, and I wanted her as a very few people have wanted me—I wanted her and me to own and control and run the city we lived in, to staff the hospital I knew would mistreat her, to drive the transportation system that had betrayed her, to patrol the streets controlling the men who would murder or disfigure or disrupt us, not accidently with machines, but on purpose, because we are not allowed out on the street alone—

Have you ever committed any indecent acts with women? 285

Yes, many. I am guilty of allowing suicidal women to die before my eyes or in my ears or under my hands because I thought I could do nothing, I am guilty of leaving a prostitute who held a knife to my friend's throat to keep us from leaving, because we would not sleep with her, we thought she was old and fat and ugly; I am guilty of not loving her who needed me; I regret all the women I have not slept with or comforted, who pulled themselves away from me for lack of something I had not the courage to fight for, for us, our life, our planet, our city, our meat and potatoes, our love. These are indecent acts, lacking courage, lacking a certain fire behind the eyes, which is the symbol, the raised fist, the sharing of resources, the resistance that tells death he will starve for lack of the fat of us, our extra. Yes I have committed acts of indecency with women and most of them were acts of omission. I regret them bitterly.

Five

Bless this day oh cat our house

"I was allowed to go
3 places, growing up," she said—
"3 places, no more. 290
there was a straight line from my house
to school, a straight line from my house
to church, a straight line from my house
to the corner store."
her parents thought something might happen to her. 295
but nothing ever did.

my lovers teeth are white geese flying above me
my lovers muscles are rope ladders under my hands
we are the river of life and the fat of the land
death, do you tell me I cannot touch this woman? 300
if we use each other up
on each other
that's a little bit less for you
a little bit less for you, ho
death, ho ho death. 305

Bless this day oh cat our house
help me be not such a mouse
death tells the woman to stay home
and then breaks in the window.

I read this somewhere, I wasnt there: 310
In feudal Europe, if a woman committed adultery
her husband would sometimes tie her
down, catch a mouse and trap it
under a cup on her bare belly, until
it gnawed itself out, now are you 315
afraid of mice?

Six

Dressed as I am, a young man once called
me names in Spanish

a woman who talks to death
is a dirty traitor 320

inside a hamburger joint and
dressed as I am, a young man once called me
names in Spanish
then he called me queer and slugged me.
first I thought the ceiling had fallen down 325
but there was the counterman making a ham
sandwich, and there was I spread out on his
counter.

For God's sake I said when
I could talk, this guy is beating me up 330
can't you call the police or something,
can't you stop him? he looked up from
working on his sandwich, which was *my*
sandwich, I had ordered it. He liked
the way I looked. "There's a pay phone 335
right across the street" he said.

I couldn't listen to the Spanish language
for weeks afterward, without feeling the
most murderous of urges, the simple
association of one thing to another, 340
so damned simple.

The next day I went to the police station
to become an outraged citizen
Six big policemen stood in the hall,
all white and dressed as they do 345
they were well pleased with my story, pleased
at what had gotten beat out of me, so
I left them laughing, went home fast
and locked my door.
For several nights I fantasized the scene 350
again, this time grabbing a chair
and smashing it over the bastard's head,
killing him. I called him a spic, and
killed him. my face healed. his didnt
no child *in* me. 355

now when I remember I think:
maybe *he* was Josie's baby.
all the chickens come home to roost,
all of them.

Seven
Death and disfiguration 360

One Christmas eve my lovers and I
we left the bar, driving home slow
there was a woman lying in the snow
by the side of the road. She was wearing
a bathrobe and no shoes, where were 365
her shoes? she had turned the snow
pink, under her feet. she was an Asian
woman, didnt speak much English, but
she said a taxi driver beat her up
and raped her, throwing her out of his 370
care.
what on earth was she doing there
on a street she helped to pay for
but doesn't own?
doesn't she know to stay home? 375

I am a pervert, therefore I've learned
to keep my hands to myself in public
but I was so drunk that night,
I actually did something loving
I took her in my arms, this woman, 380
until she could breathe right, and
my friends who are perverts too
they touched her too
we all touched her.
"You're going to be all right" 385
we lied. She started to cry
"I'm 55 years old" she said
and that said everything.

Six big policemen answered the call
no child *in* them. 390
they seemed afraid to touch her,
then grabbed her like a corpse and heaved her
on their metal stretcher into the van,
crashing and clumsy.
She was more frightened than before. 395
they were cold and bored.
'don't leave me' she said.
'she'll be all right' they said.
we left, as we have left all of our lovers
as all lovers leave all lovers 400
much too soon to get the real loving done.

Eight
a mock interrogation

Why did you get into the cab with him, dressed as you are?
I wanted to go somewhere.

Did you know what the cab driver might do 405
if you got into the cab with him?

I just wanted to go somewhere.

How many times did you
get into the cab with him?

I dont remember. 410

If you dont remember, how do you know it happened to you?

Nine
Hey you death

ho and ho poor death
our lovers teeth are white geese flying above us
our lovers muscles are rope ladders under our hands 415
even though no women yet go down to the sea in ships
except in their dreams.

only the arrogant invent a quick and meaningful end
for themselves, of their own choosing.
everyone else knows how very slow it happens 420
how the woman's existence bleeds out her years,
how the child shoots up at ten and is arrested and old
how the man carries a murderous shell within him
and passes it on.

we are the fat of the land, and 425
we all have our list of casualties

to my lovers I bequeath
the rest of my life

I want nothing left of me for you, ho death
except some fertilizer 430
for the next batch of us
who do not hold hands with you
who do not embrace you
who try not to work for you
or sacrifice themselves or trust 435
or believe you, ho ignorant
death, how do you know

we happened to you?

wherever our meat hangs on our own bones
for our own use 440
your pot is so empty
death, ho death
you shall be poor

The most blonde woman in the world

The most blonde woman in the world
one day threw off her skin
her hair, threw off her hair, declaring
"Whosoever chooses to love me
chooses to love a bald woman 5
with bleeding pores."
Those who came then as her lovers
were small hard-bodied spiders
with dark eyes and an excellent
knowledge of weaving. 10
They spun her blood into long strands,
and altogether wove millions of red
webs, webs red in the afternoon sun.
"Now," she said, "Now I am expertly loved,
and now I am beautiful." 15

"Carol and"

Carol and
her crescent wrench
work bench
wooden fence
wide stance 5
Carol and her
pipe wrench
pipe smoke
pipe line
high climb 10
smoke eyes
chicken wire
Carol and her

hack saw
well worn 15
torn back
bad spine
never - mind
timberline
clear mind 20
Carol and her
hard glance
stiff dance
clean pants
bad ass 25
lumberjack's
wood ax
Carol and her
big son
shot gun 30
lot done
not done
never bored
do more
do less 35
try to rest
Carol and her
new lands
small hands
big plans 40
Carol and her
long time
out shine
worm gear
warm beer 45
quick tears
dont stare
Carol is another
queer
chickadee 50
like me, but Carol does
everything
better
if you let her.

"Slowly: a plainsong from an older"

Slowly: a plainsong from an older
woman to a younger woman

am I not olden olden olden
it is unwanted.

wanting, wanting 5
am I not broken
stolen common

am I not crinkled cranky poison
am I not glinty - eyed and frozen

am I not aged 10
shaky glazing
am I not hazy
guarded craven

am I not only
stingy little 15
am I not simple
brittle spitting

was I not over
over ridden?

it is a long story 20
will you be proud to be my version?

it is unwritten.

writing, writing
am I not ancient
raging patient 25

am I not able
charming stable
was I not building
forming braving

was I not ruling 30
guiding naming
was I not brazen
crazy chosen

even the stones would do my bidding?

it is a long story 35

am I not proud to be your version?

it is unspoken.

speaking, speaking
am I not   elder
berry   40
brandy

are you not wine before you find me
in your own beaker?

do you not turn away your shoulder?
have I not shut my mouth against you?   45

are you not shamed to treat me meanly
when you discover you become me?
are you not proud that you become me?

I will not shut my mouth against you.
do you not turn away your shoulder.   50
we who brew in the same bitters
that boil us away
we both need stronger water.

we're touched by a similar nerve.

I am new like your daughter.   55
I am the will, and the riverbed
made bolder
by you — my oldest river —
you are the way.

are we not   olden, olden, olden.   60

"I am the wall at the lip of the water"

I am the wall at the lip of the water
I am the rock that refused to be battered
I am the dyke in the matter, the other
I am the wall with the womanly swagger
I am the dragon, the dangerous dagger   5
I am the bulldyke, the bulldagger

and I have been many a wicked grandmother
and I shall be many a wicked daughter.

"My name is Judith, meaning"

My name is Judith, meaning
She Who Is Praised
I do not want to be called praised
I want to be called The Power of Love.

if Love means protect then whenever I do not 5
defend you
I cannot call my name Love.
if Love means rebirth then when I see us
dead on our feet
I cannot call my name Love. 10
if Love means provide & I cannot
provide for you
why would you call my name Love?

do not mistake my breasts
for mounds of potatoes 15
or my belly for a great roast duck.
do not take my lips for a streak of luck
nor my neck for an appletree,
do not believe my eyes are a warm swarm of bees;
do not get Love mixed up with me. 20

Don't misunderstand my hands
for a church with a steeple,
open the fingers & out come the people;
nor take my feet to be acres of solid brown earth,
or anything else of infinite worth 25
to you, my brawny turtledove;
do not get me mixed up with Love.

not until we have ground we call our own
to stand on
& weapons of our own in hand 30
& some kind of friends around us
will anyone ever call our name Love,
& then when we do we will all call ourselves
grand, muscley names:
the Protection of Love, 35
the Provision of Love & the
Power of Love.
until then, my sweethearts,
let us speak simply of
romance, which is so much 40
easier and so much less
than any of us deserve.

The land that I grew up on is a rock

I.

From my mother, a rock,
I have learned that rocks give
most of all.
What do rocks do? They hold the
forces of the earth together and 5
give direction. They interrupt
the mindless sky in its total
free fall.
Rocks turn the monotonous winds
from their courses and bring down rain 10
before the all-collecting sea
reclaims it—so you and your friends
can have some, too.
A rock is a slow, slow
cooled-off flame, and a cradle, both. 15

They are like bone, the rocks. They frame.
They remain. They hold you.
They grind together to make digestible dirt.
Because of their slow lasting
nature, they are said 20
not to feel tangible hurt.
We were star-struck, my father and I.
We ate fast intellectual pie.
And we made fun of her, my mother;
she made material, actual pie. 25

But once, in a flash of insight,
he said of my mother: "Without her,
people like you and I would fly
right off the earth."

He made a gesture of his hand helplessly 30
sucked into the sky (like a navigationless bird).
He knew she was a rock
and so did I. He knew the worth
of gravity and certain repetition,
the safety of enclosure. 35
I knew the mute, the flame-charred
female wall, the dam
of granite rock between one's child self
and the molten family core,
the hell of terror, the inner and the outer 40
fire: my father's ire.

II.

"You never listened to me."
Unexpectedly my mother weeps, recalling
how we never took her on our flights of thought
or left her, her own falling-out time. 45
How we locked her from our patch of
significant sky (that she was holding still for us)
my father and I,
as though she were a sheer wall of will
to be mined 50
to mill
and to grind and to be there
with or without our care.
It is so shocking for us
to see her now, a rock 55
weeping.

She is rocking
in her rocking chair
a little madly, deliberately deaf
to our star-struck talk. 60
She is chalk.

III.

This lasts only a moment, a few years,
for my mother's tears
quickly evaporate and
return to their own mother, the sky 65
who weeps intermittently over everything,
renewing
without care,
and with the greatest care,
especially over the rocks, 70
bathing and cooling them
who by their basalt nature
cradle their feelings for the
longest time and most profoundly,
taking continuous 75
though sometimes secret, pride
in what they give
and giving the most of all.

Whether we (sky divers) care to learn
how to share this treasure, 80
my mother's spirit will return and return
teaching us. Whether my father and I

will learn, or not.

"Your mother is a saint," he says.
He means, 85
the center of a rock, particularly
the one we live on,
is molten like a star, the core
is light,
enlightening, giving of 90
intelligence.
Stretched far into the cold unwieldy sky
my father and I
in reaching for a star,
we nearly overlooked the one 95
that pulsed, all that time,
there (beneath us)
under our floating feet, and *in* us,
in the person of my mother,
rocking sometimes somewhat madly 100
in her brilliance-giving vision,
as the earth,
a rock, a star.

History if I could put you

History if only I could put you
in my little bowl,
cherish for your real self
you, source of what follows
and goes before. 5

Flama. Name. Story.

History if I could smoke you,
suck you up into my brain's blood
like a memory
of what really happened, 10
all the sides of it
the middle, top and bottom
including the beautiful
the boredom
including the painful burning parts, 15
my own part,
wrong, right and indifferent;
wisdom and war, love and foolery.

History, little golden glow

of understanding 20
let me blow and blow
on your heart
Tell me something.
Tell me truly.

Queen Helen

A queen am I
Queen Helen is my title.
As the sun shines so shines Helen
most beautiful.
I am what ever is 5
the weaving tree
and Mother of my people

I was Sovereign of my homespun folk
with their sheepshorn woolly garments.
We were considered most ascetic, 10
most athletic and democratic,
and I was entirely settled in my queendom
with my husband and my child,
when one day a young man came by
and I was undone. 15
He had won a contest
with the gods. I was the prize.
I was the golden apple
he had won. He, Paris, took me home
to his own land. 20

"Husband I am leaving,"
was my song.

> Husband I am leaving you,
> have left. And my homeland,
> child, and precious people; 25
> all the wild, wild island
> of my queendom.
>
> I believe it was a matter of the
> time, of Fate, a cosmic binding
> and unbinding. 30
> Ties I felt to go
> pulled harder than the ties
> I felt to stay.
> Had my power been slipping?

> Did you get the message I had 35
> pinned for you to see:
> "I want my full measure of reality,
> I don't want the numb illusion.
> Only sightfulness can make us see.
> Only freedom makes us free." 40
>
> Foolish words probably,
> of a queen wrenched from her earth,
> a queen taking to the air,
> a queen flying.
> Yet I feel a new fertility... 45

I moved my queendom and my court,
my ladies and my special looms I brought
with me as well as the hearthfire
that was my totem,
"Heart of the sky," 50
and heart of the house
of Helena at Sparta.

"Lilanna," Queen of sheep-folds
they called me,
who causes the earth to quake. 55
Mother of the temple
and of the people,
Nana.
A Queen am I
Queen Helen and a Sovereign, 60
Flama. Shaker
alike of earth and of the heavens.

Without his heart he ranted
thinking it was me he wanted,
thinking that he could not live 65
or rule without me.

And the women I left knitting
at his palace
needled and poked incessantly,
until his pride bled 70
and his whole brain broke.
Who does Helen think she is, they said,
to go among strangers,
and to let herself be prized
so highly, to be called "the fairest." 75
Haughtiest of dames and proudest,

has she never heard of "modest"?
Sitting in the Trojan tower,
does she think she has such power,
does she think she is a goddess? 80

Here is what I know:
Even the most golden
golden apple sometimes
rolls down the long wand limb
and lands in the lap of fire. 85

In ships he came to me,
in ships surrounded.
I was dumbfounded.
A thousand ships, so many! 90
where had he gotten them?
They filled the harbor
like a bobbing forest.
I was almost proud;
I stood on the ramparts of the city 95
and exclaimed out loud.

None of us knew the war would
last so long
and be so boring.
None of us knew we women were already
in prison. We sat in the weaving room 100
month on month, winding the distaff,
working the shuttle,
with only our own housebound prattle,
with never anything fresh, not air
or news or love or food. 105

We entertained each other
with bawdy jokes and stories
and a tapestry that told the progress
of the war. We comforted the new
widows. The bone-torn mothers. 110
Subject we were to every nervous stew of
scary rumors. No one danced.
Almost, we lost our glow. Ten
years passed. At least the men
had action—however many bodies paid for it. 115
And we all held fast, somehow.

In the tenth year it was clear
that those from the ships
had lost. They quarrelled

and skulked and bled. 120
Stench of the burning dead
came to our noses even in
the weaving room.
And they had stopped singing at night
or calling out my name 125
in derision or admiration
or lust.

They had lost, their shoulders sagged.
They won battle after battle without
taking the city or getting near me. 130
We no longer lived in so much dread.
We waited for surrender to be said.
But they were unjust.

And they won it finally with a lie,
hypocrisy, 135
the offer of friendship
with soldiers in its belly.
They won it with
the lie, hidden under honey
like a razor in the bread. 140

I too fell for the lovely painted horse,
with his wide nose flaring.
I too wished to have a party and be daring.
Queen of morbid siege was I,
Queen only by my title, 145
and I too grabbed for the sudden win,
the grinning, golden bridle.
Forgotten were the lessons
of want and pain,
the bodies dragged round 150
the walls of our emotion.

He was glinting like the sun
or like an apple. He was
neither; he was a bomb exploding
in the last battle. 155
Years of boredom
and regret blanked out as
I reached to embrace, to bind,
to pull him nearer with his
sparkling, blinding cargo. 160

We cheered when we had got him
all the way in. And then he flamed

into a torch and tortured;
seared the city down to ash and
rubble twenty centuries could 165
not even find.
And I began to live the recent
history of my kind.

All that night
we clung in tiny groups together 170
watching Paris and every
other Trojan man
die, too shocked to cry.
Thousands of corpses, so many!
such a limp crowd. I stood on 175
the ramparts of the tower and
exclaimed out loud.

So Helen fell like a pretty city
into the lap of war, a husband's war
against her. 180

A queen am I, Queen Helen
is my title.
Queen at the heart of the greatest
Western battle—
they have said was all on my account. 185

They have said the war was on my account,
my "beauty," they said, as though beauty
is something someone else can capture.
As though the Flame transfers.

I went out a Queen 190
a Sovereign, Mother of my people
and a lover—

I came back a captive.
My husband had gone out
a King, a Sovereign 195
and a soldier.
He came back a tyrant,
a master of slaves—
and I came back a slave.

For the first time 200
when he put his hands
upon me, I was afraid.
I was positively filled
with fear. He chased me

through my own halls, 205
even into my temple. I
crouched like a frightened
dove, passing my nights
on the edge of my bed.

Never had anyone felt so ugly. 210

I hardly recall the remainder
of the story; it dragged
past like a sluggish drug.
No one in the country used the
word "civil" anymore. 215
In the aftermath of theft and war
came more war, more blood
and sudden changes.

My sister had murdered her
child-killing husband on his return. 220
No woman blamed her, none
except her daughter Elektra.
And that was the one who mattered.
Elektra goaded her brother
'til he broke with rage and slaughtered 225
his own mother.

And me. I was not only a slave,
I was a murdered slave, by my own
sister's children. The old maternal
order flooded in blood the day 230
the two conspirators climbed
the steps to my jail tower.
It was my worst hour, and I hardly
remember it. They have said that
I did not die normally, but flew 235
into the heavens and became a star.
Venus? was it? Beauty.

I have been trying for centuries
to recall exactly why
I left my original queendom, 240
was it on such shaky ground?
Downward bound?
Why was I dragged back
into such a state—
Do I lie sleeping? 245
Will I wake?

A Queen am I. Queen Helen
and a Sovereign.
Flama. Shaker alike of earth
and of the heavens. 250
a queen am I
Queen Helen is my title.
As the sun shines so shines Helen
most beautiful, most blamed.
I am what ever is, 255
the weaving tree
and Mother of my people.
and I shall be
the Mother of my people.

The Queen of Wands

And I am the Queen of Wands.
Okay.
Here is how the world works:

It is all like nets.
ever golden, evergreen 5
the fruits fall
into hands-like-nets
the fish are hauled
into jaws-like-nets
the insects crawl 10
into claws-like-nets

and the thoughts fall
into minds-like-nets
it is all like nets.

On the other hand 15
a spider lives in the topmost branches of a pine,
her house a god's eye gleaming among the needles.
On hot days
she pays out her line and
twirls on down 20
to the surface of the lake or pond
to get a little drink of water
and to wash her face. She's such an
ordinary person.

The trees line the earth, great and small, 25
dogwood, plane, maple, rubber,
the elegant palm. The scrubby oak. The elm.

We're ordinary persons, too. We have our
long time friends across the distances,
our urgent messages and our differences. 30

And we have our parties.
We sugar up our petals just to get the probes of bees in us.
Most green ladies love everything the whipping wind can
give them.
The avocado tree hung with her long green breasts, 35
she aches for fingers pulling at her;
the cherry, peach and nut trees bent with swollen balls
long for hands and mouths and claws;
the fig tree with her black jewels tucked between her
hand-shaped emerald leaves, is happily 40
fondled by the dancing birds, wild and raucous and drunk on
natural fig wine.

almost any summer morning
sun beams fall into my arms like lovers
giving me everything they've got 45
and they're so hot oh honey
I take it all

give it to me, baby
is my song

And I am the Queen of Wands. 50
The people honor me.
I am the torch they hold over their own heads
as they march march like insects
by the billions
into the bloody modern world, 55
over discarded corpses of their ages past,
always holding me, aloft or in their arms,
a flame in the hand of the statue,
a bundle of coals
in their inflammatory doctrines, calling me 60
a chalice of fire,
essential light,
the Flama
and the stuff of which their new world will be made.

Sophia (Helen) they call me, enlightenment, 65
"God's light," wisdom, romance, beauty, being saved,
"Freedom" and the age of reason.
Progress, they call me, industrial revolution,
"People's rule," the future, the age of

electronics, of Aquarius, of the common man and woman, 70
evolution
solar energy and self-reliance. Sexual self-expression.
Atomic fission, they call me, physics, relativity,
the laser computations in an endless sky of mind,
"science," they call me and also emotion, the aura of 75
telepathy and social responsibility, they call me
consciousness, "health," and love
they call me, bloom of Helen.
Blush upon her face, and grace.

And here I am a simple golden shower. 80
and here I am only a spider
webbing their minds
with pictures, words, impulses
feelings translated into moral imperatives
and rules for living, like leaves 85
upon a tree, spread to catch the sun's attention.

They (the billions of people)
dance like Fairies on my smallest
twiggiest branches
whistling in each other's ears, 90
collecting and dispersing
seeds, wearing gold and
pretty clothing, worrying and not
really noticing all the other worlds
around them 95
how the sun center of my eye sews them
how the silver dream filaments direct them,
how their own thoughts connect them, how
the baton smacks their knees to make them
move their feet, that baton 100
at the end of the claw
of the Queen of Wands

And I am the tree
with candles
in its fingers 105
the tree with lights
Menorah
Yule-flame
tree of life

the tree-shaped 110
candle-holder
on the mantle

on the altar
on the flag of being.

And I am the Queen of Wands 115
who never went away
where would I go?

the flame is central
to any civilization
any household 120

any bag of bones. Any motley mote
you've got, of
little mustard seed can grow
into a yellow spicy flame
as you must know. 125

The sun is a weaver
and the rock earth her instrument.
Slender-fingered threads of light
and heat, dance like birds
shuttling. 130
Winds and the rain,
seeds and feet and feathers
knit the knot
making the great coat,
the coat of all colors. 135

The coat of all colors;
over the whole earth, a caught fire
of living logs, brown and red,
tan and white, black and yellow
bobbing like a forest; 140
each a magic stick with
green flame at its tip

a green web
my leaves, my green filaments
like fingers spread 145
to catch the sun's attention, spread
to catch the sun like thread,
like sexual feelings, like
the gleam from an eye, or an idea.

and I am the Queen of Wands 150
I am who stands
who always will
and I am who remembers
the connections woven, little eggs

along the message line. 155

I remember giving dinosaurs
to the tall unfolded ferns to entertain them.
and immortality to the cockroach.
I remember the birthday of the first
flower, and the death of so many furry 160
animals and kinds of people, and a star
that fell. I remember a continent
of green
green wands of grass
burning into the knees of 165
buffalo queens, a landlocked
ocean of fire. Replaced by the
picket fence. Almost equally complex.
Sky scrapers like spikes.
But that's another song. 170
And I am the Queen of Wands
who burns, who glows, who webs
the message strands,
who stands, who always will.

Helen in Hollywood

When she goes to Hollywood
she is an angel.

She writes in red red lipstick
on the window of her body,
long for me, oh need me! 5
Parts her lips like a lotus.

Opening night she stands, poised
on her carpet, luminescent,
young men humming
all around her. She is flying. 10
Her high heels are wands, her
furs electric. Her bracelets
flashing. How completely
dazzling her complexion,
how vibrant her hair and eyes, 15
how brilliant the glow that spreads
four full feet around her.

She is totally self conscious
self contained

self centered, 20
caught in the blazing central eye
of our attention.

We infuse her.
Fans, we wave at her
like handmaids, unabashedly, 25
we crowd on tiptoe pressed together
just to feel the fission of the star
that lives on earth,
the bright, the angel sun
the luminescent glow of someone 30
other than we.
Look! Look! She is different.
Medium for all our energy
as we pour it through her.
Vessel of light. 35
Her flesh is like flax,
a living fiber.
She is the symbol of our dreams and fears
and bloody visions, all
our metaphors for living in America. 40

Harlowe, Holiday, Monroe

Helen
when she goes to Hollywood
she is the fire for all purposes.

Her flesh is like dark wax, a candle. 45
She is from any place or class.
"That's the one," we say in instant recognition,
because our breath is taken by her beauty,
or what we call her beauty.

She is glowing from every pore. 50
we adore her. we imitate and rob her
adulate   envy
admire   neglect
scorn. leave alone
invade, fill 55
ourselves with her.
we love her, we say
and if she isn't careful
we may even kill her.

Opening night 60
she lands on her carpet,

long fingered hands
like divining rods
bobbing and drawing the strands
of our attention, 65
as limousine drivers in blue jackets
stand on the hoods of their cars
to see the angel, talking

Davis, Dietrich, Wood
Tyson, Taylor, Gabor 70
Helen, when she goes to Hollywood
to be a walking star,
to be an actor

She is far more than a product
of Max Factor, 75
Max Factor didn't make her
though the make-up helps us
see what we would like
to take her for

her flesh is like glass, 80
a chandelier
a mirror

Harlowe, Holiday, Monroe
Helen
when she went to Hollywood 85
to be an angel

And it is she and not we
who is different

She who marries the crown prince
who leads the processional dance, 90
she who sweeps eternally
down the steps
in her long round gown.
A leaping, laughing leading lady,
she is our flower. 95
It is she who lies strangled
in the bell tower;
she who is monumentally drunk and suicidal
or locked waiting in the hightower,
she who lies sweating with the vicious jungle fever, 100
who leaps from her blue window
when he will, if he will, leave her

it is she and not we

who is the lotus

It is she with the lilies in her hair 105
and a keyboard beside her,
the dark flesh glowing

She whose wet lips nearly swallow
the microphone, whose whiskey voice
is precise and sultry and overwhelming, 110
she who is princess and harlequin,
athlete and moll and whore and lady,
goddess of the silver screen
the only original American queen

and Helen 115
when she was an angel
when she went to Hollywood

Spider Webster's declaration: He is singing the end of the world again

He is singing the end
of the world again,
he has sung it before.

When he flattened Troy to the ground, seven times,
left Carthage salted like a fat old hog, 5
Africa, "conquered," he said, he announces,
he is singing the end of the world again,
millions burned in Europe, butchered in
Africa, millions blown to bits in China,
Russia and now in Central and South America, 10
thousands of tribes
and villages destroyed, the matrix
of whole peoples, cultures, languages, genetic
pools, ways of describing, gone, gone,
apparently, according to his song, whirled up into 15
his description of the past.

He is singing the end of the world again,
he has sung it before.
Americans fly over their world and its ghosts,
Americans stare at their own ghosts without 20
recognition. Invisible the Indian ancestors,
invisible the Mayan-centered
feather industries, invisible the
great buffalo and the buffalo queens,

old ladies of the hip high buffalo grass, 25
invisible the engineering systems, amphitheaters,
philosophical wholeness in the old
civilizations of the mind.
Occasional sulky sacred bears
stare from the cages of zoos 30
refusing to acknowledge men as their children.

He dwells in threats of fire, Armageddon, Hiroshima, Saigon,
and Tyre, Berlin, Gomorrah, Hell itself,
the story of fire, his theft of it. "Put
a large wad of flame on 35
the wand's tip. Wave it,
shouting: Fire, Fire."

The whites of their eyes stare
back at him.
There was a city *here* once, once 40
there was a city (and now there
is another)

There was a tribe
and now there is another,
there was a nation here once 45
and now there is another.

He is singing the end of the world again.
He has his song
and I have a long, long
wand like memory. 50
I remember five worlds
and four have ended.

I see (I can't help it)
buffalo faces in the gloomy white
people of Iowa, waiting slump shouldered 55
for the light to change,
chanting, "We used to rumble the earth here,
once, with the charge of our electrifying
hooves. Now in the midst of the stolen
golden corn 60
standing in their fields like sacred groves
surrounded by plenty we are oddly depressed."

He is singing the end of the world, again.
Reincarnated bears
prance and sway in the lowlife bars of 65
this place calling itself a nation; they

lean, pissing, on the wall in Dallas,
Detroit, Charleston, Denver, hold intellectual
discussings in great roars,
knife each other, make predictions. 70
They await the Bear god, the Bear Maiden. They
are not concerned with the form this will take,
it is their form, they will take it.

Dancing birds leap out of the young faces
kissing on the streets of San Francisco, Salt 75
Lake City, Memphis, leaping with an urgent
sky-message; and the lovers call what they
are feeling, "love," "desire," "relationship."
They do not know to call it,
"Birds dancing." 80
Birds *do* dance, and so do
ghosts, and buffalo.
Spirits line shoulder to
shoulder on the highways shouting
Maya Azteca Aztlan Olympus 85
Mississippi Valley Seneca Falls Cibola
Shangri-La, The River Niger, Hollywood,
Tibet. Atlantis. Eden.

There was a nation here, once
and now there is another. 90
Business people pat each other's pinstripes,
putting their own names on the ancient remedies and
products, systems and understandings. "Let's
design a rocket out of here. Don't forget to
bring the queen of buffaloes. It gives me such 95
satisfaction knowing she is mine. Let's pretend
that we are doing this for sex,
for money."

He is singing the end of the world again
he has done it before. 100
He has his firebrand
and his song.
I have a long, long
wand like memory.
I remember five full worlds 105
and four of them have ended.

Helen[1] you always were / the factory

1.

Spider:

Helen you always were
the factory

Though almost wherever you sat placid,
bent at your creative toil,
someone has built a shed around you 5
with some wheels to oil, some owner
has put you in the shade to weave
or in a great brick box, twelve stories,
twenty, glassed, neonic and with cards
to time your time. 10
Though he has removed you from your homey
cottage industry, and made you
stranger to your own
productions, though he titles you his worker,
and himself your boss, himself "producer" 15

Helen you always were
the factory
Helen you always were producer

Though the loom today be made mechanic,
room-sized, vast, metallic, thundering; 20
though it be electric, electronic,
called a mill—a plant—a complex—
city of industry—

still it is a loom, simply, still just a frame,
a spindle (your great wand) pistons and rods, 25

heddle bars lifting
so a shuttle can be thrown across the space created
and the new line tapped down into place;
still there is a hot and womblike bucket
somewhere boiling up the stuff of thread 30
in cauldrons, and some expert fingers dancing
whether of aluminum or flesh; still there is
a pattern
actualized, a spirit caught
in some kind of web 35
whether it's called a system
or a network or a double breasted
cordless automatic nylon parachute

still it is a web and
still it comes from you 40
your standing and your wandish
fingers, source, your flash of inspiration,
your support, your faith in it
is still the fateful thread, however it is spun,
of whatever matter made. 45

And still it is the one true cord,
the umbilical line
unwinding into meaning, transformation,
web of thought and caring and connection.

Just as, Helen you dreamed and weaved it 50
eons past, just as your seamy fingers
manufactured so much human culture,
all that encloses, sparks
and clothes the nakedness of flesh and
mind and spirit, 55
Helen, you always were the factory.

2.

Hannah:

Flames were already eating
at my skirts,
and I heard one of the girls
behind me screaming just how much 60
burning hurts. I could see the
people gathered on the sidewalk.
Eight stories high
I stood on the ledge
of the Triangle building[2] 65
and exclaimed out loud.
Then I took my hat
with its white and yellow flowers
and flung it out, and opening
my purse, I scattered the coins 70
I had earned
to the shocked crowd.
Then, I took Angelina's hand in mine.
I thought we should go down
in style, heads high 75
as we had been during the strike
to end this kind of fire.
I grabbed Ellie's fingers to my right;
her clothes were smoking

like a cigarette, my little sister, 80
so serious, seventeen,
actually gave me a clenched smile
just as we leaped, all three
into the concrete sea.
We fell so far. 85
We're probably falling still.

They say a hundred twenty
thousand workers
marched on our behalf;
they say our eulogy 90
was delivered in a whisper;
they say our bodies
landed under the earth,
so heavy we became,
so weighted as we spun down; 95
they say safety conditions changed
after we were killed.
Because we fell so hard
and caused such pain.
Because we fell so far. 100
We're falling still.

3.

Spider:

Helen you always were
the one enticed

The one consigned
to leave your pile of clothing 105
by the river while you
bathed your beauty
and were stolen. Always
you are the one thrown over
the shoulder, carried off, 110
forced to enter the car, the plane,
the bed, at swordpoint; lined up,
loaded onto the ships and
shanghaied, tricked
out of your being, shafted, 115
lifted and held hostage,
taken for a ride.
Always you are the one
coerced to sign the bad
contract; ordered to work past sundown; 120

the queen riding the stern
of her once proud ships,
serving two or ten or twenty years
before the mast,
cheated of all pay at last, 125
and thrashed by the birch rod,
the cat-o'-nine tail wand.

Helen you always are
the coals stoked
and taken from the hearth, 130
the precious flama
spilled upon the floor
and blamed and blamed
for the uproar
when the whole house 135
goes up in smoke…

4.

Nelda:

We were marched to the coast
where the ships waited.
I remember their masts, tossing,
—the pain of loss, 140
of being lost—
like spikes, through our hearts.
On the passage over
we were stacked like logs
below the deck, our fragile 145
and our sick
thrown to the fiery sea.

My whole family died.
My husband, my beloved child;
my village, my past life 150
became a dream.
I barely existed
when I arrived.
For who was "I" to be alive?
Like a lone star 155
through the blue sky
falling netless
to a new world. What
was new about it was our terror.

But we kept our memories. 160

We kept our peoplehood, our past.
And oh good god
we stood. We stood in
water to our knees, to plant the
seeds, we stood in ashy fields 165
and picked the ill-gotten
tobacco and the cotton and
the sugar beets and all the sweet
sweet meats we could never eat.
The sun a dragon. 170

We spread out
a network to Detroit, Chicago,
Newark and LA, all over the land
for the assemblyline work,
getting blistered in the oil-slick 175
city streets, scalded in the kitchens
and the laundries, fired in the
fires of hard times. But we did
much more than just survive; we scarred
and healed and sealed and shared and spieled 180
and blared and smoldered,
joining—however knotty it may be—
our memories
our dreaming and our wand-like hands,
to burn together like a great black 185
brand. A dance of fire.

"Remember dreams, remember Africa,"
we sing, and what we mean
is freedom, wholeness,
that integrity of being 190
that chooses its own time, its
own kings and queens.

5.

Spider:

Helen you always were
the bag of life

You with your carriage, 195
the yoni-weaving basket
with the belly-drag,
the well-used pouch,
the cookie jar indefinitely
filled and emptied. 200

Helen you always were
Santa's fat sack,
full of little worlds
to hang on the great
green tree, so prettily. 205

Helen you always were the belle
of the ball and the ball
of the bell
with the golden heart,
the egg yolk 210
of we human folk.

The singing music box
composing magic children
with their sticky
democratic fingers 215
in your eyes like wands
in water.
The ship's hold stuffed with cargo,
a carving of your image on the bow;
the white sails strung along your arms 220
like everyday laundry.

Helen you always were
the honeycomb
the honey and the honey jar
kept open by the bear's claw 225
and the words, "we need her,"
and sometimes even, in your nightmare,
the harried wasp who hurries
to lay her hungry eggs
before they hatch inside 230
and eat her

Helen you always were
the factory
Helen you always were producer

6.

Nancy:

Do you see the boys lined up 235
to board the ships
to ride the tanks
around the walls?

The flint-faced fathers

with their scanners 240
and their maps,
the saplings on the firing
line, woven in the mat
of war, to be rolled out
on any shore 245
to batter after
every door,
to lie in lifeless lines
across the warehouse floor—
is this the pattern 250
that I labored and I bore,
the blood for blood, the arms
for arms, the heart
torn out
to hurt some more 255

And who am I

if it is me
they say
they do it

for? 260

7.

Spider:

Helen
you always were
the egg laid
by the golden goose,
the full pot, the fat purse, 265
the best bet, the sure horse
the Christmas rush
the bundle he's about to make;
the gold mine, a house of our own
the ship come in, the next stake, 270
the nest egg, the big deal, the steal—
the land of opportunity
the lovely lady being
luck and love and lust
and the last chance 275
for any of us,
the reason that he's living
for, Helen you're always
high card, ace in the hole and

more, the most, the first and best, 280
the sun
burst
goodness   quenching every thirst
the girl of the golden golden golden
West, 285
desire that beats
in every chest

heart of the sky

and some bizarre
dream substance 290
we pave streets with
here in America

8.

Annie Lee:

Oh hell yes! I stand,
have stood, will stand;
my feet are killing me! 295

This tube of lipstick
is *my* wand,
this pencil and this emery board,
this mascara applicator
brushing black sex magic 300
from a bottle
these long fingernails aflame
with hot red polish, and
these pins, these sharp
spike heels, these chopsticks, 305
this letter opener
this long handled spoon,
this broom, this vacuum
cleaner tube, this spray can
and this mop, 310
all these cleaning tools
for sweeping, for undoing knots,
these spools and needles, all
these plugs and slugs and soldering
irons, these switchboards and 315
earphones and computer boards,
these knitting tools for
putting things together,
these are my wands.

In the parade I'm the one 320
in bangles and short skirt
twirling the rubber-tipped
baton; this is my umbrella,
and my parasol, my fan,
these are my wands 325
and oh hell yes I stand

I am who stands
I am also who sits
who greets who wipes
who notices, who serves, 330
who takes note
and I am who stoops
who picks and sorts
who cuts and fits
who files and stores 335
who seals and bonds

and I need my wands
and oh hell yes I stand,
have stood, will stand,
in lines, in queues, in rows, 340
in blocks, in crowds, in basic
traffic pattern flows.
I have my wands, my hands,
my ways of understanding
and my family strands. 345

And here in the sunset
is where I like to hear
the singing
of the loom.
The strings of light 350
like fingers and
the fingers like a
web, dancing. It has
all the meaning
we have made of it. 355

9.

Spider:

And still it is a loom, simply,
still just a frame, a spindle,
heddle bars lifting
so a shuttle can be thrown across

the space created 360
and the new line
tapped down into place;
still there is a hot and womblike bucket
somewhere boiling up the stuff of thread
in cauldrons, and some expert fingers 365
dancing…

Still it is the one true cord,
the umbilical line
unwinding into meaning,
transformation, 370
web of thought and caring and connection.

Just as, Helen you dreamed and weaved it
eons past, just as your seamy fingers
manufactured so much human culture,
all that encloses, sparks 375
and clothes the nakedness of flesh and
mind and spirit,
Helen, you always were the factory.
Helen you always were the factory.
Helen you always were the factory. 380
Helen you always were producer.
Helen you always were
who ever is
the weaving tree
and Mother of the people. 385

Notes

[1] In Greek mythology Helen, the daughter of Leda and Zeus, was married to Menalaus of Greece. She was kidnapped by Paris and taken to Troy, which caused the Trojan War.

[2] On March 25, 1911, a fire started on the eighth floor of the Triangle Shirtwaist Factory, a sweatshop in New York City that employed primarily young immigrant women. Most of the workers on the eighth and tenth floors escaped, but the workers on the ninth floor were trapped.

Mental

one

That she could be on the street
in the rainy season, that my mother
could so easily be one of the butterflies
curled into a misery cocoon
under the bright plastic, color of a painted 5
suburban swimming pool, vivid blue shroud
heaped over the sleeping body
on the sidewalk
stained grey with water, stained with ice

that this could be her dear distressed face 10
struggling to the surface of one more day
among the million dollar apartments

butterflies die out when their habitat is destroyed

but it's all in the head,
it's mental, 15
isn't really real, isn't happening
not on our streets, not in this
civilized and monumental era
no, it isn't really happening that our streets
are crawling with bugs, with cocoons 20
with someone (showing signs of malnutrition
in his knobby elbows

I mean is *that* what it is?) leaning, bending down
shouting as though to voices talking to him from
under a car or maybe the license plate *is* broadcasting 25
maybe it's the government
propaganda
news about the war?

no, it's all in our heads, it's mental

he isn't really bending and listening to voices 30
he isn't really walking around in a state of
malnutrition on our streets
saluting the parking meters
listening to fenders
among the million dollar apartments 35

two

Mickey and me were on the Sixth Floor Lockdown Ward B
until we were seventeen,
we were such great friends, we had so much to talk about
in spite of everything being so closed in, and
one day we escaped! yes, we ran out through the gate 40
gowns flapping
while no one was looking and we ran across the highway,
a broad white street with a bunch of trees and beautiful grass
in the center, we outran all the cars zigging and zagging
it was so much fun! 45
and we ran up to the biggest brownest greenest tree
and threw our arms
around the trunk, we just hugged and hugged that tree
giggling and yakking,
we loved it so much, 50
Mickey and me,
we hadn't seen one
for so long for years, we couldn't stop the hugging
and the yakking, and the loving
and the laughing 55
we stayed there for the longest time.

and then they came
and then they took us back.

So we were dancing gaily round a tree
and then confined again, constrained with drugs 60
and straps but not whipped as back in the 14th century
when England's Bedlam, originally
called *Bethlehem,* a place meant to care for the down
and out became a house of torment for the "mad"—
and so judgmental: 65
"Hey," people said, "they don't work, they are
possessed and erratic,"
meaning: demonic, meaning bad

three

the mental health workers don't believe them
they think they are making it up, to shirk. 70
to avoid work.
it's all mental they say,
it's in their heads

they don't realize that if she thinks there are
bugs crawling on her skin, it's the same as if 75
there *are* bugs crawling on her skin

because it is, it is mental
and it's mental, so
if we think our streets
are crawling with the mentally ill 80

it's the same as if our streets
are crawling with the mentally ill

four

when your parent has schizophrenia
the parent is like a like a butterfly when they come out
but mostly what you see 85
is the cocoon, grey and spinning spinning
making a coat of protection
from *what* you wonder? but the cocoon
can't speak, its all internal, separated
and preoccupied 90
you knock and knock, the child wanting
a response, realizing you can't get in
they can't get out
and just when you give up

here comes: a butterfly 95
so gorgeous, delicate and full of love
          your heart opens up
        and delight makes life seem real.
      and probable and magic.
   You stretch out your hand, 100
thinking you see a parent,

and it's gone
the cocoon returns, the inner spinning spinning
you can hear that much is going on in there
the munching of the larva, the devouring business 105
but it's secret
it's mental
you don't have access

sometimes you can see
that it's horrifying or dreadfully frightening 110
and you want to protect your parent
the vulnerability

sometimes you are just mad because no one
ever. answers the door

well it isn't like any of that 115
what's the use trying to describe
what can't be known,
still, we have to try
and anyhow I am about a quarter butterfly
myself, and I know what that cocoon can feel like 120
though I've never had to live there all that long.
It's like being a porcupine with the quills turned
outside in.

and once, (or ok, more than once) I experienced the full blown
hallucination of horror, the distortion of senses that takes over. 125

This happened on a trip to the tropics, I was taking
Mefloquine for malaria prevention and hadn't read
the label that said if mental illness runs in your family
don't take this stuff.
It can make you crazy. and it did make me crazy, 130
the sensation was overwhelming, of paranoia,
the fear was a heart throbbing inner gigantic bug
the certainty I knew what was causing the fear, and
the absoluteness of how wrong I was,
though still picking up on something no one else could sense 135
and then the pervasive, invasive
inability to focus, to follow the plot of conversation
or procession.

I couldn't tell one end of the elephant from the other.
No wonder my mother couldn't tell what street we lived on 140
or how old we were if this is what preoccupied her life.

Worst were the physical hallucinations,
the revolting sensation of someone dear kissing me,
with lips that became writhing worms, long, thick, twisting,
lip-colored, way too alive. I could feel the worms 145
and I could *see* them from inside myself, where everything
is mental. I didn't tell anyone this because it was so
horrible, and I didn't want to be offensive. Just withdrew.
So that was a clue about my mother's mind and what she
went through all the time. What she contended with. 150
Inside herself. In that cocoon.

When I figured out the medication was the problem
and then remembered that malaria would wreck my liver
and possibly kill me:

"I don't care," I said, "I'd rather take the risk than feel like *this* again" 155
even though it isn't *real*
it's only mental

five

the sidewalks are the skin of the city, any city
has a grey skin like that and look! how it crawls
with bugs, people who are bugs! they are bugs! 160
in cocoons in the doorways, crawling on the skin
of the city and the city is panicky, pushing its hands
up and down its long grey arms, pushing and scratching
at the people who are bugs, trying to shake them off,
to squash them, make them go away 165

where shall they go?
to the jail, to the hospital
to the street

where shall they go?
to the jail, to the hospital 170
to the street

where shall they go?
to the jail, to the hospital
to the street

or hooligans may come in the night 175
where they sleep in their cardboard shacks
to mock and beat and set them on fire

As during the Inquisition and its witch hunts
and during the continuing struggle afterwards
for a rational science 180
any expression of disparate energies was suspect,
epilepsy for example,
grounds for conviction of possession by evil spirits
women especially examined for the malady,
and diviners of all kinds arrested and tortured. 185
Even excessive joy was of the devil,
a symptom named "enthusiasm"
as recorded in the bible of the witch hunters,
the Malleus Maleficarum.
On holidays crowds came to deride and 190
mock the antics of those afflicted.

Shock and awe the mediation of choice,
everything from force feeding with cayenne pepper
to being thrown into a pit of snakes.

then came attempts to be more compassionate 195
so then came lunatic asylums, then drugs
then notions of rights and freedoms
so, turned out on the street
free as bugs

six

my mom can't get treated, they say they have so many 200
so much worse off than her, so take her home.
But I know how this goes, I've seen it six times before,
it's developmental, she will get much worse and then
I can't get her in,
I can't get her back to the clinic 205
she won't go, she's too afraid, she's so afraid,
she thinks it may get—experimental,
then I must call for help and the authorities will come
and someone could get hurt,
they could hurt her, she could hurt somebody, 210
I'm thinking of Saturday, I turned my attention
to my niece for just one minute and during that time
my mother called 911,
next thing we knew the tac squad at the door
forcing their way in with rifles and those looks, 215
so departmental.
She said he was murdering us all,
'No,' I told them, 'it's her illness.' And so glad she didn't
threaten them, they didn't shoot her.

And then taking her to the clinic 220
I don't need to hear a lecture on how much worse off
the others are, out there in the streets.

She's as worse off as she needs to be to get the treatment
if only they would believe me, I am the daughter,
I am her primary caretaker, 225
as I have been most of my life,
so I know, who knows her better than I?

they are afraid, so afraid, so irrationally afraid

seven

they hallucinate, they think they see a threat where there is none

as when the young man suffered an emotional breakdown 230
and stood in a theater
with a knife, his girlfriend called the police for help
and they shot him forty eight times shot forty eight times shot forty
eight times shot forty eight times shot forty eight times
they thought they saw Godzilla, giant dark crazy devil axis of evil 235
they thought they saw the great satan, yes that was surely him,
eating the entire city, sticking all the downtown buildings
into his gigantic mouth
(he's the mother of all bugs)

And his mother. She sued the hell out of them. 240
(and so they said they got some training)

What if we don't need to choose
between lockdown asylums and the streets
what if we create a geography of disparate spirits?
what if space were set aside for behaviors like these: 245

dance on one leg, sing for hours off key,
scream and roll around,
hold your breath, accuse the universe of crimes
listen to essential messages from bees
rock all day pace all night 250
recognize strangers but not your family
pound your furies into the stalwart bodies of trees
say the weirdest ideas right out loud, fly into a cloud,
no need to fear your hysteria will bring chains
or a ring of whitecoat people terrified of being sued, 255
or a ring of bluecoat people terrified. unto death.
and shooting. you. you-shooting-you.

eight

think what a butterfly does to our life
that's elemental

there is nothing substantial about a butterfly 260
it doesn't feed you or give you a bed
it doesn't remember what street we live on or how old you are
There is nothing about a butterfly we would want
to take to the insurance adjustor, nothing incremental.

But think what a butterfly gives us 265
of delight,
think what surprise in that flutter of life
and how amazing the colors, way beyond
ornamental, who would ever have imagined
such combinations as a butterfly takes for granted 270
in its short display of light play
and that sacramental face, those sensitive antennae
connecting to our inner eyes.
There are dances, notions and inspirations
we can't know except for butterflies 275

that we can't know when there are no butterflies
when life is detrimental
and when the habitat, the habitat of butterflies
is so destroyed
what is the covenant 280
we must have with butterflies.

not that I'm really talking about butterflies,
not that they aren't dangerous at times
and crawl from their cocoons onto an entirely different
landscape than any we can imagine 285

remember my mother threw an iron into my face
when I was four; who knows what monster she saw,
some reports from deep in those cocoons tell us
their babies turn into Satan or a hairy watermelon
or God gives them specific instructions from His boombox 290
and so they drop him out the window or in the Bay or run over her,
that baby, that writhing bucket of snakes.

a mother may try to kill you in a number of ways.
and then there were those kittens unexpectedly dying,
my father and I sobbing, she so still with no expression on her face. 295
My mother was willful, once at the hospital for a routine physical
the confident doctor insisted on giving her an ekg
she didn't want, so she said no, (her no is a no)
he said ho ho ho
and hooked her up anyhow 300
as soon as she was alone she shredded the connections,
five thousand dollars damage, and innocence, whimsical,
let's hear how "she's so sweet"

now imagine being her daughter or her son, trying to hold
onto your sense of balance, your space, your clothes, your kittens... 305
your friends and the minor matter of lunch and dinner

and ferocious fear…that someone will come and take her away…
or that they won't……or that they will….or that they won't…..
and then they don't.   So you don't have   exactly a mother,
you're left with sort of a child. Occasionally, wild. 310

and you don't speak about this, as there is no one to hear you

Everyone thinks schizophrenic means helpless and locked up for life
but lo! there are a lot of functional folks with the illness and they have
jobs and families, some have children, just imagine being five or nine and
taking care of the parent with the condition that no one can talk 315
about or think about,
that comes and goes, because he is mostly stable, except for episodes,

and meantime everyone thinks he is so sweet, they tell you,
they rather insistently tell you,
"Your father is so sweet," and you are thinking 320
why does everyone say that
except his children?

those children secretly, obsessively scurrying from one definition
of sanity to another, trying to sort.

it's like being from an unknown country, always astonished 325
at everything everyone does, because after a while it all seems
like cocoon life to you, it all seems equally irrational,

this may give you quite a sense of humor
and people will say that you are a bit quirky, even fay.
you won't have an answer for this.   you won't say. 330

nine

They are demented and so
are likely to kill the children
or otherwise terrify them.

Sent back for a third time, a third deploymental decision
omygodomygod my ticket is up 335
soldier you were given instructions to fire upon civilians
to protect yourself

how now will you live with this
how *will* you protect yourself? from this:

given amphetamines to keep you up up up 340
til you can't tell friend from foe,
instructed to kill whatever comes near

your vulnerable lethal humbug vehicle
how now will you exist with these ghosts
how will you protect yourself 345
from those curled little lumps staining the backseat

you could smell their stillness when the noise settled
in back of the bloody windshield
what shield will protect the tender eye of your memory
from child, student, old man, pregnant woman 350
terrified driver trying to back up the car

what will protect you from the screaming mothers
how now will you live with these nightmare memories
of the car that goddammit didn't blow up even after you shot
everyone in it 355

the country sends you like bad thoughts from its house of bugs
all dressed up in the pretty camouflage
and not quite enough exoskeleton armors
eyes wrapped in the dark rhomboid lenses
bugged, bugged, bugged, we are all bugged 360
the arrogant cocoons in such big white houses, plotting
and frothing, bugging everyone,
listening to God broadcast from little black boxes
about the end of his regime

urging the people to be 365
flag wavingly sentimental
seeking purification in self fulfilling
delusions of Armageddon
as the fundamental hallucination of
virgins, angels and dragons 370
dancing on the heads of missiles
a thousand times the numbers required
for annihilation of the lovely little blue planet
to get to states of transmogrification
for true believers where nothing is mental 375
it's all moral

it's all moral so we can lie about everything
as millionaire men of powerful super nation
super superiorly fearful

being so instrumental 380

and you, the soldier, the one who joined because
you wanted to rescue someone, or felt you had no better choices
your father was a soldier and this is a caste system
you had no idea it would be like this, you only wanted some money
you didn't know you would want to kill everything 385

on a very particular singular cocoon-feeling day

blown out of your mind with grief
seeing your friends melt to just bloody bones
and you not even scraped
(and you as far as you can get from home) 390
you didn't know your buddies would go mad with bloodlust
and rape you
in the fog of butterflies
whose habitat has been destroyed

and so you will live on in the *street,* babe 395
you will live on the street like a *holy man*
owning nothing but your beard and the visible *pinkscabs*
eating away your hands like infectious *beetles*

and your eyes like ponds in a meadow of *nowhere*
    as you feed the pigeons the last of your trust in *anyone* 400
        owning no gas guzzling cars no *property*
            nothing that calls for AK Kalashnikov to guard the pearly *gates of*
                    owing nobody *nothing*
and so they will call you that strange and *traveling word:*

that word of prophets, murderers, and *survivors* 405
that word that sets you apart from them that *accomplish* things:

craaaaazy

they will call YOU *craaazy*

To the Mother of All Bowls

(for Luisah Teish)

some bowls are cool
to the touch
some bowls are full of stew
some bowls don't hold
too much 5
what kind of bowl are you

though made of porcelain
some bowls last tens of centuries
though made of solid gold some bowls
change in a flash meltdown 10

some bowls age in penitentiaries
some begging bowls sit out on the ground
some bowls sing.......
some bowls get passed around
for everyone to drink 15

some bowls get smashed
in the kitchen sink
some bowls stand still in the old bowl museum
some bowls go to every pot luck

some bowls overflow 20
some bowls suck it up
some bowls clutch ash in the mausoleum
some bowls hold hospital suffering

circling bowls alleviate
envy 25
water bowls consecrate
nativity
burning bowls emulate
eternity
flower bowls re-create 30
proclivity
red garuthi bowls
soak up soak up soak up
negativity

some bowls spill out in offering 35
some bowls transform
some bowls bring about a sea storm

some bowls say bowls
witness everything

She loves all bowls 40
She makes

all bowls break
all bowls return to Her

the Mother of all bowls

dishes up love, 45
that's why the love is
unconditional
unconditional love
belongs to bowls.

FICTION

From *Mundane's World*[*]

Remembering Is One Way Of Writhing In The Clutches Of Three Large Aunts

In a city of dreamers the women say they dream babies into their bellies from spirits and the men dream of hunting animals who no longer live around the vicinity.

Off the street within the walls of a small workyard of the Snake clan, the clan of healing and balancing, a female child is neatly unobtrusively playing. Her elder cousins are all grown up and gone to work as shepherds. She herself has dark brown skin and kinky black hair near her head, a sturdy body with a slightly round stomach and large hands, large eyes and heavy eyelids. She has one eye set straight in her head, the other eye wandering off to the left. She is squatting and arranging ceaselessly a wide variation of small bottles and jars on the ground in front of her, and is mumbling to herself; and is very serious and is called: *Ernesta.*

She had turned her head to the right to listen to a donkey arguing with someone in the distance but when she is called: *Ernesta,* she turns her head to the left, so that her eye wanders up even more, seeming to be staring straight at the sky; and anyone looking is tempted somewhat to laugh but controlling it, then seeing the rest of her face, the solid-featured heaviness of it, anyone puts away their laugh and takes the face more seriously than they would if it did not have a wandering eye, which is a form of justice.

"Mama?" Ernesta asks, although the caller steps out of the shaded doorway and is not exactly her mama being rather her aunt, Aunt One, whereupon the eye wanders more and is huge.

Aunt One knows that Ernesta was first in a line of girls from various clans who recently escaped a perilous situation with a mama lion who had nearly undone them, being perhaps even the notorious Lion of Mundane.

Knowing this lengthens her square face of concern. She says, "What are you doing out here? You aren't using any more water are you?"

"Oh, I'm just waiting for something to happen," Ernesta says. Actually she has been remembering five girls walking in a line three days before; she has been lining up the pots and jars on the ground before her naming them, "First there was me, then Jessi-ma from the Bee clan, then Fran-keen from the Lion clan. Next was Dee. No, next was Margedda who is such a weird person and then Dee was last, and both from the Tortoise farming people." This arranging of jars was helping her remember who was who and how it had all gone that day when everything changed.

Aunt One moves with a soft-footed marching motion, she wears a long dull red dress of filmy material of her own making with pins holding it together at the shoulder. Her niece wears a faded red skirt with no top and very little bottom.

*[*Editor's Note*] Rather than selecting the first few or last few chapters of the novel, I've assembled these selected chapters to represent a single plot line—without 'giving away' the novel's ending. I've chosen the cooking-themed plot to coordinate with the cooking chapter of *Blood, Bread, and Roses.*

Aunt One's hands are full of dried plant fibers, yellow and tan which she calls her wickers.

"Waiting will not cause something to happen," she says sharply. "Nor prevent it either."

She crosses the courtyard to a place with a bowl of water where she sloshes her wickers. Aunt One is making a basket, she sings while she does this.

Aunt One often sings. Everyone sings for many reasons, Aunt One often sings for her own amusement. She sings to remind herself what she is doing. She sings to placate the spirits of noncreation. Today Aunt One's song is about a crane who stood for so long in one place on one leg that she hardened into that position, and was unable to lay eggs or get about at all until a supple green snake came along who she persuaded to stiffen itself and be her second leg, whereafter she could walk with not so much trouble although everyone made fun of her and called her a green legged crane.

The entirety of Ernesta's clan, the Snake clan, is happy these days, everything is in harmony with their ways, nothing is in dissension with them. By midsummer's eve their own major clan workyard will have a complicated tile mural picturing some of their more important stories. These included a story of Aunt One and her three sisters and their mother Mundane importing fig trees in a procession carrying the tree bundles from the sea side dock and transplanting them into one of their medicine gardens. Soon the story of the procession would be part of a brilliantly colored mural, glazed and shiny with a permanent record of Snake clan power, the power of certain people to effect transformations on living matter.

Aunt One and two of her sisters had brought the mural matter up with the council of elders recently wrangling it through with no problems except a slight argumentation from the Bee clan. The wonderful story tiles would be baked by the Bee clan as was proper and then set into place in the wall of the major workyard by the time for the midsummer festival.

The tail end of Aunt One's basketmaking song includes this current information which she sings loudly as she weaves her wickers. The more recent version of her song has forty-two verses taking the better portion of one hour to sing and she enjoys every one of them.

Ernesta does not hear the end of the long song. Her attention has returned to her rows of little baskets and jars, miniatures of the ones used by adults, made long ago when she was a small child, each one a child's size with a child's contents of dust or selected pebbles or barley meal leftover from the cooking larder.

Ernesta has made variations of the mixtures, and the discovery that sprinkles of water mixed with dirt and grain and left in the sun for a week or so renders a baked mass that will neither go in nor out of any jar, and is ugly looking besides. Information so useful it never needs to be remembered again yet having something to do with learning the nature of cooking. Memory is important to Ernesta and so is cooking. In Ernesta's clan, cooking and the making of chemical mixtures are one and the same thing.

How Cooking Took A Long Time To Learn

Ernesta knows that cooking took a long time to learn because she herself is a primary example. Ordinarily many people do the cooking together but one time left to her own devices in the kitchen, she had put honey in the vegetables and salt in the fruit. She had boiled the milk and left the bread dough nearly raw, just lukewarm. Her relatives had threatened to make her eat the whole composition by herself, all of it, to better appreciate her own creativity.

"I didn't burn anything," she protested. They were not impressed by this.

Ernesta's family have a thorough understanding of how cooking took a long time to learn, because they invented it, or so they say; the entire hundred-thousand-year-long process is analoged in their songs with many variations including the difficulty of combining fire with water.

When Ernesta had put so much salt in the fruit her mother had said, "Ernesta has imagination."

"Not so," Aunt Two said, "that's not imagination. She just doesn't pay attention when she is taught. Ernesta has only a scattered memory, therefore she makes things up as she goes along."

Ernesta worried about this a great deal, for in her family a good memory was an imperative. She worked on her memory, reciting avidly when no one was looking: salt for vegetables and curing; salt for cheese but not for teas; honey for bread and open wounds, honey for milk only in the morning or when someone has a stomach ache; onions and garlic for nearly anything though not for melons or rashes. She worked on her memory when she was very young and anxious until it became a habit with her mumbling to herself the litany of whatever she might be in danger of forgetting. This habit gave her an excellent memory which her doubting aunts tested her on considerably.

"Smell this," Aunt Three would say, holding a little jar of crushed petals under Ernesta's nose. "What is it called? What foods is it used in and what medicines? How much do you use, where does it come from? If you boiled it with cloth, what color would come out?"

"Feel this powder, Ernesta," Aunt Two would say. "What liquids does it mix with? What did I tell you about it yesterday, where does it come from?"

A puzzle remained to her for some time about cooking, why some things are never eaten raw, like barley, and some are never cooked, like lettuce. Beer appears only at festivals, berries only in the early summer. Why don't you put butter on *everything,* for instance oranges. Why can't you ever put onions in the apple cider. Why are there a hundred ways to eat squash but only a few ways to eat melons when in the fields the squashes and melons look almost the same. These things are peculiar about cooking; these and thousands of other details Ernesta had to learn concerning mixtures which took a long time in the beginning as well as presently.

In the meantime she lined up her jars, a thin one for Jessi-ma, a heavy one for Margedda, a short one for Dee. She was not so much playing since she had actually outgrown this sort of toy as she was trying to puzzle out a thought. She put in place in the little line an unpainted jar to stand for Fran-keen and then a most interesting and decorated elder one first in the line, for herself. Then she reconstructed her memory.

Here they were walking up the trail from the river where they had pulled each other out soaking wet. She scratched a long slender mark beside the line of jars for the trail; she scratched other marks off to the left where the foundation for the new temple was being built by the Bee clan; and then down the center she made a wide scratch for the river road, past where everyone now knew a dead woman had been found that same afternoon, three days before. She laid a short woman-representing stick on the spot with reverence.

An enclosed space in a city with light and air is for young children; in this city the walls of every four ground-floor rooms form courtyards of many sizes. These are often with trees or shrubs for shade and company, more often they are with gardens and henyards.

There are four clans in the city altogether, the yards of this particular one are lined with pots and plots of herbs and nursling plants. Ernesta's clan being the healing people always smell of sharp powders and spices they use in their processes. All her babyhood she has played with old or imitation powders and has been warned sharply away from the places in the area where the Aunts and her mother Donna keep their more volatile drugs and venoms. Fear that their babies could eat the leaves of overly powerful plants have caused the women of Ernesta's clan to build a sturdy formal moon temple with a plant nursery on the second floor, guarded by heavy doors that can not be pushed open by little fingers easily.

The four clans altogether in the city of Mundane are: The Snake clan, of transformation, balance, healing and mixtures. The Bee clan, of constructions, water bearing women, and the keeping of measurements. The Lion clan, of animals, movement, transportation and trading. The Tortoise clan of farming, provision, distribution of necessities and the keeping of records.

In addition are the pan-clan societies of which the largest are the Spider Society of predictive women and the Arrow Society for crafty men. In a city of dreamers the clans are held together by a mutual knowing of numerous natural powers and especially one whose name they usually call: *Ana* and who is a lady of many faces, some other names and a great deal of body.

Handiwork Is Just Another Name For Manual Labor

Anyone who makes baskets all day long for several days will get blisters, but not Aunt One. Aunt One has hardly callused hands and is an expert. The thin green branch of a willow tree wound around in a circle and woven together with itself by skinny water-soaked strips of long sharp wicker leaves will eventually form a sturdy basket but almost anyone who makes baskets all day long will get blistered. Except Aunt One, who has made so many and who is however annoyed at the amount of work it takes to make a good midsummer festival. She has sworn not to make any more containers though everyone knows she will anyway because her two younger sisters can always think of more things to put in them. Aunt One wonders if it is wise to have sisters with so much imagination.

Aunt One has been working on the same basket for six months. It is now so tall that only the black top of her hair shows as she stands inside of it, working. She hums a song to help herself along and also to breathe a good spirit into the container. She wants nothing to ever rot secretly at the bottom of it, she wants nothing to ever leak out of its sides. She has incorporated a pattern of red and black into the walls, intermittently a long wavy snake figure and a crane with red body and black legs and head; there are nine of these figures all the way around. The head of each crane is as large as the palm of Aunt One's hand. They stand for transformations of the spirit, something which their designer is hoping for herself, who has been depressed lately on account of arthritis in her hands, and is dreading the chill of winter.

Even a Snake clan woman of transformations can be in need of transformations. Ernesta does not know that her first aunt is depressed by what is happening to her hands; she believes that Aunt One's new gnarly knuckles and oddly bending fingers are an invention of her person, Aunt One's creating of a variation in her own form. She is amazed by this, for she herself even practicing cannot get her hands into such positions; it seems to her a further proof of Aunt One's complete control over her own physical matters.

Ernesta fixed her wandering eye on Aunt One's head, barely showing. Aunt One had told her that meeting a lion on the trail was the reversing of a perilous situation, and from then on that was how she remembered it. It was important to Ernesta that she had been the first in a line of girls who reversed a perilous situation because she had been the one called on to think up the solution. She wondered if this being first in line would happen to her again, was that the kind of person she was.

All the people of the Snake clan of transformation have great control in physical matters, in this family they have learned much of it from Ernesta's grandmother, the great Mundane, who is currently on a lasting journey. She has left behind her five children in the city, four women and a man, Blueberry Jon. Of the four sisters the youngest is Ernesta's tender-hearted mother Donna and the elder three are her formidable aunts.

Ernesta examined the pattern of jars and scratches she had made to help herself recall what had happened on the particular day. There was one element missing, something so mysterious she had discussed it with nobody, not even her mother who sometimes listened or appeared to be doing so, under her lowered eyelids and nodding skull.

Of all the dreamers in the city Ernesta's mother Donna was the most unusual. While other women dreamed their children from stars, domesticated plants or people, she had dreamed hers from a strange wild bush growing deep in some rocky hills east of the city. Someday Ernesta would meet this plant, who was called by her mother a spirit mate and called by her aunts a greedy little weed.

[...]

How Cooking Took A Long Time To Learn

Ernesta can tell that cooking takes a long time to learn because lately she has been spending so much of her time watching her aunts cutting up onions. Sitting next to each one in turn night upon night or in the middle of the day she has seen their peculiarities. She has noticed that although the little pungent piles of cut up onions are similar as they sit stacked near the bowls or hot pans ready to be swept away into the recipe, nevertheless they have their serious differences. She has noticed that these serious differences have to do with the philosophical meanings of the onions, and this depends entirely on which aunt has done the cutting.

Aunt One's white piles of cut up onions are often soggy with water drops and have great potential for stinging the eyes. Aunt One says onions have such potential for stinging the eyes that she always cuts them holding them in a bowl under some water so they can't get out to her and sting her. She slices them first in half making a crisscross pattern on the flat half of an onion she then cuts across horizontally, causing a dozen or so neat little squares of white flesh to fall into the bottom of the bowl of water at a time.

Aunt Two says there is only one way to cut up onions and that anyone knows this, and she herself knows it the best. She says the onions might sting some people's eyes and this shouldn't bother anyone least of all her. She prefers a chopping method of approach, first cutting the onion into slices while holding its round body down with the other hand and then holding one end of the knife down with her same holding hand while the cutting hand rapidly slaps the blade up and down with a swift swiveling motion that reduces the onion to hundreds of parts of itself in a little minute. Her piles of onions are always rapidly moving, sometimes so rapidly that it is nearly impossible to see them, and she sweeps them rapidly also, sweeping them into the bowl or the hot pan of waiting oil to get them all at once into the recipe.

Aunt Three says there is every way to cut up an onion and it really doesn't matter which one anyone uses. She says they do not sting a person and are the world's most wondrous vegetable. Sometimes she just puts the whole onion or two halves of an onion into the recipe without cutting anything at all, or she might sit carving large chunks from the whole, or other times she once in a while meticulously chops them into tiny bits in something of a flurry. Parts of Aunt Three's onions sometimes end up on the floor, under furniture or even up her wide sleeves and never do make it to the recipe in time for dinner. Her piles do not sting the eyes much nor do they move rapidly. They do tend to lie around in odd places occasionally turning grey or causing a slipping sensation if someone steps on one of them.

What Ernesta loves best is to be sent into one of the storerooms hung with ropes of onions woven together into a braid by their long dried stems, gleaming and wrapped in their tight crisp golden skins with the remnants of their roots curled against their bottoms like little old beards.

Ernesta can see how cooking took a long time to learn from the heavy work of rolling barrels and jars up from the cellars and onto the wagons being done now by her grown cousins. Lifting the packed containers in their striped robes and weathered, friendly faces the men are sweating even in the early morning. Deep in the barrels are fish who were smoked before their packing in layers of salt. Ernesta remembers those days of salt and herring with her nose wrinkling every time she thinks about preservation, the strings of onions and garlics hung to dry in knobby bundles and the piles of peppers and apricots spread out on racks for weeks where no one can walk and she must fan the flies away for days waiting for them to shrivel and be preserved.

Ernesta's nose wrinkles even more recalling vinegar days, the pleasant in the beginning and then increasingly uncomfortable smell of the cucumbers, fish, pork, hardboiled eggs, onions, bits of melon and wild fruits pickled and pickled and pickled in vinegar and spices, brine and rock salt until everyone's hands were pickled too, shrivelling from the minerals of the preparations and everyone's eyes too had watered from the gasses and the smoke and the concentrations of acids and odors, and everyone's hands had wrinkled and everyone's nose had wrinkled as though these too were preserved. Once out of the storeroom however and back in the fresh morning air her nose unclenched and when she came back into the kitchen with the rope of onions she had been sent to fetch the time had come for her to go to her mother's room to get dressed for the festival and for her mother to fix her hair.

Ernesta's Head Forms Its Own World

Ernesta's head forms its own world; coils out on springs that make it a bush, a growth of its own kind. Dirty, it merely darkens or greys; wet, a thousand eyes look out. Wet, it catches the water and rolls the drops into a thousand lights or phosphorescent insects. Oiled, Ernesta's hair catches the blue black mineral colors of the world and reflects them to each other; every hair a mirror for every other. Anything lives in Ernesta's hair, everything loves it there; leaves, fluff, bits of string move in as if the hairs themselves invited them. Birds had been known to take things from Ernesta's hair for their own purposes, and almost everyone at some time wanted to put their hands into it, to play it like water turned into thin strands of musical wire, to want feeling like that, in Ernesta's hair. All of it moves in one piece, a bouncing motion; combed all the way out it stayed there; left to its own devices it coiled deeper and deeper into itself as though to go back into her head. Often she ran a belt around the crown of it, just off her forehead, letting the main bulk of the bush push up out of the top like a loaf of lava rock.

On the morning of the first day of the festival Donna washed Ernesta's hair for her, holding a mirror so she could see how the round water eyes sparkled out like thousands of stars from between the hairs all over her head. Then, even though Donna is a slender small person and Ernesta has grown to be so tall lately, Donna grabbed her and lurched outside holding her upside down laughing and shaking her so that water flew everywhere and they could see how the drops of it fell and then stayed in perfect gleaming globes in the dust under their feet. Then Donna set Ernesta down top side up on the rug in their room, and rubbed oil into her hair, all over her face and down her arms. The oil had been soaked in saffron petals.

"Phew," Ernesta said, "that smells too strong."

"Not for a festival," Donna said. "Don't you want everyone to know that you're there?"

Ernesta thought they would not have any trouble doing that. Her mother began spreading a green powder around Ernesta's eyes, who scraped some of it off examining it on the end of one finger.

"Don't rub that," Donna warned. "It might get into your eye." People often spread the powdered green malachite around their eyes in the summer for it not only kept flies away and kept the ambitious creatures from walking on children's eyeballs, it also prevented eye infections. Ernesta had a habit of rubbing her wandering eye if she became self-conscious for any reason and so often in the summer she had a greenish streak down one cheek.

Donna hung two silver earrings from the perpetual holes in Ernesta's ears while finishing painting her with slender white and red stripes on her cheeks, nose and chin.

"See how you look?" She flashed the mirror as Ernesta laughed in delight.

"I'm a green-eyed zebra."

"You're a fire-dragon child."

Aunt Two appeared in the doorway, her hands dripping suds from washing her own hair and that of the other aunts. She waved one hand with suds flying. "Zebras don't drag their stripes on the ground," she said. Ernesta hitched up her skirts, which were pleated and made with yards of brightly dyed material.

[...]

Two Who Watch Out For Each Other Are Related

If a fly is created by odors it is also true that what is created creates in its own turn. Once a form is created it creates other forms and not just those like itself, often it creates other forms unlike itself in order to give itself limits, company and composition. As the bright eyes of a mama mouse watch from the mounds of straw on the floor of the stable, so a white chested owl dreams on a rafter near the roof of the stable. The two are related especially in the time they spend thinking about each other. The mama mouse thinks about the owl dreaming on its rafter above herself and her large family about thirty percent of the time, more thought than she often has time to give to her grown children although they will soon number in dozens. Since the owl thinks about the mouse and her children about seventy per cent of the time, together they are thinking about each other one hundred percent of the time.

Living together as they so often do in the stable, the owl sits working on a beam near the ceiling while the mouse works below gathering goods into collections keeping them stored in a number of places. The two watch out for each other. The owl watches out of her huge flat eyes below her for the least motion or displaced shadow and the mouse watches out of her shiny round eyes above her for the similar motions, and she also watches the floor for any changes in the shadows of intent dropping. While the two were watching out so closely for each other they have forgotten to watch for a third entity who has appeared in the form of an immense, chubby determined stalking person named Margedda.

Trying to be unlike her own mother Margedda was determined never to cover her tattoos or be happy with a plain white dress of effort and gratitude, and never to go stalking in the woods or wild meadows for secret joy and not for mushrooms as her mother did. Instead she would stalk crouching in the stable, and she determined as she did this never to like farming as her mother had finally learned to like farming, bending and stooping, squatting and hauling, but rather to be a wild dancer and a gatherer of dreams and predictions. And today she would squat in order to be a gatherer of mice and other delicacies to take care of the baby owl her mother's lover Jon had brought her from the river.

"His mother is obviously dead," Blueberry Jon had said. "This little baby needs a patient person to take care of him." And for this task of patient care she must be wily. And she must grow up to be a wily woman.

For her part the mama mouse has already grown up to be a wily woman. The little present-minded children that she had trained ran around the edges of the objects in the stable as she herself did growing large and thickly furred while the little absent-minded children she forgot or decided not to train ran across the middle of the designated spaces directly one by one into the course of the owl's shadow of intent and rapidly dropping flight and nails and beak and stomach.

Because of her habits of trembling without moving the mouse has taught the owl to do a great deal of sitting and of dreaming it would not otherwise be doing. Because the mama mouse has habits of working at night the owl has been given plenty of night vision and silent, rapidly dropping flight in order to fall down on her from above. Falling down on a mouse from above is something the owl has practiced a great deal involving air currents and the precision of foot muscle releasing and gravitational diving. And because of this dropping flight of owls the mouse keeps always to the edges of the objects of her environment in the stable or anywhere, moving always in geometric lines as though drawing pictures of a space by running all around its parameters. For their part the owls have learned to think of other things extensively with their big eyes open for otherwise the waiting is all too boring. Waiting for a mouse to move within a given space so you can suddenly drop down on it from above is boring, even apparently paralysing unless you are excellent at finding other things to ponder.

For a mouse to have so many babies at a time as she loves to do she must have someone to give some of them over to and for this reason her kind have thought up the family of owls and dreamed them into existence. With their bright mouse eyes gleaming and jerking they dreamed and thought them up, with their noses pointed into a circle of each other around the scattered grain pile, the sharp whiskered noses of the mama mice and the imitative smaller noses of the children mice and the jowlfaced noses of the men mice. They thought them up, the few birds who do not live at all like mice at the scattered grain pile but who rather live on the succulent bodies of mice and who constantly ponder the smell and the feel and the possible every movement of mice.

Though most birds live on grain and fruits and twitter and play and tremble and live somewhat like mice a few birds do not do this, they do not twitter or quiver but perch and hover for long periods, sitting in the rafters or the tree limbs hour upon hour of their lives worshipping mice and pondering the subjects related to waiting for mice and how and just exactly when to drop down from above onto the sweet grainy bodies of mice. They do not do much more than this, and because of it the mice can produce plenty of hot little pink children knowing there will never be too many, and knowing that now there can also be great feathered creatures with large dreaming eyes who can never be disconnected from mice. For their part owls give a mouse more than one thing at a time to think about, so it is never boring to be a mouse. It is very exciting to be a mouse, so exciting she trembles and quivers continually from having different possible events to think about and different places to go that she might not come back from.

[...]

Some Mice Are Born Over And Over Again

Inside the stable a village of born over again mice lies mainly sleeping in their nests, young and grown ones mixed together with their furry bodies touching. In the newest nest a pile of furless pink infants lie mixed together in a pyramid formation.

A mama mouse whose alert eyes peer from the straw has nests and gathered stashes everywhere in the stable. She has found by staying near one gathering place of floor all kinds of usable objects will fall from the bodies of passing animals and humans. What she likes to gather in her stashes are feathers, bits of bone and leather, things dropped by the humans such as old biscuits, string and shiny pins and beads, even a heavy metal ring that took so much long neck stretching to carry.

All these usable objects she put in several places of storage along with large chunks of vegetable greens growing on stalks around the stable door and most of all the continual grains that so often dribble from the perpetually chewing mouths of donkeys who live in the stable. Her grown sons from the first litter live in their own bachelor nests or sleep in the daytime with their sisters. Her daughter mice have nests of their own or sometimes come to sleep with her and her newest born infants.

For herself the mama mouse is exceptional at digging, at hollowing, at hiding and at finding. She is very good at squealing. She is somewhat good at climbing and very good at looking after her children, at cleaning and at storing. She is extremely good at shredding. She is not at all so good at weaving, at pounding, at pouncing or at growling. In her village inside the stable she likes to make a lot of paths, she likes to have a lot of nests to sleep in and a lot of storage. She does not care so much for open spaces except on mating nights when she loves to run

wild and dancing in the open where she can be certain to be chased and where she can make certain that the mate chasing has enough running enthusiasm to be advantageous to future mice.

The mama mouse was a careful self-contained individual who enjoyed washing her face while sitting in the early morning sunshine and running up the walls to find interesting high perches. She loved to eat the greens that grew outside the door of the stable. She was never so foolish about what to bring home for storage as her brother mouse who ambitiously attempted one night to drag away a donkey by its hock, and who was mashed under the hay for the enormity of his vision. The mama mouse lived for a period of two years and three months, and bore an average of eight babies every two months following her own two-month childhood, totalling ninety-six new mice of whom fifty-four were females, eleven of those living to have babies and each of them producing a number of daughters though only one lived as long as their original mother did.

By the end of her life the mama mouse had been already responsible for contributing 2,916 of her own kind to the world, some two hundred fifty or more pounds of mice, most of whom had made a wealth of living for the various barn owls, shrews, voles and moles, hawks, frogs, snakes, ants, wasps, beetles, cats and weasels who pass through stables and other mousely places. Many of those she fed depend so thoroughly on her provision that her habits have completely formed their body shapes, eyesights, hearings, sleeping patterns, body movements, stances, attention spans, habitats, digestions, nervous systems, states of mind, and relative positions in the world. In return they gave her their undivided attention and plenty of reason for living.

Of this her second litter, thirteen babies had been born. One was immediately dead which she pushed out efficiently along with the turds, uneaten scraps and other trash. The rest of the new babies pleased her immensely not so much yet as individuals as a moving warm conglomerate with pretty pointed pink faces sucking milk from her breasts and twittering with cries that she left only after the second day and then only for the water she could extract from a melon rind dropped by a passing human.

The new babies were five days old when Margedda's fingers found them, folded all around themselves to form a ball with a labyrinthian middle in a similarly round house of straw and shredded apron left hanging over a rail by a stable hand from the Lion clan, to judge by its blue color. The blue fibers mixed attractively with the straw bundle surrounding the twelve who lay in a softly padded hollow with their big sister sleeping curled around them. The sister mouse who was half grown and covered with bright straw-colored fur did not squeal but ran out of the house when Margedda's monstrous hand lifted the outside layer of shredded hay with her big fingers reaching in to gather three of the stretching clean warm babies.

"It's only me, the human owl," she whispered, carefully replacing the nest with its curled outer sheath and topping hay. As she reached her fingers holding one pink naked infant toward the little triangle of owl beak showing through bedraggled fluffy facial feathers she remembered that Blueberry Jon had said he thought the mother owl might chew up the baby's food before feeding her. Margedda's own face recoiled in horror at this possibility, and she was greatly relieved when the little beak opened and the little mouth closed over her offering. "That's a good baby," she murmured, offering a second helping. When the owl did not accept the third naked mouse she wondered if she had been too hasty in taking three at one time.

"Margedda, Margedda," suddenly she could hear her mother calling her along the street outside the stable. She could tell it was her mother not only because her name was being publicly called and who besides her mother ever called her name? In addition, she could tell because her mother Gedda had a way of pronouncing words that differed from everyone else in the city, differed from Blueberry Jon's words and even differed from her daughter Margedda's words.

She jerked to her feet with the birdcage bobbing against her arm. Gedda would not appreciate her long disappearance and the search she had to make to find her daughter. She would not appreciate, Margedda felt certain, her crouching in a stable in her festival dress hunting for mice. Most of all, she would not appreciate the precious pink mouse infant clutched in her palm like a piece of fig candy, nor were there any pockets or secret places in the ceremonial dress.

"I'm keeping this for you until later," Margedda whispered fiercely to the startled ball of owl clinging to the side of the slatted box, and then she popped the warm little body into her mouth where it lay quietly sleeping between her tongue and cheek.

How Cooking Took A Long Time To Learn

"The bread of Ana," Ernesta heard someone say and someone else handed her a bread cake. This had been made, she knew, by the Tortoise clan in their public bakery ovens, the dough mixed and endlessly mixed with great paddles in ceramic troughs to be poured into bread molds six inches long shaped into Ana with crescent horns coming from her head, bread the shape of Ana who had made so much variety of life possible, to remind them that the earth is quiet until someone knows to turn it over as the wind and rain turn it over; that grain is inedible grass until someone knows to swell and tend and harvest its seeds and how to dance to them and talk to them and tell them about human problems of digestion and chewing and desirability of texture and cooking.

In her Ana-shaped cake she knew the powers of Ana were being personified and remembered in the millions of women on the earth stooping over their fires and their fields and their wild meadows who had accumulated and passed on the shared knowledge of how and why to make bread; how and why to control small pieces of fire, how and why to grow the grain heads, and to soften them, grind them, mix them, form them, bake them in the heat. All this reminded them that bread is not a free form occurence but is a collective labor, a cooperation between themselves, the earth and sky, a willful body of knowledge they called Ana.

Ernesta began to think of such things as she chewed the first dark sweet bite of her bread cake, having strong feelings when she looked at the figure with her arms raised bent at the elbow and her tiny bread breasts bared in the position of veneration and nourishment she had seen her mother and her aunts do so many times.

Ernesta decided to eat her Ana cake from the feet upward so she would take the longest time to kill her great body and her face, though sneaking looks at Jessi-ma next to her in her paint and mass of black and yellow Bee clan robes she saw her friend begin with the hands first, then the head; then one breast. She also saw when Jessi-ma dropped her entire cake on the floor, snatching it back quickly to wipe it on her robe hoping no one would notice. And when she met her eyes the giggles welled up again and she had to turn away or choke on her joke with Jessi-ma instead of paying attention to the bread cake of Ana.

As Ernesta bit into the belly of the bread cake she saw across the room sitting with the Tortoise clan women Dee a girl who had been with them when they spent the day recently at the river, and she watched her as she stuffed all of her cake into her mouth at once, then pulled some of it out sticky with saliva and not a bit self conscious that she had so grossly overreached herself. She was standing nearly naked, a white and yellow tortoise painted on her stomach with sun rays coming off the shell and the nose pointed in an upward direction, toward the north of her mouth. In her nakedness she looked much younger than she really was.

The adults, Ernesta noticed, chewed their cakes carefully, wiping their fingers on the insides of their clothing, their faces intent with strong feelings and memories, and she tried to imitate their motions as she chewed the remainder of Ana's head.

In a while there was some chanting while the room filled with the heavy smell of smoking incense. People began standing and moving to the fires for the offerings. Her mother Donna was already bending over a small flame with a long handled silver skillet in one hand. Smiling in understanding into Ernesta's watching eyes Donna took a pouch from her belt, drawing open the strings and taking from it five greenish black seeds she had gathered from her spirit mate during the midnight trek she and her daughter had gone on so recently.

So many other things had happened Ernesta had nearly forgotten her meeting with the hairy weed of midnight, and her mother's promise, as she pulled the seeds from their sticky flower pods, "I'll take care of these." Now here she was keeping her promise, arranging the five plump seeds in the long handled offering skillet held over the fire of Ana.

Ernesta wondered just how pleased the scheming weed would be to see her seeds hopping and frying and turning blacker and blacker putting off charcoal odors in the skillet of her mother's loving attention. Certainly they were turning blacker than they ever would have turned ripening on the bush of their origination, and smelling far differently besides.

Ernesta herself was not so concerned with these matters, she was more interested in going outside to a major festival gathering where people were preparing for the dancing. In the center of the courtyard of the Sun temple the men had built the largest fire of all, a blaze surrounded by watching people of all the clans plus outlanders. Ernesta saw that her uncle Blueberry Jon and another man were carrying Aunt One's basket, and she became very excited wondering what they would fill it with, would they fill it with bread of Ana, and would they now be eating cakes every day of the year, or would they fill it with food from the carts standing all around steaming and creating flies and people fanning.

Aunt One stepped near the fire while everyone grew silent.

"I wish my basket to be an idea of baskets," Aunt One said, and so saying she helped the men place the tall basket in the center of the largest fire the men had made in front of the temple of Ana, with all the people watching who could see through the crowd of shoulders. To Ernesta's complete amazement Aunt One filled her basket with fire while everyone watched as it blazed out in a flame so hot that the whole basket caught fire all at one time. When this happened the exact shape and structure of the thousands of fibers and wickers and all the different colors and pattern of cranes and snakes woven into the basket were outlined in brilliant white flame, like an idea shell of the basket's entire self.

This idea shell burned out of the basket and into the eyes and the memory of all the onlookers. All the people watching through the crowd of shoulders saw the basket burn into their own memories as the appropriate size and shape of baskets.

From this event on whenever anyone in the city went to make a basket or describe one out loud or brag about or hold their arms in the shape of one, Aunt One's tall burning basket was the idea that came to mind.

The consequence of this is that the size of the people's baskets grew larger as so did their expectations since much more material substance was required to fill the new size than the older smaller sizes. More material substance came into the possession of the people since they had now more storage in the form of larger baskets and the town increasingly materialized with objects and substances unbeknownst before. Aunt One was given credit for these increased material matters of the city at the speeches each year on midsummer's eve and asked to rise and sing her basketmaking song with fervor which she did. Thereafter Aunt One's basket burning was remembered as the most significant event of this particular year's midsummer festival.

Ernesta wondered what all this had to do with cooking. Was cooking the same as ripening on the limb. Was burning in the fire the same as cooking. Was shaping into a form the same as making. Was producing the same as mothering. Was receiving the same as worshipping. Was eating the same as valuing. Was looking the same as eating.

All these questions about cooking passed through Ernesta's mind as she ate the Ana bread and then as she watched Donna's fingers crumble ashes of the scheming weed's precious seeds and then as she watched huge-eyed while Aunt One's idea basket blazed into the minds of the people.

[...]

How Cooking Took A Long Time To Learn

Ernesta knew that cooking took a long time to learn because it took so much effort for Aunt Two to make the largest of her cooking pots. She began working on this one afternoon after talking a long time with her mother Mundane, coming out of the straw house with a long measuring line she and her sister Lattice held, drawing off the dimensions for a large pot in the courtyard on the opposite side from Mundane's house and at right angles to the oak tree.

First constructing a sapling frame which her sisters cut and put into place for her, Caddis next wheeled carts of clay and water from the river in to the courtyard location and set to work with clay up to her elbows and all over her face from wiping the sweat that came to pour down her face of intense working.

Ernesta noticed that she and Margedda were not allowed to help with the new pot although many others were, instead being told to stay in the straw house with Mundane and learn more chants.

One day as she was winding her way through one of the longer and less interesting of the chants Ernesta began talking to her friend Jessi-ma, who was standing in front of her just on the other side of the pig outside the straw house.

"We had to walk such a long time just to get to the ship," Jessi-ma said, "I was afraid we wouldn't get back in time."

"What have you done to your hair," Ernesta said, and just then Margedda stopped saying her own less interesting chant and looked over at her.

"It's the same as it was yesterday," she said. "Why?"

"No, I didn't mean you," Ernesta answered, "I meant *her*," suddenly leaping out the door and looking around, but Jessi-ma wasn't there any more.

"I saw Jessi-ma," she said, feeling strangely bubbly inside her solar plexus, while Margedda stared at her with large eyes and Mundane's broom-shaped head with its white re-coiling though still somewhat fly-away hair bent casually to put more herb leaves on the little pile of coals in her cooking pot.

All month long Aunt Two supervised work on the great pot in the courtyard, a pot shaped like Ana lying on the ground, with a narrow waist and two swollen chambers like a queen bee mother. Ernesta also noticed women from the other clans helping Caddis, as well as gathering wood, huge piles of it stood under the oak tree waiting.

"What's going to get cooked in that huge pot?" Ernesta asked, and her grandmother laughed and tugged on her hair. "Maybe you are," she joked.

Ernesta laughed too though later she felt uneasy when Margedda said to her, "You've never heard of the Snake clan eating young women, have you?" and pretended she had only been joking when Ernesta scoffed, "No, of course not, don't be silly."

They both noticed extra cooking going on in the kitchens, even the bakery people seemed busy these days and they wondered if winter was expected early, was the city stocking up for hard times.

One morning on her way to Mundane's straw house for her morning of enchanting, she was stopped by Margedda, who often got up very early to go roaming by herself, and who had arrived first.

"Guess who's here?—Jessi-ma is back." Margedda was too excited by the news to play a good round of guess-again.

"Where is she?" Ernesta said, whooping with surprised pleasure.

"I saw them down at the dock unloading. They're going to be purified from their voluntary exile and allowed back into the city. The Spider Society is down there smoking and enchanting them now."

Ernesta knew that if the Spider Society waved smoke over the returning exiles their magnetic field would be changed so they could fit back into the city without bitterness on anyone's part. She felt bubbles in her solar plexus again, and when she saw Jessi-ma walking past the Snake clan house that evening she was not surprised to see that her hair was totally changed. Instead of a large fuzzy mass sticking out of her head like a lively beehive her hair now wound around her head in metrical coils and then hung in three dozen tight shining braids with elaborate beadings at the ends of each strand.

Jessi-ma was glad to see her and her hair was impressive in its new design but she looked tired and sad. "We had to walk so far to get to the ship we almost missed it," she said.

"I know," Ernesta said. "You came to me and told me."

"I didn't know if I would get back in time."

"In time for what?" Ernesta asked but Sonia and Jon Lilly came by just then and came to give her a hug of greeting.

Three Can Come Back If They See Cooking As Dreaming

"Mama sent Jon after them weeks ago," Aunt Three explained. "She didn't tell any of us. He hooked a ride on a commercial fishing boat clear down to the metropolis of Celeste and just asked around for days until he found them. Sonia was doing fairly well, living with some relatives, though of course not as happy and active as she was here. Getting that temple built here has become her whole life's focus, the focus of her entire priesthood."

Aunt Two snorted as she lifted breakfast cakes from her flat cooking grill. "I can't understand what Mama is up to. She certainly doesn't want a stone temple built here. She thinks the Bee clan is entirely too single-minded in their measurement. She says they're only seeing lines and forgetting spaces. She says one creature's line is another's space."

"She told Jon to tell Sonia that if Jessi-ma would undergo the blood ceremony with Ernesta everything would fit into place for them to come back." Aunt Three chuckled. "Then she had to give the Tortoise clan practically everything she brought back from her trip to get them to listen to her plan. They agreed to stop cursing Sonia, though, just as they agreed for us to take on Margedda and prepare her for the Spider Society."

Ernesta drew in her breath and her aunts looked at her where she stood in the doorway to the common kitchen still in her nightclothes. "I found blood in my bed," she said, and an endless hush followed by electric ripples of excitement fell into the room as though from a great distance.

Certain Events Of Cooking Take Time To Dress For

Ernesta threw the beads back into the bowl in disgust letting the desultory impatient braid uncoil once more in Jessi-ma's long fingers of friendship and oil and the sharing of style. "This doesn't feel right at all," she exploded, "I don't think it's going to work for my hair. Besides, it's taking all day long."

"Well of course it takes all day," Jessi-ma said with a newfound patience that irritated Ernesta.

The beads of Jessi-ma's hair have such mathematical significance of measurement and counting as to be breathtaking in their coordination. Blue, red and black beads of emotion for the heart, head and overall strength and certainty of feeling lay along the careful spiral coils of fascination on her head and down her neck. The journey she had made by ship was present in a set of parallel coils that led to a diamond shaped bed of beads on the crown of her head.

In addition, as she explained to Ernesta, the shapes and colors of the beads have significance. Triangle, round and rectangular beads gave indication of the shapes and figures she would use in her life as a Bee clan woman of architecture and a shaper of numbers of material matters. Blue beads indicate hundreds, red tens, and black means zero if it occurs in the bottom row, or one if it occurs between rows. In addition, she explained, each placement of each bead means a syllable in the language of the singing priesthood of the metropolis that is the place of origin for the Bee clan, before they made their sojourn to Mundane's world to mark a geodetic center for measuring the surface of the earth. "Certain spirits are honored by certain configurations," she explained.

"The beads just don't mean the same things in my hair as they do in yours," Ernesta told Jessi-ma. "They don't even want to stay there."

Since Margedda had also begun to bleed, just a few days after Ernesta's first showing of menstrual blood, the aunts had explained that the great pot in the oak tree courtyard was for the menstrual initiation that all girls undergo in the city of Mundane. Since two other girls, Dee and Fran-keen, had also begun to bleed and were scheduled for sponsorship by the pan-clan Spider Society rather than the more local women's societies within their own clans, everyone waited only for Jessi-ma's womb to release the full wash of its adulthood for the blood ritual to begin.

"You'll spend four days in the pot with the other girls," Mundane explained to Margedda and Ernesta, "dreaming together on a bed of hot rocks."

"So you do have a way of cooking us," Ernesta said.

"Yes," her grandmother laughed, "We have a way of cooking up girls into women."

Margedda was sure she could predict the very hour that Jessi-ma's periodic bleeding would start, hardly letting her out of sight so she could readjust her current predictions as needed. The three girls spent hours together each day now, preparing their clothing with the help of Ernesta's aunts. They took lots of time to hunt for special feathers and flowers to dry, for shells at the river's edge and other valuable decorative items. Margedda watched her owl companion like a hawk, catching each discarded bit of down for use in her dress, that had tufts of feathers woven over the front to attract the power of birds of prey. No longer living in a slatted box the owl preferred standing on furniture dropping tiny feathers in a welter of fast scratching.

Ernesta found two perfect buzzard tailfeathers lying in a bush on a shale beach near the river that had changed shape since the night of flooding. They were as though waiting for her and she put them on the end of the sash she had woven for herself on Aunt One's small belt loom, along with some acorn shells given by the oak tree.

"The oak tree offers her acorns to all and sundry," she said, "but for a buzzard to give me these feathers is a rare event, for they are stingy with their feathers."

For Ernesta the clothing was not at all difficult, she easily chose the heavy brocaded dress that her mother had worn for her own blood ceremony, and Aunt One altered it for her. For Ernesta the difficult part was deciding on a configuration for her hair that would suit the bearing and the balance of her being.

"How you wear your hair has to do with how you wear your own life," Aunt Three said, and everyone else agreed.

Margedda easily arranged the tendrils of her populated wilderness hair and sat for two days out on the roof carving a ceremonial comb to wear of fragrant sandalwood using Aunt Three's carving tools and Aunt Two's pottery polishing stones. She had no trouble arranging the power of her hair, however her dress was another matter, nothing she could think of made sense for her to wear.

Sonia had made her daughter Jessi-ma a yellow, blue and black dress with geometric designs for this occasion years ago and many commented her hair had never looked better than with the rearrangement of it that Sonia now did at great length, of twenty-eight moon braids spiraling from the crown of her head with beads signifying names, facts and measurements of time according to the geodetic time keeping in the temples of the Bee clan of architecture and measurement. Jessi-ma spent her preparation time worrying about her residual childhood clumsiness and making up musical songs to accompany the Celestial star stories told in her beaded hair, as her first blood began to come down on the morning following a dream Margedda had had of seeing drops of blood on fingertips that resembled the silver surface of the moon.

Boys at the Rodeo

A lot of people have spent time on some women's farm this summer of 1972, and one day six of us decide to go to the rodeo. We are all mature and mostly in our early thirties. We wear Levis and shirts and short hair. Susan has shaved her head.

The man at the gate, who looks like a cousin of the sheriff, is certain we are trying to get in for free. It must have been something in the way we are walking. He stares into Susan's face. "I know you're at least fourteen," he says. He slaps her shoulder, in that comradely way men have with each other. That's when we know he thinks we are boys.

"You're over thirteen," he says to Wendy.

"You're over thirteen," he says to me. He examines each of us closely, and sees only that we have been outdoors, are muscled, and look him directly in the eye. Since we are too short to be men, we must be boys. Everyone else at the rodeo are girls.

We decide to play it straight, so to speak. We make up boys' names for each other. Since Wendy has missed the episode with Susan at the gate, I slap her on the shoulder to demonstrate. "This is what he did." Slam. She never missed a step. It didn't feel bad to me at all. We laugh uneasily. We have achieved the status of fourteen-year-old boys, what a disguise for traveling through the world. I split into two pieces for the rest of the evening, and have never decided if it is worse to be thirty-one years old and called a boy or to be thirty-one years old and called a girl.

Irregardless, we are starved and so decide to eat, and here we have the status of boys for real. It seems to us that all the men and all the women attached to the men and most of the children are eating steak dinner plates; and we are the only women not attached to men. We eat hot dogs, which cost one-tenth as much. A man who has taken a woman to the rodeo on this particular day has to have at least $12 to spend. So he has charge of all of her money and some of our money too, for we average $3 apiece and have taken each other to the rodeo.

Hot dogs in hand we escort ourselves to the wooden stands, and first is the standing-up ceremony. We are pledging allegiance to the way of life—the competition, the supposed masculinity and pretty girls. I stand up, cursing, pretending I'm in some other country. One which has not been rediscovered. The loudspeaker plays "Anchors Aweigh," that's what I like about rodeos, always something unexpected. At the last one I attended in another state, the men on horses threw candy and nuts to the kids, chipping their teeth and breaking their noses. Who is it, I wonder, that has put these guys in charge. Even quiet mothers raged over that episode.

Now it is time for the rodeo queen contest, and a display of four very young women on horses. They are judged for queen 30 percent on their horse*man*-ship and 70 percent on the number of queen tickets which people bought on their behalf to "elect" them. Talk about stuffed ballot boxes. I notice the winner as usual is the one on the registered thoroughbred whose daddy owns tracts and tracts of something—lumber, minerals, animals. His family name is all over the county.

The last loser sits on a scrubby little pony and lives with her aunt and uncle. I pick her for a dyke even though it's speculation without clues. I can't help it, it's a pleasant habit. I wish I could give her a ribbon. Not for being a dyke, but for sitting on her horse well. For believing there ever was a contest, for not being the daughter of anyone who owns thousands and thousands of tracts of anything.

Now the loudspeaker announces the girls' barrel races, which is the only grown women's event. It goes first because it is not really a part of the rodeo, but more like a mildly athletic variation of a parade by women to introduce the real thing. Like us boys in the stands, the girls are simply bearing witness to someone else's act.

The voice is booming that barrel racing is a new, modern event, that these young women are the wives and daughters of cowboys, and barrel racing is a way for them to participate in their own right. How generous of these northern cowboys to have resurrected barrel racing for women and to have forgotten the hard roping and riding which women always used to do in rodeos when I was younger. Even though I was a town child, I heard thrilling rumors of the all-women's rodeo in Texas, including that the finest Brahma bull rider in all of Texas was a forty-year-old woman who weighed a hundred pounds.

Indeed, my first lover's first lover was a big heavy woman who was normally slow as a cold python, but she was just hell when she got up on a horse. She could rope and tie a calf faster than any cowboy within five hundred miles of Sweetwater, Texas. That's what the West Texas dykes said, and they never lied about anything as important to them as calf roping, or the differences between women and men. And what about that news story I had heard recently on the radio, about a bull rider who was eight months pregnant? The newsman just had apoplectic fits over her, but not me, I was proud of her. She makes me think of all of us who have had our insides so overly protected from jarring we cannot possibly get through childbirth without an anesthetic.

While I have been grumbling these thoughts to myself, three barrels have been set up in a big triangle on the field, and the women one by one have raced their horses around each one and back to start. The trick is to turn your horse as sharply as possible without overthrowing the barrel.

After this moderate display, the main bulk of the rodeo begins, with calf roping, bronco riding, bull riding. It's a very male show during which the men demonstrate their various abilities at immobilizing, cornering, maneuvering and conquering cattle of every age.

A rodeo is an interminable number of roped and tied calves, ridden and unridden broncos. The repetition is broken by a few antics by the agile, necessary clown. His long legs nearly envelop the little jackass he is riding for the satire of it.

After a number of hours they produce an event I have never seen before—goat tying. This is for the girls eleven and twelve. They use one goat for fourteen participants. The goat is supposed to be held in place on a rope by a large man on horseback. Each girl rushes out in a long run halfway across the field, grabs the animal, knocks it down, ties its legs together. Sometimes the man lets his horse drift so the goat pulls six or eight feet away from her, something no one would allow to happen in a male event. Many of the girls take over a full minute just to do their tying, and the fact that only one goat has been used makes everybody say, "poor goat, *poor* goat," and start laughing. This has become the real comedy event of the evening, and the purpose clearly is to show how badly girls do in the rodeo.

Only one has broken through this purpose to the other side. One small girl is not disheartened by the years of bad training, the ridiculous cross-field run, the laughing superior man on his horse, *or* the shape-shifting goat. She downs it in a beautiful flying tackle. This makes me whisper, as usual, "that's the dyke," but for the rest of it we watch the girls look ludicrous, awkward, outclassed and totally dominated by the large handsome man on horse. In the stands we six boys drink beer in disgust, groan and hug our breasts, hold our heads and twist our faces at each other in embarrassment.

As the calf roping starts up again, we decide to use our disguises to walk around the grounds. Making our way around to the cowboy side of the arena, we pass the intricate mazes of rail where the stock is stored, to the chutes where they are loading the bull riders onto the bulls.

I wish to report that although we pass by dozens of men, and although we have pressed against wild horses and have climbed on rails overlooking thousands of pounds of angry animalflesh, though we touch ropes and halters, we are never once warned away, never told that this is not the proper place for us, that we had better get back for our own good, are not safe, etc., none of the dozens of warnings and threats we would have gotten if we had been recognized as thirty-one-year old girls instead of fourteen-year-old boys. It is a most interesting way to wander around the world for the day.

We examine everything closely. The Brahma bulls are in the chutes, ready to be released into the ring. They are bulky, kindly looking creatures with rolling eyes; they resemble overgrown pigs. One of us whispers, "Aren't those the same kind of cattle that walk around all over the streets in India and never hurt anybody?"

Here in the chutes made exactly their size, they are converted into wild antagonistic beasts by means of a nasty belt around their loins, squeezed tight to mash their most tender testicles just before they are released into the ring. This torture is supplemented by a jolt of electricity from an electric cattle prod to make sure they come out bucking. So much for the rodeo as a great drama between man and nature.

A pale nervous cowboy sits on the bull's back with one hand in a glove hooked under a strap around the bull's midsection. He gains points by using his spurs during the ride. He has to remain on top until the timing buzzer buzzes a few seconds after he and the bull plunge out of the gate. I had always considered it the most exciting event.

Around the fence sit many eager young men watching, helping, and getting in the way. We are easily accepted among them. How depressing this can be.

Out in the arena a dismounted cowboy reaches over and slaps his horse fiercely on the mouth because it has turned its head the wrong way.

I squat down peering through the rails where I see the neat, tight-fitting pants of two young men standing provocatively chest to chest.

"Don't you think Henry's a queer," one says with contempt.

"Hell, I *know* he's a queer," the other says. They hold an informal spitting contest for the punctuation. Meantime their eyes have brightened and their fronts are moving toward each other in their clean, smooth shirts. I realize they are flirting with each other, using Henry to bring up the dangerous subject of themselves. I am remembering all the gay cowboys I ever knew. This is one of the things I like about cowboys. They don't wear those beautiful pearl button shirts and tight Levis for nothing.

As the events inside the arena subside, we walk down to a roped-off pavilion where there is a dance. The band consists of one portly, bouncing enthusiastic man of middle age who is singing with great spirit into the microphone. The rest of the band are three grim, lean young men over fourteen. The drummer drums angrily, while jerking his head behind himself as though searching the air for someone who is already two hours late and had seriously promised to take him away from here. The two guitar players are sleepwalking from the feet up with their eyes so glassy you could read by them.

A redhaired man appears, surrounded by redhaired children who ask, "Are you drunk, Daddy?"

"No, I am not drunk," Daddy says.

"Can we have some money?"

"No," Daddy says, "I am not drunk enough to give you any money."

During a break in the music the redhaired man asks the bandleader where he got his band.

"Where did I get this band?" the bandleader puffs up, "I raised this band myself. These are all my sons—I raised this band myself." The redhaired man is so very impressed he is nearly bowing and kissing the hand of the bandleader, as they repeat this conversation two or three times. "This is *my* band," the bandleader says, and the two guitar players exchange grim and glassy looks.

Next the bandleader has announced "Okie from Muskogee," a song intended to portray the white country morality of cowboys. The crowd does not respond but he sings enthusiastically anyway. Two of his more alert sons drag themselves to the microphone to wail that they don't smoke marijuana in Muskogee—as those hippies down in San Francisco do, and they certainly don't. From the look of it they shoot hard drugs and pop pills.

In the middle of the song a very drunk thirteen-year-old boy has staggered up to Wendy, pounding her on the shoulder and exclaiming, "Can you dig it, brother?" Later she tells me she has never been called brother before, and she likes it. Her first real identification as one of the brothers, in the brotherhood of man.

We boys begin to walk back to our truck, past a cowboy vomiting on his own pretty boots, past another lying completely under a car. Near our truck, a young man has calf-roped a young woman. She shrieks for him to stop, hopping weakly along behind him. This is the first bid for public attention I have seen from any woman here since the barrel race. I understand that this little scene is a re-enactment of the true meaning of the rodeo, and of the conquest of the West. And oh how much I do not want to be her; I do not want to be the conquest of the West.

I am remembering how the clown always seems to be tall and riding on an ass, that must be a way of poking fun at the small and usually dark people who tried to raise sheep or goats or were sod farmers and rode burros instead of tall handsome blond horses, and who were driven under by the beef raisers. And so today we go to a display of cattle handling instead of a sheep shearing or a goat milking contest—or to go into even older ghost territory, a corn dance, or acorn gathering—

As we reach the truck, the tall man passes with the rodeo queen, who must surely be his niece, or something. All this non-contest, if it is for anyone, must certainly be for him. As a boy, I look at him. He is his own spitting image, of what is manly and white and masterly, so tall in his high heels, so *well-horsed*. His manner portrays his theory of life as the survival of the fittest against wild beasts, and all the mythical rest of us who are too female or dark, not straight, or much too native to the earth to now be trusted as more than witnesses, flags, cheerleaders and unwilling stock.

As he passes, we step out of the way and I am glad we are in our disguise. I hate to step out of his way as a full-grown woman, one who hasn't enough class status to warrant his thinly polite chivalry. He has knocked me off the sidewalk of too many towns, too often.

Yet somewhere in me I know I have always wanted to be manly, what I mean is having that expression of courage, control, coordination, ability I associate with men. To *provide*.

But here I am in this truck, not a man at all, a fourteen-year-old boy only. Tomorrow is my thirty-second birthday. We six snuggle together in the bed of this rickety truck which is our world for the time being. We are headed back to the bold and shaky adventures of our all-women's farm, our all-women's households and companies, our expanding minds, ambitions and bodies, we who are neither male nor female at this moment in the pageant world, who are not the rancher's wife, mother earth, Virgin Mary or the rodeo queen—we who are really the one who took her self seriously, who once took an all-out dive at the goat believing that the odds were square and that she was truly in the contest.

And now that we know it is not a contest, just a play—we have run off with the goat ourselves to try another way of life.

Because I certainly do not want to be a thirty-two-year old girl, or calf either, and I certainly also do always remember Gertrude Stein's beautiful dykely voice saying, what is the use of being a boy if you grow up to be a man.

Green Toads of the High Desert

My mom giggles like a little kid who has gotten away with something naughty when I ask her whether she has stopped writing to everyone or just me. I haven't gotten a note from her for three weeks, and I don't tell her I am worried, I just ask the question and then listen to the giggling. She is taking open delight in not writing, that much I can tell, even over the telephone.

"Who is this?" she asks after we exchange a few more how are you's. Usually I respond, "Judith," which with her particular hearing problem is almost guaranteed to make her guess "Edith?" She says the name very slowly, like "E-space-space-*dith?*" in two ascending high whole notes. She has been talking slow-syllabled like that all year, effortfully, as though the jaw is on strike and taking over the company.

Edith was our neighbor and close family friend who has been dead for seven years, a crossing which doesn't seem to have impressed my mom. Time has become compressed for her. Or maybe she's right. Maybe it is Edith on the phone, sometimes, calling to remind her of her immortality. This time it is me.

"I'm calling from California." Let's give her a big clue.

"O—hh." I hear wheels clicking across the miles between our two minds. She's going through a short list of names that includes her older sister, who moved to Bakersfield twelve years ago. And then the explosion of pleasure: "*Ju*-dith!"

She is ninety-two this year, and busy giving up one thing or another, a matter of "going light" I should say, the way birds do when they lose weight in certain seasons. Except she is also becoming luminous and high-humored. "How's Kris?" she asks, immediately adding, "She's your other part." This was not how she was ten years ago, when I first took Kris out to meet my parents, the year before my father died. By the time Mom and I have said our half-dozen goodbye I love you's and hung up the phone, I am remembering that trip.

We'd only been together a couple of months when I wrote Mom and Dad that I had a new friend who was a mechanic and we were coming to visit. My folks live in the high desert of New Mexico and we took off in Kris' avocado green VW bus. We weren't yet living together, and full of hesitations to try it, and nothing lets you know whether you can live intimately or not as completely as being nose to nose for ten days in the confines of a vehicle.

I thought this trip would give us plenty of time to talk, as there were so many subjects we had been avoiding, but the first day's drive told me differently. With no air conditioner to mediate the August heat blast we had all windows down, a favorite way for her to drive anyhow, and in all seasons. In the roar of moving air and shrieking trucks, she put Bonnie Raitt on the tape deck and cranked up the sound till we were splitting the sky open with enthusiastic harmonics to Bonnie's sweet dark country western. Endangered by the dry oven blast, we guzzled water and citrus drinks across the chest-searing sauna that is an un-airconditioned car in the Mojave Desert in summer, and then turned south along the brilliant blue knife of Colorado River across the Arizona border.

Gila Bend is a tiny town on a blistering bit of road in southern Arizona.

It was named for a colorful and rare huge lizard which had become exotified and demonized. In my childhood, roadside sheds with screaming red and yellow signs had featured them for voyeuristic scrutiny, along with rattlesnakes and other hapless desert creatures who happen to use venom in earning a living. Tourists were enticed to stop and spend money to gape at the little dying prisoners in their cages, feeling grateful not to be stepping on them. I had always hated these displays, and still had an attitude toward the town though such misuses of creatures were now illegal.

So it seemed to me our journey turned ominous when the bus lurched and Kris guided us with a deflating tire to the exit for Gila Bend, late in what remained of the blistering August afternoon.

The station attendant was amiable, and the amount of sweat pouring off us all day had made us dull-headed so we decided to stay overnight and the gas station guy recommended a motel.

My first shock once we were in the room was noticing some kind of steam coming off the toilet water, so that for a second I wondered if I hadn't overheated my bladder and my own pee was steaming the commode like a radiator in the desert. The second shock was turning on the cold water tap and nearly scalding my hands. "What the hell is this?"

"All the water in town is the same temperature—ninety-two degrees," the motel manager reported to our inquiry. "Just don't ever turn on the hot water at the same time as the 'cold' and you won't really scald yourself," he assured us.

We watched as buckets of ice vanished into the steamy vapors of the "cold" water tap before we could get a sip to the lips. Setting down our cups, we looked at each other. The unspoken question of whether we were going to make love at this stop hung in the air for a moment, as each of us searched inside, finding the reality of our tiredness. This was a disappointing part of the trip—I had imagined that we would be steaming lusciously skin to skin in motel beds or even the bus, which featured its own bed. Instead, the trip was steaming us.

"Let's try the swimming pool," Kris suggested hopefully, so we grabbed suits and towels and followed the signs along the broiling cement driveway.

The motel had two pools, one big steamy one and a glimmering shallow wading pool. "This could be sort of like a hot tub," I suggested doubtfully. The shallow pool did look inviting with its blue and cream tiles, despite the warm mist lifting off its surface.

"Why don't we relax in warm water in the evening when it's cooler?" Okay, I agreed.

In the late evening though it wasn't what anyone would call "cooler" we put on suits and nestled together in the small pool. This was more than worth it for the rare chance to be close in semi-public, and for the added exhilaration of being outdoors under the naked sky in an intimate situation. This didn't appear to be a popular tourist stopping place. No one was around so we treated the small pool like our personal bed, the water's calm seeping like deep psychic pleasure into sore muscles, our throats opening to long cold streams from the cans of pop we drank to cool our insides. She put one arm around me and we laid our heads against the slick tiles that rimmed the luminous silky water.

Our bodies were stretched out langorously floating in that idyllic state, next best thing to sex, resting half-excitedly against each other when from the corner of my eye I saw a moving shadow and sensed a being rising from the lower depths of water. "Naw," I thought to my instantly pounding heart. "Now I'm hallucinating, the heat of the drive sure must have gotten to me." I nuzzled my chin against her shoulder and shifted so my head was leaning on her upper chest. Her breast fell along my cheek. I dropped into a doze, awakened by a sensation of a bumping from underneath, and instantly my childhood as a desert kid came skittering toward me with the Grade B-movie experience of coming eye to eye with a tarantula in the public swimming pool, or the sense my body gave of flying around the room the day the long segmented—very, very long segmented—centipede climbed out of the drain in the bathtub while I was in it.

As an adult I had used these fears to try to understand other peoples' fears of me as a lesbian. I had figured, if I can learn to get over my fear of a centipede, others can learn to get over their fears of me. Not bad reasoning, as far as it went. And I'd discovered that centipedes were good mothers, wrapping those long bodies protectively around their broods. Somehow that made me like them better. But those were real insects, not some phantom seen from the corner of a sleepy eye.

Then I believed I felt her hand approaching my midsection, and thought how daring the woman was, out here in the open to hold me and now to reach to fondle me. I opened my eyes to smile at her. Then I clutched Kris and let out a shriek, limbs flailing and neck stretched far away from a scratchy insistent and very concrete monster that had just crawled onto my stomach.

"What is it what is it what is it!" I cried out, thrashing my way out of the pool like a panicky poodle.

"I don't know," Kris said, "you tell me—I didn't see anything, my eyes were closed. I was napping." She had climbed out with me, somewhat disgustedly I thought. How undignified I must look with my eyes popping out of my head, shrieking. Oh no, she's going to think I'm a hysteric who can't be trusted in difficult situations. Calming down now that I saw the mysterious stranger was not following me, I peered back into the water. "Where did it go?"

"Where is what?" Kris still looked skeptical. Not only was it not following me, now it didn't seem to be anywhere, and I worried she would think I was the kind of woman who would wake her up every other night expecting her to explore mysterious house noises with a flashlight.

"There it is!" I pointed to a slight shadowy pale form hovering in the silky pool light, and began to laugh, then got back into the water. "It's a little toad. Must have been trying to climb out. Must be trapped in this little pool." I slid my hand under the eagerly swimming body, barely visible as an outline in its watery camouflage.

"Oh, how beautiful it is," Kris exclaimed over what has to have been the palest shade of green anyone ever wore, even the gold eyes were light as mineral shavings. I turned the little creature loose on the paving and we watched as she hopped away. "Why does it look like such a ghost?" I wondered.

"The hot water turns them pale. They live in the pipes all over town," the motel manager later said in answer to our question. "You wouldn't think they could survive in this hot water, but they do."

When we filled up with gas in the morning the gas station guy explained more about the water. "Used to be eighty-seven degrees but everybody in town believed the hotshot engineering advisors and drilled a new, deeper well at more than anyone could afford and now it's five degrees hotter. See here. The water stains everyone's teeth and erodes them away," he said, showing his own poor teeth: dark stubs in a trapped mouth. "S'ruined the town. I'd move away too, but this is my business and I can't leave it," he mourned. "Oooh," I said sympathetically.

I thought about him on the mountainous drive over the New Mexico border to the town of Lordsburg, where we spent our second night. How a person can get fatally wrapped up in what they have already done, as though life is a fishnet we weave around our own feet. This reminded me of my last relationship, how I could never please her no matter what I did. And the more I tried, the more tangled in I got. Until I was doing things I hated myself for, her displeasure the hook taking me deeper and deeper. The memory made me uneasy as I stared out the window at the saguaro forest around us.

That night once again Kris and I did not make love, despite that the motel room was pleasant and even air-conditioned. Road tiredness, I thought, though our seriousness seemed to be made of something more profound. I debated wearing the new white Levi's I had bought to impress her with, and then slid them back into the suitcase in favor of plainer travel pants. The white pants could wait, and I would know the right moment. After dinner we went for a walk, and to our delight we discovered a park. Even though it was nearly pitch dark we crossed the thin grass to a playground.

"Look at the swings," Kris said. "I love to swing." She sat down on a wooden seat and grasped the chains, which creaked. "Come on," she urged, "don't you like this? This is fun." At first I felt foolish, then I got into the swaying motion with her and forgot my self-consciousness. The creaking chains created a song I found myself examining for hidden meaning.

In the dark, she began to talk earnestly about her past relationship, how she had felt inflexibly identified. Her face was shadowed between the chains of the swing, which glinted every so often, and her voice was all the more easy to listen to because I couldn't see her expressions. I could hear the lyric qualities in it, and the basic optimism.

"I don't want to be that hurt again," she was saying. "I'm not willing to be anything except exactly who I am in a relationship."

"I'm not sure I even want a relationship," I said. Then, to fill in her overly long silence, "I mean, I'm just not ready quite yet to fall over any cliffs." I didn't say, and you don't seem substantial to me; I want someone to rely on, someone with big strong shoulders to lean against. Her shoulders are narrow, her face and neck delicate. My last relationship had worn me out too, I realized.

The moon broke through clouds in a dazzling display of directed light that enveloped us, so I felt we were in a bubble together, and also separately, each watching the other. The chains continued to creak as we rocked back and forth, and though we had resolved nothing whatsoever, a tenderness came between us. We walked out of the park hand in hand, and I was so oblivious to the earth I nearly stepped on a small shape in the road, and I hopped awkwardly over it at the last moment before the crush.

Laughing and puzzled, we turned back to find a small toad, dark olive green and fearlessly possessive of the road. "It's rained here," I said. "Look, there's another one, the town must be full of toads." I remembered my childhood in Las Cruces, how welcome and exciting the brief season of toads was, coming in the late summer rains. "They lie deep under the clay," I explained, "for years if necessary, waiting for a season of wet. Then they just explode all over town. I brought a few tadpoles home once and we put them in a tank—an old Coca-Cola case behind an abandoned store. We watched them get fins, and then legs—it was so exciting."

We walked on and suddenly car lights lit us up, with our hands linked. I cringed as a carload of teenaged boys slowed and began to holler insults. We separated and walked quickly, faces turned alertly to the threatening car. It passed, became more noisy, and swayed to turn. The boys in back were pounding on the sides of the car. I searched the road for a stone or board, anything, frantic that we had left ourselves wide open, weren't even carrying knives. And then the car straightened, and rode on. We breathed again. The insults themselves didn't bother me. They were names for who we are together, and ordinarily I love hearing them. And you could turn even the word "milk" into an ugly name if you holler it angrily enough. But, I wondered, what if they had gotten out to beat us, could we really take care of ourselves, each other, in this world? And fell asleep with this question.

We crested the mesa overlooking Las Cruces from the west around ten in the morning. We would visit my parents only a few hours, partly because in their eighties they grew irritable from too much company, and partly because Kris had to get back to work on Tuesday morning, and it was already Sunday. Whatever happened among us on this first visit would have the rarified effect of severe compression, making each moment an event and each event momentous.

My mom was outside her apartment door. She walked haltingly toward us as though on stilts that reached deep under the earth. When we were close to her she flung herself into Kris' arms. "*Ju*dith!" she cried.

Kris looked startled, hugged her back, then gently turned her and guided her in my direction. "I think this is where you want to go."

"It's me Mom," I said.

"Oh!" she said. "Oh, your hair!" Puzzled, I patted the top of my head. "Hair?" I asked.

Just at that moment Marian came out of her own apartment, downstairs from my parents'. Marian is my mom's age. She wobbled toward me, hand outstretched.

"Congratulations dear," she said, in tones she reserved for graduating students and blushing brides.

This puzzle was followed by another. Once we were each situated in seats upstairs in my parents' living room, my white-bearded father in his wooden arm chair and Kris and I on the rose couch, my mother stood up in the middle of the floor and surprised us all by bursting into tears.

"What is it?" I asked with concern. My father said nothing, just stroked his beard reflectively. He couldn't see anymore, so only his ears could tell him the course of history. My mother doesn't hear, necessitating repetition and sometimes yelling. Their twin conditions had led them to heights of cooperation unimaginable in their younger days, so that watching them cook a dinner together was like watching an intricate dance of the senses turned into two characters on stage. This trip however, we arrived so late in the day they had already accomplished the cooking, as I could tell by the delicious smells wafting from the kitchen. Meantime I was worried that Mom was going to burst out with some dire medical prognosis or other crisis.

On my third query she sobbed, "Oh, it's so awful to be old. Don't ever get old."

I was not satisfied with this, as it is her standard answer when she really cannot say what is bothering her, and since her crying persisted, so did my question. Finally she blurted out, "It's your hair, what have you done to it?"

My hair again. I looked at Kris and shrugged in puzzlement. We had both cropped our hair in preparation for the hot trip. She crops her hair all the time and much shorter than mine, a butch look I find endlessly exciting and challenging. "Don't think this means I am always the butch," she had said emphatically, early in our getting to know each other. "I don't want to be cast in stone or have my tender side overlooked."

Still baffled, I followed my no longer crying mother into the kitchen where she completed preparations for dinner. I knew "what have you done to your hair" was shorthand for something else, a shorthand she had often used when I was living under her roof. Meantime we were immersed in the mechanics of stirring the gravy and mashing the potatoes, and getting Kris to arrange the TV trays that passed for a dining room table and its trappings. My mother filled the plates to her own specifications, and then handed me a full one.

"There you are," she said. "I'll take Elmer his plate and you take Kris his plate."

For once I was the deaf one. "What was that again?"

"I'll take your father his plate and you take Kris his plate."

"Mom," I said, "Kris is not a his."

"Eh?"

"Kris is a she."

"What is it?"

"Kris is not a he—Kris is a woman—a she."

"What are you saying? I don't hear so well." As though I didn't grow up knowing this every day.

"Kris is a SHE." I could hear attentive silence from the living room.

By now I was genuinely shouting: "Kris is a SHE!" And the fifth or sixth time around my mom suddenly got it, throwing her hands to her face and rocking backwards, all the bad aura stuff leaving in a flash of lightning understanding that illuminated her face with a lively glow.

"Oh I'm so glad to hear that!" she said, her joy and relief transferring yet a new puzzle to me. "I'm so glad to hear that." Totally changed, she wiped her face with the bottom of her apron, and then peeked guilelessly as a child around the corner to peer the twelve feet into the living room, where Kris sat with a beatifically controlled face and body language that said 'later I will explode and bend over laughing, but not now.'

"I thought she looked awfully cute to be a man," my mom finished, handing me the plate of food with finality of purpose and settled accomplishment.

I could hear my father in the living room begin to laugh, a cascade that began at the throat and worked its way down to big guffaws and finally toe-rocking spasms that he enjoyed thoroughly for several minutes, until the emphysema took it up and turned it painful and he stopped, wiping water from the corners of his bright, round brown eyes and holding his chest with the flat of his hand saying, "Oh Lord. Oh Lord."

Kris stayed cool as a cucumber through dinner, balancing her plate on her knee. When Mom and I were in the kitchen finishing washing the dishes, the whole time I could hear Kris and my Dad talking, and from various words that drifted in, they were talking shop and talking about crafts and wandering off from that vantage point into their views of the world.

When I walked back into the living room, to my surprise they were both standing up, hugging, Kris the taller of the two.

Two hours later in the green bus traveling north, Kris and I continually howled with laughter over my mother, over my shouting "Kris is a SHE!" and we'd put the greater picture together: that I had written in my note to them only that "Kris was a mechanic and would be coming with me."

"The way you spell your name!" I added.

"My occupation and my haircut," she continued. "And how she thought I was you."

"And all that crying about the hair, she always used to rag on me about my hair, that was the one place where she knew that she had to socialize me and make me do it right, and be a real woman, or she would have failed her mother-mission for certain."

We decided she had been upset because if Kris was a man, how could I do anything so shameful as to drive across the country with him before we were married?

"That must have been what she herself made certain not to do, it's as though she had memorized that particular morality all the way to her bones, whereas the lesbian thing—"

"You said she talked it through with a neighbor—"

"Yes, when I was eighteen, by the time I was living with my first lover and she had met her, you know she loved Von. She took me around the corner into the kitchen after five minutes of the first visit and whispered to me: 'How can I not like her? She's just like you.'"

"Through all her socialization, your mom sees what is really there."

"Yes—except for the hair thing, and the business about riding in a car overnight without being married." As though morality settles out as a few emotionally memorized injunctions, different for each generation. They should come with labels: "Caution, in certain circumstances, this may not apply." I thought about my father wasting no time during our visit, getting out of his chair to hug my new woman after talking to her for only half an hour.

"What did my Dad say to you?"

Her face moved to the tender end of the scale, "Well—he—he said, 'I love you.'"

"My goodness," I said. "He's hardly ever said that to *me*."

"First he said, 'Kris—tell me—what do you look like? I'm too blind to see you.'"

"And you said—? You said, 'oh I look like your average handsome dyke,'" I joked.

She looked very serious. "I said, 'I look okay. I like the way I look.' Then he stood up and gave me a big hug and said, 'I love you.'"

I saw that she was very moved by this. As so was I.

Our drive north had brought us to a right hand turn, the entrance to a portion of New Mexico called La Jornada Del Muerte, The Journey of Death. A group of black vultures stood to the left of the cattle guard that marked the beginning of the dirt road. We stopped to admire them, aware that for us they did not so much signify death as transformation.

The summer rains had saturated the plain, bringing out the vivid redness of the bittersweet clay stretching out on either side, and thousands of yellow, pink, and blue wildflowers. All day our eyes feasted on the silhouettes of distant mountain ranges and the vivacity of desert sage in the middle of flowering enticement, cleared of dust by the showers, stroked by the recent thunders, burgeoning with sap under the thick skin of resistance. We ate my mother's turkey and margarine sandwiches without pulling the bus over, wanting to reach Santa Fe for dinner and rent a beautiful motel room, maybe stay an extra day and have some time to rediscover each other.

About six o'clock a broad puddle reached across the road toward us and Kris steered down the wrong edge of it, thinking it was shallow skim on hardpan. The road melted out from under her and turned pond, sluicing the bus off to the left and deep into the thick entrapping juice, stopping the engine. We looked at each other, and got out.

The red mud stretched indefinitely into the future as I looked at the depth of hub cap sinkage, seeing the white sparkle of my brand new levis in the same field of view. I had worn them this day finally to celebrate our trip, and one thing for sure, I was not going to be the one getting into the mud to dig us out. Kris was the mechanic, let her figure it out. I stood waiting, withholding myself from the problem.

She revved. The bus lurched feebly, sank deeper; she revved again, the bus swept forward, sliding further off to the left, stalled in yet deeper mud. I glowered. She was the butch, she had gotten us into this, now she could damn well get us out.

"What's your plan now?" I snapped as she gave up the driver's seat and came to join me. The sun had lowered dramatically.

"Why don't you dig us out while I steer," she said.

"Me? Me?"

"You have the shoulders for it," she observed. She handed me the little trench shovel. I bugged my eyes at her. I slapped the shovel handle with my other hand. Looked at the gathering overhead blue darkness, felt its deep quiet.

I sighed. Went through a number of inner adjustments. I gave my white levis one last admiring glance, and then surrendered. I felt the surrender all the way to the base of my spine. I wondered just what it was I was surrendering *to*. I hoped I would like it.

I knelt, looked under the car, feeling the water squeeze from the mud onto my knee and down my shin. She touched my back, ran her fingers up the back of my thigh, and when I turned my head her lips were there to meet mine and her tongue was hot and alive.

"Let's make love first," she said.

"Here on the road?" I asked, already climbing into the bus.

"If anyone does come along they'll be too preoccupied trying to drive through this stuff to notice," she reasoned, helping me off with my red-stained jeans.

"I got these pants to impress you," I laughed.

"I'm very impressed," she said, running the flat of her tongue up the inside of my naked thigh before reaching to tug off her own shirt. Her breasts tumbled out like two new friends and I spent some time getting to know them. The first star had already marked the opening of night. By the time we were sex traveling to constellations the sky was beading up millions of stars, each a glistening drop of intensity. Blessed under the blanket of their certain light pulsing in that certain dark I lay in her arms thinking about how easily we exploded together, about the stunningly beautiful visions that spontaneously appeared between us, the inexpressible pierce of her tongue on my clitoris, her underarm smell of mesquite wood, my age-deepening musk, our easy fit in the narrow confines of the vehicle, how my parents had responded to her, how she moaned my name when I slid my fingers into her.

Soon I would be under the bus sweating and swearing, my Levi's saturated in the red juice of earth, an iron smell wrapping around me, mud in my hair and mouth, mud on the sweet apple she fed me around ten o'clock to keep me going. She would cheer me on, her face smeared from hugging me, her hands sturdy on the steering wheel. I would dig with big strong motions and lie down under the back tires fitting the one palm-sized flat stone and the one foot-long rotten board we had found to give the back wheels any kind of traction in the slip-slick road. My sandals one by one would be sucked off into the cloying soup and I would dive for traction with my toes, seeking bedrock. She would drive as she had never driven before, pelvis and knees working, skillfully rocking and shimmying us forward six or ten inches at a time while thick drops spun out and splattered the windows. Her foot out the open door pushing us along. In exhilaration of the effort I would shove my weight against the rear frame timed with her shouts of "Now!" until my muscles went numb and capillary vessels burst in my hands and legs. I would lose the stone and board in deep mud, search the bus to find a glove and one tire chain to substitute, then lose them as well. We would dig and drive a foot at a time through a half mile of road, until two o'clock in the morning when we reached solid ground. And in these simple actions we would know one simple thing. We would know we could get married. We would know she could drive us through and I could dig us through, we would know just how big a distance we could go together in our lives in this avocado green bus or out of it.

For the moment I lay love-spent in her arms, cheek pressed against her sweet mouth, as, their voices rising out of small pools, the whole Jornada del Muerte began to thrum to the rhythms of light green toads, gold-eyed and piping their lovesongs to the heavens, celebrating the end of their waiting, celebrating their climb out of solitary slumber into the time of expressing and connecting. And in that holy time I felt completely enveloped in love, love arriving from every side, pouring over us where we lay together, two women in a timeless covering of the approval of red mud and live reptiles, of insensate but loving parents, and vibrant, vibrant, vibrant stars looking at us, in the certainty of their procession through the night, and exactly as though seeing us, from all around the sky.

DRAMA

The Queen of Swords
A Play with Poetic Myth

Introduction

In my earlier book *The Queen of Wands* (first of four in a series of which this is the second) I began the saga of the goddess Helen, or El-ana, variants of whose name and story appeared repeatedly in European mythology as she ran for cover under the relentless authority of the all-male monotheism that gradually replaced her worship during these last few centuries. As Queen Helen she appeared in the *Iliad* where her abduction was the cause of the great Trojan War, when her husband Menelaus besieged that city for ten years with a thousand ships to get her back from her shepherd-prince-lover Paris. She died at the end of that story, murdered by her own niece and nephew as Greece overthrew its old matriarchy in a welter of blood, guilt, and grief.

But Helen did not really die, the story continued. Rather, she "flew into a cloud"—and will return to us when we are ready. In *Wands* I placed her as a worker (as all workers) in industrial capitalism and as a romantic figure in Euro-American folklore.

Earlier in this century the poet H.D., in *Helen in Egypt,* envisioned her in a haven where she could retain her old Hermetic knowledge. In the novel and subsequent movie *Sophie's Choice,* William Styron placed her in Nazi Germany, where she was tragically asked to choose between her male and female children. More archetypally, Gertrude Stein, in "Dr. Faustus Lights the Lights" in 1938, named her "Marguerite Ida and Helena Annabel," a character who says of herself, "I know no man or devil or viper and no light I can be anything and everything and it is always always alright." Stein apparently took some of Helen's multiple names from Goethe's *Faust.*

In a different story set simultaneously with the life of Jesus, Helen and the great magician/wise man Simon Magus were worshiped together as gods under a plane tree, Simon having found Helen working in a lowly brothel. In a later and more chilling North European tale, the goddess of beauty entices unwary men into the woods by her astounding beauty; once she is certain they can never find their way back, she turns, and they see she is completely hollow inside: there is nothing there. Helen appeared many more times: as Elaine of the Celts, as Hel of the Scandinavians, as Cinderella, Snow White, Helle and Holde of the Germanic and East European tribal and post-tribal folk, as Venus of the Romans. In a worldwide context her prototype is a weaver/fire goddess of fiery beauty and creativity with such diverse names as Ashketanne-mat of the Ainu people of Japan, Oshun, the beauty goddess of West Africa, Pele, the great Hawaiian volcano goddess, Skywoman with her tree of life of the Iroquois, and Chin-nu, the Great Spinster of China.

Sumerian texts of cuneiform writing, found at the beginning of this century and dating to at least 3000 B.C., have been unearthed at archeological sites in the Tigris-Euphrates river valley. From these texts, which are just now beginning to be understood, a great cycle of epic myths is unfolding. They center on the Sumerian goddess of heaven and earth, Inanna. (In neighboring areas she was known as Ishtar and Astarte.)

Practitioners of Jungian psychology, in particular, have translated and interpreted Inanna's stories, including the beautiful, lyric accounts of her sacred marriage to her consort, the bull god Dumuzi, and of her acquisition of the sacred powers of god-hood, the *mes* (pronounced *mays*). For these stories I especially want to call attention to *Inanna: Goddess of Heaven and Earth,* by Diane Wolkstein and Noah Kramer.

I was especially fortunate when, just as I began working on *The Queen of Swords,* Jungian analyst Betty De Shong Meador joined one of my writing classes while she was translating into poetic form the text of a major saga of Inanna. This myth tells of her descent into the underworld, where she confronts its reigning queen, the goddess Ereshkigal (pronounced ER-esh-KEE-gl').

After living with this ongoing translation for several years I have no doubt that Inanna's story informed many later stories about the goddess-queen-harlot figures who are related to Helen, goddess of beauty and love. In *The Queen of Swords,* I have chosen to depict the story of Helen, a modern-day Inanna, as she confronts Ereshkigal. Ereshkigal, the Queen of Swords, is associated in the Tarot deck with air, storms, intelligence, science, piercing violence, and strength. Among people who honor the queen of the underworld she has been called Cerridwen, the Morrigan, Morgan the Faery, Kali, Hel, Persephone, Oyá, and other names representing goddesses of death, rebirth, and the spirit world. She is remembered in our times as the wicked witch, jealous queen, or evil black-garbed woman who appears in stories such as "Snow White" or in comic books such as "Little Lulu."

I found it irresistible to present the relationship between these two female mythic characters, Helen and Ereshkigal, as a Lesbian saga, setting it in an underground Lesbian bar owned by Ereshkigal. The spicy Crow characters, Nothing, and the other naggy notables of the cast followed naturally. The myth itself is so powerful, however, and so profound, that it transcends any fixed setting or easy labeling of the characters. The questions it undertakes to raise concern the nature of life and death, darkness and light, innocence and guilt; how we human beings use the trials of life to transform ourselves from mundane to metaphysical and back again.

The Sumerian story upon which *The Queen of Swords* is based tells of the decision of Inanna, queen of heaven and earth, to go to the "great below," risking everything in order to gather even more powers for the benefit of her cities. She leaves her consort, the bull god Dumuzi, her children, and all heaven and earth in order to undertake this perilous journey. "Mourn for me," she instructs her faithful female minister, Ninshubur, "tear at your eyes and mouth and genitals." Then the great goddess makes her descent to the underworld. This domain, Ganzir, is described as a desert or wilderness; it is ruled by a shamanic queen, Ereshkigal, a Kali-figure of death and transformation. She carries a drum, is naked, stamps her feet, has hair like coiled snakes and long fingernails like "copper rakes." Instead of a golden, jeweled throne, Ereshkigal has a plain wooden one. There are seven gates to her domain, guarded by a gatekeeper whose name, Neti, in Sanskrit means "nothing."

At each of the seven gates Inanna is stripped of one of her powers of office: her headband of queenship, her lapis lazuli necklace of rulership, her measuring rod, her man-enticing breastplate and perfume. Finally at the seventh gate she is judged by Ereshkigal's seven underworld judges, the Annunaki. Inanna is fixed by the "eye of death," and then Ereshkigal kills her, flays her corpse, and hangs her, like a piece of meat, on a peg. This complete reduction to "nothing" lasts three days and three nights, predating the Christian story of the Resurrection by several thousand years and giving us an arresting example of a female sacrificial myth. And in what to me is the most startling twist to the story, while the goddess of beauty hangs on her peg, the great queen of change, Ereshkigal, herself no simple figure, lies moaning in birth pains, apparently giving birth to a renewed Inanna.

Meanwhile aboveground the faithful servant Ninshubur goes to three father gods entreating their help in getting the goddess of love, beauty, and life out of the underworld. The first two refuse, saying Inanna asked for too much, and that in any event it is impossible to return from the realm of death. The third father god is Enki, god of wisdom and sweet waters. He is instantly sympathetic, and takes dirt from under his fingernails to construct two genderless creatures, Kurgarra and Galaturra. He gives them "the water of life and the plant of life" to take on their sojourn, as well as instructions for tricking Ereshkigal. They go down into the underworld, disguising themselves as a "cloud of flies" to get past the gatekeeper.

Standing before the agonized Ereshkigal, they commiserate with her, and their empathy tricks her into offering them whatever they wish. In true shamanic fashion they refuse to eat the deadly underground fruits that would prevent their return, instead choosing Inanna's corpse, and bring her back to life. Ereshkigal allows the queen of life to ascend, but only on condition that she send another down to take her place. Seven demons accompany Inanna to make sure she keeps her promise.

The demons attempt three "false arrests," including that of faithful Ninshubur herself, before Inanna takes them to her own beloved consort, the bull god Dumuzi; he is gorgeously dressed and sitting on a jeweled throne near his apple tree, not mourning or missing her. Inanna stares at him with her newly attained "eye of death," and the demons take him, though not before his sympathetic sister Geshtinanna offers to take his place in the underworld half the time. Ereshkigal accepts this compromise, and for six months of the year Dumuzi remains below while his sister descends for the other six months. Inanna again rules the world above, now with even greater powers. The myth ends with her acknowledgment of and love for the underworld queen: "Holy Ereshkigal, sweet is your praise."

Following this story closely I have set the play *The Queen of Swords* in a modern context, a Lesbian bar in which Nothing is the bouncer and bartender and the seven judges are Crow Dikes. (Crows traditionally accompany the queen of the underworld.) The play consists of three "aboveworld" scenes and seven "belowworld" gates. And in the spirit of the paganism that sustained this story for so long, I have made the play as funny as I could without losing its profound center of gravity.

The Queen of Swords*
A Play with Poetic Myth

MODERN NAMES	ANCIENT SUMERIAN NAMES
HELEN, *a modern woman*	*Inanna, goddess of heaven and earth, Venus*
THOMAS, *her husband, a scientist*	*Dumuzi, Inanna's consort, the bull god*
NIN, *Helen's friend and Higher Mind*	*Ninshubur, Inanna's minister, queen of the East*
NOTHING, *bartender, dealer, and bouncer*	*Neti, gatekeeper of the Great Below*
ERESHKIGAL, *Lesbian bar owner*	*Ereshkigal, Lady of the Great Below, goddess of the underworld*
Seven CROWS, *variously crows, dikes, Amazon warriors, motorcyclists, judges, demons*	*Annunaki, the seven judges of the underworld, also the Galla, seven demons*
PEN, *corpse of an Amazon warrior*	*Penthesilea, Greek name for the leader of the thirteen Amazons who fought at Troy*
ENKI, *god of the wisdom of nature*	*Enki, god of wisdom and sweet waters*
KUR *and* GAL, *vegetarian fairies*	*Kurgarra and Galaturra, genderless professional mourners/musicians*
GISHI, *Thomas's girlfriend*	*Geshtinanna, Dumuzi's loyal sister*

SCENE ONE: ABOVEWORLD

In a Glass House

Home of HELEN *and* THOMAS BULL. *With* NIN, *an ex-neighbor, now a friend. Nice house, nicely kept, somewhat fussy. Glass wind chimes.* THOMAS *has a telescope, set on a tripod and aimed through an imaginary window, upstage center; he looks out over the audience.* HELEN *paces behind him, sometimes looking over his shoulder,*

*[*Editor's Note*] Grahn has indicated poems that may be read separately; the downward-pointing daggers in the margin indicate the beginnings, the upward-pointing daggers the endings.

sometimes out a window at rear stage left, for her view of the skies. They are utterly detached from each other. Front door stage left. Stairs to upstairs bedrooms stage right. A collection of HELEN*'s glass horses and other glass ornaments is in evidence. As* HELEN *and* THOMAS *are talking,* NIN *knocks lightly, opens the door a crack, peeks around, then comes in. She is carrying a brightly colored pouch.*

Each of the players in this play has an everyday modern side and a timeless, mythic side. Their costumes and gestures may reflect this. They act and speak naturally, not stiffly, formally, or "poetically." Their natural speech just happens to contain much imagery and to rhyme.

HELEN
The sky is a sheet of crystal †
on a night like this.
I can almost see myself reflected
in its starry face.

THOMAS
As soon as I have this tripod adjusted,
we can see her in her evening aspect.

HELEN
I live in a glass house, with glass bells
and fine crystal,
yet I don't see myself reflected
in any of my aspects.

THOMAS
There she is; I've got her
captive in the lens—
how luminous she is!

HELEN
Venus shines expectant[1]
in the embracing sky.
A queen am I;
Queen Helen is my office—
loveliness and love
are in my province;
yet I feel a cloud across my mind, and ponder
love and beauty toward what end, I wonder?

THOMAS
She's in good clear focus tonight.
Yet—they say she is veiled,
and they are right.
Still, you'd never guess she was
twenty-five million miles away.

HELEN
Venus of what universe am I?
I live in a glass house
with glass bells
and glass horses;
how rarely do I stand face to face
with my own forces.

NIN
The stars themselves, they say, have forces.

THOMAS [*not looking away from his telescope*]
Hello, Nin. Come on in.
An electromagnetic net appears
to stretch across the sky tonight.

HELEN
An electromagnetic network
stretches across the sky—
as though space itself has a mind—
its own science…
What mind have I?

THOMAS
Some fellows in physics
postulate other probable worlds
coexist with this one—improbable, eh?
For instance, what could live on this cloudy monster?

HELEN
He has so many eyes to see things by;
he has glass eyes that magnify.
I live in a glass castle;
I feel so fragile
and unimaginative.
I have no expectations
except to shine…
I do have my beauty, my attractions,
but they're fleeting, fleeting
as the wind bleating in a wind chime…
What do I have to magnify my mind?

THOMAS
Come look, have a last look
before I set up the camera for a shot.

HELEN
I was a cherished, petted child.
I live in a place that's a crystal vision

from *House Beautiful* magazine.
I would expect to be very lively,
a vibrant person, so alive.

THOMAS
She is veiled.
You can only see part of her at a time—
a crescent, like the moon. Even so,
she is so luminous
she hurts the eyes.

HELEN
I live in a glass house
with glass bells and glass horses—

> [*She suddenly throws one glass horse to the floor where it smashes. She is instantly contrite, and bends to pick up the pieces.*]

Oh poor horse. Oh poor horse. Of course
I certainly didn't mean—
to kill you—

THOMAS [*reacting to the noise, but not looking up from his telescope*]
What was that, Love?

HELEN
Oh, nothing. A little horse fell.

THOMAS
Oh, too bad. One of your favorites?

> [*He continues making his adjustments.*]

HELEN [*returning to her own ruminations and pacing*]
Venus shines expectant
then sets too fast,
clouds erase her memory
and shroud her past.
A queen am I.
Queen Helen is my office.
Yet *trivial* is how I feel.
Venus of what universe am I?

NIN
Venus is currently traveling in Scorpio,
but you look solidly earthbound to me.

HELEN
Oh, Nin. How are you, I'm glad you came over.
The poor horse flew from my hand.

NIN
Yes, I saw how it used your fury for a motor.
I'm doing well, especially since
I moved away from here.
And I have a new vocation. Look!

[*Holds out a long deck of cards.*]

I've become a diviner of the future,
using Tarot cards.

HELEN
Oh, do a reading for me,
tell me everything that's wrong with me.

[*She and* NIN *sit one on each side of a small table.* HELEN *cuts the cards and* NIN *lays them out.*]

HELEN
Don't tell me about tonight;
tell me about tomorrow.

NIN [*examining the lay*]
The card that signifies yourself is crossed by the Queen of Swords.

HELEN [*shuddering*]
Tell me everything the reading means.
Is something awful going to happen to me?
Am I going to take a trip? I'd like to do that.
I really need some change of scenery.

NIN
The sky is a sheet of crystal on a day like this †
a person could easily fall through
into an abyss.
You could find your astrological aspects
reversed,
your path crossed, your luck
cursed—
on a crystalline day under a crystalline sun
you could fall from this
familiar life
into some other one.
You could come untied,
open one door and enter another one.
You could begin this day with
a solid position in your class,
a marriage built on tradition,
an education, a vocation and an aim,

and having no further explanation than that
you fell through a sky of glass
on a particular crystalline day like this—
have none. ⸸

HELEN [*getting up, dancing around nervously*]
You're right, it is time for me to take a journey.
And I must go, I must go wherever the wind takes me.
Perhaps out to a far mountain—to be a lumberjack!
Perhaps down to undertown, to have an adventure.
Thomas, will you wait up for me,
if I should be late?
Nin, will you still be my friend
when I return? Will you miss me?

Will the wind rattle the glass
in the window of your heart
and remind you that I'm gone?
Will you wait up for me, even if I'm late,
will you still be my friend when I return?

[*She gathers up her purse, and as though packing, stuffs it full of various things: kleenex, her checkbook, lipstick, one of her horses.*]

THOMAS [*he doesn't turn around during this speech, but takes a camera from a case at his feet and loads it, reads the directions, cleans and adjusts the lens*]
Oh Helen, don't go down †
to undertown,
if you go down
to the underground town
you'll never be found,
nor worth the finding.
You'll catch some disease—
a venereal chancre—
and then who'll want you?
Who'll even speak of you?
Don't take such chances.

Don't go down
to undertown,
you're sure to be raped
and then who'll want you?
You'll give birth to an ape
or a pig-headed monster.
You'll have experiences,
you'll age, you'll wrinkle up
around the mouth and eyes,
you'll be despised!

Oh I'm just joking, but
Helen, really, think of your position
and your beauty. Like it or not,
beauty such as yours becomes a duty.
To save your face—and mine—
you need to stay here in this place—
and simply be desired.

HELEN
Desire? And what of my desire?
And what is my desire?
Everyone wants Love to be his own,
to be her own.
But what is it that Love wants,
what does Love want to know?
Everyone wants Love to follow them
down their road;
where is it that Love wants to go?

THOMAS
Oh damn, she's almost set;
I want to take a picture.
Love, bring me the lens cleaner, would you?

HELEN [*going to stairs, to* NIN]
I'm too nervous to stay and talk.
I'm going up to bed; but tell him
I've gone for a walk, tell him
I've gone down below the horizon.
Tomorrow I think I'm going out looking for a job,
or an adventure, or something...

NIN
Be careful out there in the streets alone.

GATE ONE: BELOWWORLD

Where Nothing Lives

ERESHKIGAL'*s bar,*[2] *doorway and street stage right, bar occupying most of* the stage.

The bar is rambling, has a back stairway and other rooms evident. The bar floor has two support posts with a large crosspiece beam that overhangs facing the audience, nearly center, upstage. If the set must be more simple, perhaps a row of coathooks on the back left wall, or a large standing coatrack with a sturdy base can be substituted. The main bar is mirrored and stage rear, persons standing or sitting at the bar turn so they are facing audience, the bar curves at one or both ends so it is possible that a person sitting at the end presents a side or even front view to the audience. There are two crossed swords over the bar's mirror. There is a small table and a chair or two upstage, center. A pool table is either down stage left or off left, with sounds of occasional games played by the CROWS. ERESHKIGAL *has an instrument she occasionally strikes, a set of metal, wood or stone wind chimes, or a xylophone that gives a similar deep-toned effect.*[3] *Generally the bar is cobwebby, garishly lit, seedy, and dusty-looking.*

HELEN *has fallen and struck her head on curb or wall.* NOTHING[4] *comes out of doorway. Sign overhead says* "CROW BAR, ERESHKIGAL, OWNER." *Nothing is visible of* NOTHING *inside a long gray or black robe, no distinguishable gender, age, or, if possible, size;* NOTHING *wears a shoulder bag or purse of cloth that is obviously empty. In offerings to* HELEN, NOTHING *mimes pulling things out of the bag and giving them to her, and, though nothing ever appears in* NOTHING*'s gloved hands, material objects such as glasses of liquor, flasks, bottles of pills, drug paraphernalia, kleenex, etc. do appear on the table or bar in front of* HELEN.

The seven CROWS *play several mythic parts, including crows.*[5] *As* CROW DIKES *they are both butch and femme, aggressive, flirtatious, sardonic, very physical and expressive with their bodies.*

HELEN
Hello, anybody here?
I am alone.
I think I fell and hit my head
against that curb. I thought someone was
chasing me, some violent man. But maybe it was
just a shadow fell across me
made by the wind. You
have no idea how rough it is, out here.
Where have I landed?

NOTHING
You're not *on* land, exactly.
You're in Underland.

HELEN
I'm where?

NOTHING
Underland is not a place like †
"your land and my land," hinterland,
Herland, Thailand,
or even run-'em-out-of-here-land.
It's neither Disneyland nor Prisoner land,
nor of course Fantasy Eye-land.
It's not a movement
to go back to the land,
followed by "get off my land,

go back to your Ownland."
I know you've heard of Homeland and
Strangers in Strangeland, Wonderland,
Funland, Finland, Sunland and Overland,
and you're not in any of those places.
You're in Underland.
Here, give me your hand.

HELEN
You're not easy to give a hand to.
Where are you?
Who are you? And what are you doing in that
strange outfit?

NOTHING
You—who are you?

HELEN
I—who am I?
I'm Mrs. Thomas Bull.

NOTHING
That's more of a title than a name.
Haven't you a name?

HELEN
Well, of course, my given name is Helen.
And my name is very often given.

NOTHING
You sound as though
others often envy you.

HELEN
Yes, I think that's true.
I'm one of the privileged few;
it's no reflection on you.

NOTHING
I don't reflect easily.
Very few seek to be me.

HELEN
Well, you—who are you?

NOTHING
I—who am I?
I'm Nothing.

HELEN
You're nothing? What an awful

thing to say. How self-deprecating;
haven't you any self-esteem?

NOTHING
Being Nothing I don't need self-esteem.
I find it rather limiting.

HELEN
Where are you from, then,
who are your people
that they let you be nothing?

NOTHING
I'm Nothing, from nowhere,
and married to no one—
I live alone here in the underground,
when I'm not traveling.
I live in a room with no furniture,
lights, or heat,
I haven't even a cat.

HELEN
Oh you poor poor thing…
such a restricted life,
Why—you're nothing…

NOTHING
Didn't I just say that?
Why do you think of me as restricted
when I'm welcome almost anywhere,
I'm boundaryless,
I'm often invited everywhere;
there are so many wonderful places to go,
when you're bound to nowhere.
I live in the west, I live in the east,
I live in the north and south, the middle
and the up and down.
I'm here to be your guide in undertown.

[*They enter the bar.*]

HELEN
But to call yourself "Nothing"
isn't healthy, it's putting yourself down.

NOTHING
But Nothing *is* down,
Nothing is all the way to the bottom,

that's certainly the right direction—
it's where I can be found!

> [HELEN *surveys the bar, which also stops to look at her, the seven* CROWS *stopping their games to look at her; then* HELEN *goes up to* ERESHKIGAL, *a black-and-red-clad woman*[6] *who is ignoring her, wiping a small table center stage that has a lit candle on it, which* ERESHKIGAL *carefully blows out.*]

HELEN
Hello, pardon me, do you work here?

ERESHKIGAL
I call it work just to remember who you are.
I'm Ereshkigal, the owner of this bar.
I'm surprised you got this far.

HELEN
I'm glad to meet you.

ERESHKIGAL
You remember me, we've met before, †
you passed me once on the streetcar,
pulled your skirts away, so they wouldn't touch me.
You didn't spit, exactly, but pursed your lips,
like this, as though you meant to;
and you've seen me glaring in fury from some picture
in the newspaper, taken in some jail, you've seen me
in the grade-B movies portrayed as a Mata Hari,
or an evil spy, or Mother Kali, or a spider—
a black widow. You remember me, I played your older
sister Clytemnestra once, in a violent Greek play.[7] ⸸

HELEN
Oh I have no memory of this at all.

ERESHKIGAL
Well, you, who are you,
that can't remember where you've been?
Who is it you think you are?

CROW DIKES [*by turns and closely examining her*]
She used to be the Mrs. Famous Thomas, †
now she's Mrs. Helen Venus,
she's the sought after, hungered for,
she's the slobbered over, fought in behalf of,
she's the overly desired, envied, resented, bought,
she's the traded, stolen, lied and murdered over.
She's everything a woman ever wants to be, and more. ⸸

HELEN
I may be everything a woman
ever wants to be, and more,
but at least I'm not a bar owner,
or a madame, or a boy or a whore[8]
or whatever it is you do here.

ERESHKIGAL
Speak, Helen, speak into my ear!
Speak until your mind is clear.

HELEN
I'm from a nice townhouse uptown,
married to a wonderful man who holds
a good position in science, and this place
makes me a little nervous, however
I mean no offense, I'm sure you're very nice…

ERESHKIGAL
Now listen, Helen. Listen with your inner ear.[9]
Be quiet, Helen! You talk too much![10]
Try listening, instead of such
a smokescreen of babble as you emit
to cover up your ignorance.

HELEN
I have a certain problem with my memory,
perhaps you could help me, perhaps we have met
somewhere before, in some other bar?

ERESHKIGAL
Look, Helen! Look into your mind!
If yours is foggy, look into mine!
You were a goddess in Christ's time,
worshiped with Simon Magus under a plane tree,
doing miracles and acting like a Shakti,
and before that you were only a whore,
a working girl, a street queen,
found in a brothel where Simon set you free,
he and you together were considered gods—[11]
but before that you were just a whore—
and before that you were a real queen,
fought over in a great war; you were what
they fought it for…

HELEN
Never, never, never mind. No use trying to remind
me. I don't have a memory of that awful time.

I live in a pretty house, full of glass bells,
I live with a man who does everything well,
it's just that I feel so trivial...
and I have a terrible time with my memory...
I set out to get better mental recall,
and to see something of the world,
and it's too early for me to go home.
Thomas would make fun of me
and then he would take care of me.
He must be worried, but I'll only be
a little while.
I want to go back—in style.

ERESHKIGAL
Deny, deny, deny, deny.
Seven venial virtues cloud her eye.
Her first venial virtue is that she thinks she's
something, when less than Nothing is what she is.

HELEN
How can you possibly say I'm less than nothing!
I'm the goddess of love and beauty.

ERESHKIGAL
Because Nothing is at least employed,
Nothing is in great demand,
and popular. Much more popular than you.

HELEN
Well, I have to work at what I do!

ERESHKIGAL [*dancing with* NOTHING]
It isn't easy being Nothing †
it isn't simple being down
but someone has to do it—
for the sky to turn around.

We can't all be in our places
in an orderly form;
someone has to be chaotic
for the sky to turn around.

The wind is Nothing's true lover;
where the wind lives
is Nothing's true home,
out on some street corner picking up crumbs;
high on some mountain, down in the dumps.

Where the wind lives is order,
what the wind leaves is chaos,

what the wind does is blow.
What Nothing does is hold the place
completely still, for Zero.
It isn't pleasant being no one,
the eye in the eye of the storm;
but someone has to make the spaces—
or the sky would never turn around.

[*Meanwhile the* CROW DIKES *steal* HELEN'S *things.*]

HELEN
Oh help! Oh heaven!
Someone has stolen my money,
someone has stolen my credit cards!
Someone has stolen my identification!
Someone has stolen my coat!

CROW DIKE CHORUS
Five minutes ago she was a rich girl.

CROW
Mrs. Famous Thomas, wasn't it?

CROW
Lived on a hill.

CROW
Now she's a poor girl, no one.

CROW
Only has a first name.
She'll have to invent the other one.

CROW
Helen—Venus, isn't it?

HELEN
Someone has stolen my shoulder bag!
Someone has stolen my picture!
Someone has stolen my fame!
Someone has stolen my position!
Someone has stolen my name!
Oh help! Who am I?
Oh heaven! Who can I be?

ERESHKIGAL
Well, what can you do?
We haven't much use for a pretty face here—
to stand around and look at you.
We're all pretty enough as we already are.

Can you dust?
Can you make beds others have rumpled
or do you just grumble?
Can you clean another's mess
and do it without a fuss?

HELEN
Well, it isn't that I can't dust.
I just never thought to be doing it for a living.
A servant—Beauty isn't a servant—
trapped in housework—how can
I assert myself in the world?
Still, in this condition, I can't go home.

ERESHKIGAL
Listen, Helen. Listen with your inner ear.
Listen till your mind is clear.
Helen, you've been called Inanna,
a goddess, queen of heaven and earth.

How can you rule the seas
if you can't bait a hook?
How can love pour from your fingertips
if you can't cook?

How can you expect to
rule heaven
if you can't make a bed?
How can you affect stubborn earth
if you can't even bake it into bread?

How can you keep the order of nature
if you can't keep a simple house?
How ride the great breast of the wild wind
if you can't even dust?

HELEN
I wish I knew what you're talking about.

ERESHKIGAL
Look, Helen! Where is your memory?
Look into your mind!
If yours isn't working, then look into mine!
You were a goddess in Christ's time.
And how can you be a goddess
if you can't even dust?

It doesn't matter what you sing—
as long as you can sing something;

and though it matters what you make,
it matters more that it be whole, some
entire thing, oh it really doesn't matter
what you can do as long as you can do
some things useful to yourself and others,
and the first thing
I want you to do, Helen Venus,
is to go get something for Nothing.
Then you'll be an underground Maid.

CROW DIKES
Maid in the Shade.
Yes, go get something for Nothing,
get it without being heard or seen.
If you can get something for Nothing,
you'll be a genuine underworld queen.

HELEN
Oh no you don't, you can't fool me.
I'm not going to work for Nothing!

ERESHKIGAL
There is no use trying to think that way,
because here in Underland
you do have to work for Nothing and that's
because here is where Nothing matters—
offer her something, Nothing.

NOTHING
Welcome, welcome, welcome here.
You'll have a great time being nowhere.
Have a drink, have more
till you're falling on the floor,
have a drug, have a score
till you're crawling up the door.
If you don't want to go so fast,
I gladly deal in more gradual obliteration,
to the resultant obfuscation of obligation,
and the ultimate consummation of degradation.

ERESHKIGAL [*playing her wind chimes*]
It isn't as easy as it may seem
to poison the apple of self-esteem,[12]
and Nothing is the best there is at this,
Nothing does the job better. Nothing is tops.

CROWS
Because Nothing matters! Nothing matters!

Nothing matters!

ERESHKIGAL
Nothing is sacred!

NOTHING
Nothing makes a difference!

CROWS
Nothing is important! Nothing is important!
Nothing is important!

[HELEN *holds her hands over her ears as the* CROWS *dance raucously around the bar with* NOTHING *while* ERESHKIGAL *rings her brass wind chimes.*]

GATE TWO: BELOWWORLD

The Nature of Nature

ERESHKIGAL'*s Crow Bar, slightly neater than it was in Gate One.* HELEN, *feather duster in hand, sits at the bar;* NOTHING *is behind the bar.* ENKI *comes in, gets a beer from* NOTHING, *steps forward and addresses audience. He is dressed in a gardener's outfit and carrying a rake and a duffle bag with clothes in it. He changes clothes during the course of the Gate to a woman's garb, makeup, wig; or perhaps he only puts on a long skirt, or a woman's hat.* CROW DIKES *are sitting or standing around, playing pool and the like.*

ENKI [*to audience,* HELEN, CROWS, *and* NOTHING]
Where is when— †
ever notice that?
When you go somewhere
has everything to do
with where you are
when you get there,
whether you're there again,
or for the first time.
It's evident
that place is time.

When is where—
ever notice this?
When you go too long
and too far
to remember where you are
or you try to meet
someone somewhere
in a particular space
and miss each other

by minutes
it becomes clear again
(or for the first time)
where is when
and time
is place.

HELEN
I know where I am.
Here is where I am stuck in this underground bar.

ENKI
Not only that, now is *when*
you've been stuck here in this underground bar.

HELEN
I've been left here with nothing.

CROW [*to* NOTHING]
Is she complaining?

CROW
We do have Nothing to offer her.

NOTHING
You'd think she would be used to me by now.

CROW
She can't help it.
Nothing bothers her.

HELEN
It seems that all of humankind
has walked away with me behind.
How long I've been abandoned here
even nature doesn't care.

ENKI
Who sits there
describing her own sorry state of mind
while crediting all of humankind?

HELEN
Nature doesn't give a damn[13]
if I'm not or if I am.
All the sounds of life I hear
sound the same without my ear.

Yet stars affect me just the same
as if I were affecting them;

and I love no less the sea
for its never loving me.

Butterflies and birch trees
are unaware of pleasing me.
Earth needs no love to give.
We love. What other cause to live?

CROWS
CAW CAW CAW CAW

CROW
What other CAWS to live?

CROW
I CAW CAW CAWS to live.

ENKI
Who's to say what Nature loves
and does not love?

HELEN
Oh I wasn't talking to you.
I was simply feeling blue.
I long to get away from this ugly place
to go somewhere nice—to the country.
But I can't.
I'm reduced to nothing.

CROW [*to* NOTHING]
Are you reducible, too, Nothing?

NOTHING
Absolutely.

HELEN
I have lost everything,
my name and position. I have to stay here
and be a servant.

ENKI
That's what nature is—a servant.

HELEN
You—who are you?

ENKI
I am Enki, at your service.
I'm a gardener, of sorts, that is to say
I look after the natural world. You might say
I help to make its templates.

HELEN
You're a very strange man, if that is what you are,
and this is a very strange bar.

ENKI
I like this place myself.
Why would a beauty such as yourself
descend alone to a place she despises?

HELEN
Oh, because I'm more than a beauty,
I'm supposed to be in charge of beauty,
but somewhere along the long line
I believe I lost my own mind,
so recently I set out to do more than stand alone
in some admiring bask,
I set out to do the harder task,
to break, to ask,
to fall all the way down,
and eventually to understand.
And I know I'm not entirely alone—
Nature loves me, this I know,
as she loves the flowers that grow.
You, a gardener, understand
how Nature holds us in her tender hands.

ENKI
Beware of little eggs that fall
from Nature's hairy horny paw.
What if it simply isn't true
that Nature gives a royal damn
if you're not or if you am.
Who do you suppose you'd be
if Nature didn't care at all?

HELEN
You say this to be shocking me,
you must be drunk, but I'll be
understanding—since you can't be
nice, I'll do it for you. And I
can't imagine who I'd be, if Nature
didn't care for me.
It's bad enough to live in towns
where mankind's evil brings me down—
the smoggy air, the ugly roads,
the huge inhuman buildings,
and the violence of criminals—

I couldn't stand never to sit
under a tree or to climb a grassy hill.
I get my strength from the wild land
and the wild sea, and my inner sense of
harmony.

ENKI [*to* CROWS]
Correct me if I'm wrong
But didn't she just say
She takes the strength from the wild land
to make up for her own weakness?
Did I hear her say that?
I've always called that stealing, haven't you?

CROWS
We CAW CAW CAWL it CROWING.

ENKI [*to* HELEN]
Nature's all around a place—
a country home, a city space—
freeways have a nature of their own.

[*To* CROWS:]

These humans strum a gloomy song.
They live in towns and run them down,
spin the gold from underground,
and then they say the area isn't Nature—
but it is—it's *their* Nature.
They simply have an ugly one.

CROW
This is Wisdom declaiming on the Nature of
Nature to someone who doesn't believe he *is*
Nature.

CROW
Not only that, he's declaiming on the nature
of beauty to someone he doesn't know *is* Beauty.

CROW
I don't believe in Beauty, either. I think it
happens only in the mind.

CROW
I don't believe you have a mind.

CROW
Well then I believe it happens only in the bowel.

CROW
You are a singularly foul fellow.

HELEN
You haven't a woman's sensibility.
What could you know of Nature?

ENKI
Perhaps I haven't any sensibility
except I know my nature and my name
and besides, in a way I AM Nature.

HELEN
Oh what are you saying, you're lying,
who are you?

ENKI
I'm the god of wisdom and wild lands
and fertilizing waters.

HELEN
But look at you, in women's clothing,
boozing it up in this ugly place,
look at you—you're so *un*natural.

CROW
Who's unnatural?

CROW
Nature.

CROW
Well, that's only natural.

CROWS
She's finally getting some sense.

CROW
What could be more unnatural than Nature?

CROW
Always interfering with the course of my life.

CROW
Always coming in here to drink beer and make a mess.

CROW
Always changing everything, ever notice that?

HELEN
Men are so violent.

Woman is more like Nature.

CROW
women are not violent †

CROW
and I am not violent

CROW
and the Queen of Swords is not violent

CROW
and violence is violet

CROW
and Americans are not violet

CROW
and the wind is never violent

CROW
and the sea, the sea is not violent

CROW
and nonviolence is not violent

CROW
nonviolence is inviolate

CROW
and the earth is not violent

CROW
and a shooting star is not violent

CROW
and a volcano is not violent

CROW
and war is not violent

CROW
and violet is not violent

CROW
and nice is not violent

CROW
and nice is not viola

CROW
and men are not violent

CROW
and mice are never violent

CROW
and the deer are not violent

CROW
except in the woods

CROW
where they live

CROW
but in the movies they are not violent

CROW
and the woods are not violent

CROW
and puking is not violent

CROW
and death is not violent

CROW
and cars are not violent

CROW
and Americans are violas

CROW
and violas are sometimes violent

CROW
And violas are sometimes violet ‡

ENKI [*to* HELEN]
It's your modern human nature to construct an ugly place †
and then dislike it.
You weren't always like this.
Why do you go to the city of trees to help
restore your soul, why not do it in your own
city? Take a look around—
Here's Nature! Here's you!
Here's Nature and you!
It seems to me, at least presently,
and I have a number of opinions,
naturally, but currently
at least, it seems to me
that a beehive is a bee's Nature, ‡

a stand of trees is a tree's Nature,
mountains have a rocky Nature of their own.
This bar here and this industrial city,
this is modern human's Nature,
you take your Nature everywhere you go.

HELEN
Oh you don't know.
How could you?
How dare you say cities are natural,
how dare you say I have no right to trees.
You—who are you!
You're only a gardener! A materialist!
Rooting around in dirt!
What do you know of beauty?
I AM beauty.

[*Exit* ENKI.]

Nature loves me, this I know,
as she loves the flowers that grow.
Nature loves to give and give
and Nature loves—
what other cause have I to live?

CROW CHORUS
CAW CAW CAW

CROW
What other caws to live?

CROW
I caws to live.

CROW
I live to caws.

CROW
I love a just caws.

CROW
I love a righteous and good and just caws.

CROW
I loathe any kinds of caws.

CROW
I prefer first caws.

CROWS
CAW CAW CAW

CROWS
We prefer last caws.

CROW
I prefer long drawn-out caws.

CROWS
CAAAAW CAAAAAAWW CAAAAAAAWWW

CROW
I like edible caws.

CROW
The caws of peas.

CROWS
CAW CAW CAW

CROW
The caws of corn.

CROWS
CAW CAW CAW

CROW
The caws of war.

CROW
CAW CAW CAW

CROW
The caws of contemplation.

CROW
Contemplation has no caws.

CROW
The BEE caws—

CROWS
CAW CAW CAW

CROW
The BEE caws—

CROW
bee caws of you—

CROW
there's a song in my heart—

CROW
bee caws of offal—

CROW
Bee caws of offal? That's awful!

CROW
Bee caws of offal there is food.

CROW
Bee caws there is shit—

CROW
there is grit—

CROW
bee caws there is dirt there are trees—

CROW CHORUS
the mother of trees is dirt
the mother of feel good is hurt
the mother of all is none
the mother of found is gone
the mother of talk is breath
the mother of laughing is death
the mother of do is been done
the mother of enough is waste
the mother of more is must
the mother of go somewhere is place
the mother of beauty is memory

HELEN
The mother of beauty is memory?[14]

ENKI [*returning with another bottle, and by now even more cross-dressed as a female,*[15] *addressing* HELEN]
You're wrong you know, that is, you're wrong
in this particular place at this particular time
and given who you're speaking to—
the Wisdom and Nature god.

HELEN
Nature god? perhaps you have a thought or two
on the nature of the Beauty god of Love and Life?

ENKI [*dancing*]
If you would be a goddess of beauty
try first being a frog,
something wet and green and viscous,
something growing in a bog.

First you need a tender belly
and an all-consuming throat,

fingers touchy as the top of jelly,
an ability to float—

HELEN
Let's see if I have this straight.
You're advocating
nature as a building
and beauty as a frog?

ENKI
I'm advocating nearly everything,
and quite a bit of Nothing.
What forms would you prefer we came in?

HELEN
Something pinker and more austere—
something traditional, stars or
sea anemones, or flowers…

ENKI
You see flowers as austere?
You miss their rank indecency.
I see a flower in its fullest blooming
thickly musky
as a woman with her legs spread
for any lover,
or a man with his stem sprung
standing nude in the sun or street
for anyone or dog to tweak.

HELEN
You aren't the kind of nature I adore.
And my once precious view of Wisdom
is hopping greenly out the door.

ENKI
We see things differently, obviously;
through different lenses…
Would you like to borrow my glasses?
You see, on the one side is observation,
and on the other—a crystal lens,
for looking out and then for looking in,
and not confusing the two of them.

[*He holds out his glasses, she puts them on, then reels around the stage, examining people, walls, floor, liquor in bottles, her own hand, etc., reacting strongly, alternately shrieking, laughing, leaping, jerking, weeping, howling, in a rapid succession of extreme impressions. Exhausted, she wrenches the glasses off.*]

HELEN
What *are* these things—
they see absolutely everything,
from every point of view,
from lowest pit to highest summit.

[*Puts them on again.*]

Ugh. From many-headed microbe
to the interior of Nothing's robe.

[*She shrieks at what she sees in* NOTHING*'s robe and jerks the glasses off again.*]

ENKI
Aren't my glasses wonderful!

HELEN
They give me a giant headache,
and turn my stomach.
What are these things made of?

ENKI
Lenses of the eyes of beetles and flies,
a dozen of each.

HELEN
I have to give them back to you.
Oh Enki, I can't see from so many
points of view,
one is enough, or at most two—
I'd go mad if I had to bear witness
as thoroughly as you do.

ENKI
I'm only trying to offer
a little clarity of vision.
Would you rather try my eyeball than my glasses?
It has a little more focus—eight miles, like an owl!
And you can see clear as a blowfish underwater—

HELEN
No thanks, no thanks, no thanks.
I really have nothing more to say to you.
Nothing! Absolutely nothing!

NOTHING
You're calling me again?

HELEN
Oh, I can't stand this crazy place.

[*Exits to right.*]

CROW
Nature offended her.

CROWS
CAW CAW

CROW
She's a little coo coo.

CROW
And you're a little dodo.

CROW
And you're a little doo doo.

CROW
And you're a little ka ka.

CROWS
CAW CAW

CROW
She can't stand being in this CAW-razy place.

NOTHING
With Nothing!

CROWS
Absolutely Nothing!

ENKI
It simply isn't the nature of her nature!

[*The* CROWS *exit one by one pretending to be huffy, high-handed, and insulted by each other, while enjoying it immensely.* ENKI *drinks a toast to* NOTHING.]

GATE THREE: BELOWWORLD

Descent to the Butch of the Realm

Interior of the Crow Bar with ERESHKIGAL, CROW DIKES, NOTHING, *and* HELEN, *who leans her elbows on the bar facing the audience while others carry on their usual bar business, pool playing, dancing cheek to cheek, playing cards, etc. Sensual music on the juke box fades out so we can hear the dialogue.*

HELEN
I hate you all.
I came here with love, and goodwill.
Now I feel nothing.

CROW DIKE [*to* NOTHING]
She feels you.

NOTHING
How sensitive of her.

CROW DIKE
Do you think you're being objectified?

NOTHING
Absolutely.

ERESHKIGAL
What is it you say? Speak into my ear.

HELEN
I said, and I think I said it loud enough
that even you could hear me,
I came here with curiosity and goodwill
in my heart, but now having been here
a while, and being unable to leave,
I have nearly come to hate all of you.

ERESHKIGAL
Oh, you can't hate us.

HELEN
I can't? Just watch me.

CROW DIKES
You can't hate us.

HELEN
I can't hate you?

ERESHKIGAL
You can't hate us.
We're Lesbians.

CROW DIKES
You can't hate us.
We're Lesbians.

HELEN [*fuming and then laughing*]
I can't hate you, you're Lesbians—
what are you talking about?

Of course I hate you.
And of course I don't hate you.
And of course I *can* hate you.

ERESHKIGAL
No, not here in the underworld.
Here in the belowworld Lesbians are loved,
and Lesbians love.

HELEN
And what do Lesbians love?

CROW DIKES [*by turns*]
Lesbians love
to talk
to sing
to walk
to cling
to balk
to sting
Lesbians love to do anything,
and to do nothing.

NOTHING
Not without my permission they don't.

HELEN
Actually it isn't hate I feel
but endless curiosity.
What do Lesbians do?

CROW DIKE
What do Lesbians do?

ERESHKIGAL
Yes, what do Lesbians do.
Go ahead and answer her,
answer her true.

CROW DIKE
Lesbians love to do.

CROW DIKE
Lesbians love to dance.

CROW DIKE
Oh, Lesbians do love to dance.

CROW DIKES [*by turns*]
Lesbians love to dance

†

inside the thunder.
Lesbians love to dance
outside in the rain
with lightning darting
all around them.
Lesbians love to dance
all night in any
kind of weather, love
to dance up close
their arms pulled tight
around their partners'
backs and hips and
shoulders. Lesbians love
to dress in lace
and leather and
to court each other
(and each others' lovers).
Lesbians love to be so
bold and getting
even bolder, their fingers
love to linger
inside tunnels.
Lesbians love to dance
indoors and under
covers, Lesbians love
to dance inside
mountains and
to watch their lovers' faces
as they come and come and come
completely undone.
Lesbians
love to dance together
in the pouring rain, in
summer.
Lesbians love to dance
inside the thunder,
sheets of water
washing over their whole bodies
and the dark clouds
boiling and roiling like a
giant voice calling.
Lesbians love to answer
voices calling like that.
Lesbians love to
dance without their clothing
in thunderstorms with

lightning as their partner.
Screaming, holding hands
and turning soaking faces
skyward in tumultuous
noise and yearning. Lesbians
love to see each other
learning to completely
rejoice. Lesbians love
to feel the power
and the glory they can dance
inside of, in a storm
of their communal choice. ⸸

HELEN
Well, that's all very nice for you.
But what do Lesbians do that has anything
to do with me?

ERESHKIGAL
Look, Helen! Look into your mind!
If yours is scrambled, look into mine!
You were a goddess before Demeter's time,
Lady Venus of aboveworld form,
Inanna by name, Sumerian born—
you passed through seven gates of the underland
to deliver yourself into my hands,
into Ereshkigal's hands…

HELEN
And you—who are you, really?

ERESHKIGAL
I am your wild cherry sister, red and †
black sheep sister of the unkempt realm.
I am the Butch of Darkness and the Lady
of the Great Below.
I have a nickname: see if you can guess it.
Thistles in my fur are twisted
taut as wily wires of gristle.
You won't find me sitting home in front of TV
drinking beer, not me—I'm outdoors
prowling midnight. Nor do I march
to take back the night with other women
for I never lost it. My name is Shadow of the Wolf,
I woof and I whistle.
My usual companion-lover's name is "Destiny."
She had it tattooed
on my upper arm. She is, of course,

a Dike.[16] She chews me down to something honest
on a weekly basis when I let her.
Oh! But I have plenty of time for you
and your bright beauty—
yes, I have plenty of room for a Venus-type
such as yourself
in my chamber.
Remember me now whenever
you hear the phrase "wild cherry."

Oh descend
Descend to me
to my exhilarating gaze
and my desiring
Yes it is true—I am who wants you
and I hear you have chosen
to come down to me.

Strange to everyone but me that
you would leave the great green rangy
heaven of the american dream,
your husband and your beloved children,
the convenient machines,
the lucky lawn and the possible
picture window—to come down here below.
You left your ladyhood, your queenship, risking
everything, even a custody suit,
even your sanity, even your life. It is
this that tells me you have a warrior
living inside you. It is for this
I could adore you.

Now I want you to enter my stormy regions.
My gatekeeper will guide you; where
do you think you
want to go? Just ask his howling
hollow center.
His name is "Nothingness."
I want you to stand as I stand before you,
tremulous with expectation
as I reach to tangle all my fingers in your hair
to rip away the veil of your
perpetual smile, and then to strip
off your scarf of limitations, even
the birthright of your long hair itself.
Do my stark eyes surprise?
My name is "Naked of Expectations."

And I want to bend you
as I am bent to nip your neck, unclasping
your lapis blue necklace. Ever notice how it
keeps you from talking? You are going to do
a lot of talking. And no small amount of yowling.
Are you certain you should have come?
I may never release you.
Oh descend
Oh lower yourself to love
in the underground, the union
of a woman to one other
woman, not self to self
but self to other
self.

Slap your feet flat on the earth now,
heel first preferably, thrust
your pelvis forward.
You see I am about to change
your center of gravity.
As for those explanatory notes and diagrams
tucked under your arm—put them down.
You won't need them.
You will be too busy with your own internal
computations, as I lick between
your fingers, slipping off the golden rings
of definition and adherence.

Oh descend to me
lower yourself into yourself
as I go down
and go down
and go down to you.

I want you to fall, as I fall
heavy lying next to you, your twin egg stones
happy underneath my hands, the
pearl-pearl buttons I'm unsnapping,
then that thick-ribbed brassiere that gives you
all the cleavage you have used to
get your men to hope and grope
bearing gifts and favors.
You are your own gift now,
and you have chosen to come to me.

I of the snarled hair, the one earring
and the brassy metallic nailpolish,
I am your wild cherry sister. I am savage,

living in regions ruled by laws
that to you just happen.
When you say "just happen"
you will remember me.

I want you to crawl
unravelling
as I crawl over your dancing belly
to unbuckle the belt of willingness,
last obstacle before you splay your doorway
to my doorway. Reveal to me.
You have a secret self, don't you?
Can you bear your heart to be split
open and to lie so naked
in the sight of
either one of us?

Oh descend to me
mound on mound of Venus meeting
maddened Earth to be unbound on.
Fix your gaze upon me
while I find and flay you
with my fingers and my tongue.

My tongue is nicknamed
"Say Everything."
She's appealing enough
at first until she nails you fast
to solid dirt of the fat earth
and ends your fantasy.

You will moan, Inanna
you will cry.
Everyone you ever were
will die,
while you go down
and go down
and go down
on me.

Hanging helpless on a peg of feeling
as I bear you to your
new and awe-ful place of being, locked in
dead heat, we will argue. We will
fight. Your heart will ooze like red meat.
I will suffer too, to birth you,
to transform and finally release you.
I am cruel, yes. Exacting and not
possibly fooled.[17]

Pain opener. You want pity for your
little yellow egg of being
broken on my greasy griddle.
I am pitiless. And stirring
I will sear you, so when
next you say "you puking, putrid
lying self-conceited wretch you"
it is my face you will see,
my name you screech out "Oh! I'll Kill!
That Rotten! Bitch!"

Yes, I am the Butch of the Realm, the Lady
of the Great Below. It is hard for me
to let you go.
When next you say "you bitch"—"wild cherry"—
and "it just happens"—
you will think of me
as she who bore you to your new and lawful
place of rising,
took the time and effort
just to get you there
so you could moan Inanna
you could cry
and everyone you ever were
could die.[18]

[*A pause.* ERESHKIGAL *and* HELEN *embrace, then are surrounded by the* CROW DIKES, *who hum a love song to them. All collapse to floor.*]

GATE FOUR: BELOWWORLD

Amazon Rising from the Dust

ERESHKIGAL'*s Crow Bar as before.* HELEN *is alone center stage. The bar looks somewhat better than it did in Gate Three, a little decorated and not exactly cheery, but at least neat and clean. She has been washing the bar and mirror with rags, a bucket, a spray bottle. Her hair is tied up in a scarf. She is tired from her efforts, and primps in the bar mirror, then goes to sit at the table upstage. Just as she starts to sit down, she is startled to see a large waddy-looking mass just right of center stage.*

HELEN
What dreadful thing is lying there
as though growing from the floor?

[*Corpse of* PEN *gradually rises from the floor. She looks like a 3,000-year-old corpse, yet underneath the torn flesh, rotten garments, and protruding bones,* PEN *is actually quite handsome and would be appealing to* HELEN *if she were an entire being. She rises, holding one arm up first, fist clenched, and then the first shoulder while she braces herself with her other hand, teeth wrenched over her tongue, the flesh pulled tight over her skull to form a human face.*]

PEN
I am not graceful in this first movement.

HELEN
You—who are *you?*

PEN
I have been the Amazon †
in the dust.
From dust all things arise.
I'm a little awkward getting up.

HELEN
Don't bother, then.
Just sit where you are,
at least until you have your face on.
You look like a pile of bones
from some garbage pit.

PEN [*sarcastically, and rising anyway*]
Thanks a lot.
The last time we met
was during the great war.

HELEN
The First World War?

PEN
Not that one,
the earliest one, the war at Troy
three thousand years ago.
You had gone there to be with Paris
of your own choosing.
We guessed some bitterness of life
in hard-mouthed Sparta drove her queen of sexual
intelligence and beauty to make such a down-bound trip.
Then they simply could not rest
until they forced you back, stripped of your
protectors, stripped of your freedom, stripped
finally of your life. Just the day before
we Amazons arrived, they had killed Hector,
Troy's best warrior, next to me of course.

HELEN
And who did you say you were?

PEN
Penthesilea, Amazon Queen, who went once
to war to save Queen Helen (that was you).
"Able to make men mourn" my name signifies,
supreme Amazon speeding to the neediness of Troy,
leader of twelve good warrior maidens,
battle-scarred
and with fierce reputation. We were the last
hope that queenly Troy could keep intact
and reachable, the greatest beauty in the world.

> [CROWS *begin entering one by one; they lounge around the bar casually; then as* PEN *and* HELEN *speak they act out battle scenes; they are Amazon Warriors though some take the parts of male Greek warriors in the fray*]

HELEN
I remember that day.
The sky was a sheet of crystal
and the wind was still.
I ran to see your arrival
from my windowsill.
You were like Artemis to us,
you arrow-carrying bear-dikes.
I could tell how Hector
and the other men had learnt
some of their skill from you,
and then too, what can confuse
a man more than a naked female
breast with a bloody ax behind it?

PEN
You and I met before the fight.
I rode into the hall
on the great long-legged stride
my mother prized me for.

You turned almost at once
to look me up and down.
My cheeks burned with pride
though inside
I felt more like a clown.

HELEN
The Amazons were coming!
To fight on our side!

We women were electrified.
You looked strange to us
but exhilarating.
I was especially electrified
by you.

PEN
I knew it too, that moment
at least, when our eyes met across the room.
I was your last battle ax
and you threw it.

HELEN
By then, with the war in its tenth year,
I don't think I cared much
whether I stayed with Paris
or my husband won and took me home.
You put up the hardest fight they ever saw,
carved their gullets and split their craws,
set them mewling in their own fear,
pinned to the ground with their own spears.
I had never seen men die of terror.

PEN
You flew into a cloud of dust, Helen,
you withdrew.
We didn't know what slavery of your beauty
stood on the other side
of my downfall.

HELEN
I remember that day.
During the fight
some of us thought
we should run outside
to help you, stand beside
with shield and mace and other weapons.
Someone reminded us,
you trained all your life
for this—we are different,
built to carry a different burden,
stand in a different place.

PEN
I don't know how you are or are not built.
I know you were watching
when Achilles killed me.
I know it affected you horribly.

HELEN
I wanted to turn my face
and couldn't.
I was transfixed.
No one imagined
you could ever be beaten,
let alone raped
and dragged around like a dishrag.
Everything fractured then
as the sword clubbed and then went in,
not just the ribs and skull,
the full picture
went to pieces, I saw the
world break like a dropped egg.

PEN
Helen your beauty
and your godlike features
cracked like shell
after my own cracking face
and graceless fall.
Oh god Helen, we lost the war;
we lost each other in the war.
I was your tooth
and they pulled it
I was your dagger
and they tore it
from your hand.

AMAZON CHORUS
She was your voice
and they slit your throat;
she was your breath
caught like a duck in a gill net.

HELEN
I stood with all
the women on the wall, watching,
hands clutching
as you lay on the sand
blood-drained and stiffening.

PEN
I was your arrow
against the foe
I was your backbone
bent low

oh lady of sorrow
I was your bow.

AMAZON CHORUS
Helen, your arrow—
where is it?
Is it hidden
in your pocket?
Is it long like a rocket,
or is it round as a locket?
Is it a bee sting?
Is it stored in a quiver,
or under your disgust for slimy things?
Helen—your arrow,
do you have it?

HELEN
How horrible that this happened to you,
how horrible what they did to you.

PEN
They did it to you, too.
We have to move through memory
as the wind sifts through dust, examining
everything for clues.
My corpse self was crow-eaten
and discarded, my power stolen.
I have to move through that scene
to another, to the dream remembered,
a dream of wild horses
of women's fingers tangled in the manes,
and tangled with each other,
in a dream of what we do with horses
when we do it all together,
when we do it with one motive.

HELEN
Oh yes, I'd rather talk of horses.
At home I have a shelf of lovely glass horses.
And I've heard of Amazons with horses.
I've heard you do the most
amazing things with horses.

AMAZON
Horse my pelvis, horse my thighs,
horse the thunder in my eyes…

HELEN
What *do* you do with horses?

AMAZON CHORUS
As for what we do with horses †
it's none of your business,
it's none of your knowing
what rides we mounted
what circles rode, what songs shouted.

It's not for your understanding
what fires we kindled
in autumn darkness,
what flames we handled
when the moon was
breathless.
        As for what
we did in tandem
it was the bonding of warriors,
as for what we did of ritual
it was what you now call: actual.

As for what we learned in shadows
it's not of your fathom,
it's deep as molasses
or a parade of motorcycles,
it's the well-waxed chassis
with eighty horsepower
and electromagnetic fuel injection.

As for what we do with horses
we ride them like forces,
as for what we do with forces,
we tug them in closer.
As for what we do with borders
we cross and uncross them,
as for what we do with curses,
we put them in purses
and fling them to blazes.

As for what we do with horses
we fondle their noses
we drape them in roses
and race them on courses,
it's a great-hearted outpouring
with the whole crowd cheering,
it's not for the artless,
it's the marriage of speed,
the finest run on the finest steed,

it's what we whisper in their ears,
it's how their hoofbeats whisper up
to us, "Destiny, destiny, destiny…
rides on opportunity."
It's the brave heart churning,
to nearly bursting,
it's the pent blood pressing
the hot breath
to the hotter neck,
it's the hand slapping and the wet flank
slapping back against the hand,
as for what we do with horses,
it's the rush of our great trying,
it's the tension of our lunging
it's the love of promising
it's the flesh imagining itself flying
it's the flash of light before thundering,
it's the dark ring of opening,
it's the way we have of living
in the dust of the wind.

HELEN
That's not anything I've ever done with horses.

PEN
After the fall of women's power,
in the dust whirl of dream
I lay for centuries hardly moving,
paralyzed,
recalling only the last act, the rape
that Achilles bent to vent himself on me.
I thought I would never be free of it,
until at last I began to live again,
and again, to hang at the corner of the ceiling
and recall who I had been.
I saw myself a Roman soldier
on the march,
saw myself a Viking on the Normandy coast,
I saw myself a tender-hearted soldier
in the First World War.
Saw myself at last reborn
in my own killer's form.

HELEN
You have lived over and over
in the bodies of men?

PEN
When he took our Amazon strength
to be his own he became a soldier; women
such as you and I hung high on a peg, burning.

HELEN
Like Joan of Arc! Hung on a stake!

PEN
Yes, high on a peg, and then down
to the scorpion ground. I have been down
to the bottom of the ditch;
I have been down overcome by my own corpse-stench.
If you could just join forces with me now
you would find the awesome power of nothing
you've been looking for.

HELEN
I don't want awesome nothing
and I don't want dust,
I certainly can't join forces
with you, I'm not
part of your war.

PEN
My war?

HELEN
I stood apart from everyone,
I stood on the ramparts of the wall,
while men on the inside warred
with men on the outside,
and you manlike Amazons
mixed it up with the worst of them.
I stood on the wall; I fled on the stair;
I was hardly there at all.
I hid out in Egypt,
keeping the occult sciences that once
belonged to me;[19] I have no part of war.
I live in a glass house, with glass horses;
I hardly ever come face to face with my own forces.

AMAZON CHORUS
Helen, the nature of your strength,
what is it?

HELEN
Everything I have or am
I give to men now,

they fought and won it,
isn't that correct?
Besides they are so strong,
and losers mushy-chested
and contemptible.

AMAZON CHORUS
Strong, there are so many kinds
of strong.
Men are steadfast
in what they want,
that is one.
Amazon strength
lives in the wind,
in a dust-particle dance of transformation.

HELEN
And Helen's strength, what is it?
Is it the strength of love?

AMAZON CHORUS
Helen, your strength
is in your memory.

HELEN
And is my memory my mother?
What are my memories?

AMAZON CHORUS
Memory is the mother of truth;
and truth is the mother of beauty;
and beauty is the real mother
of real science.

PEN
Helen. I was your tooth,
and it rotted.
I was your knife and you dropped it
from your hand.
I have endured every humiliation of the battle-lost,
the war-torn. I have sometimes wished not to be born.
I have been called every vile name,
and worst of all, you have seen,
and feared, and scorned, and shunned me.
But names are only identity games, and suffering ends
in toughness or death, what I have never been
is a slave, only the side that lost the war.
Yet without me as the dagger by your side,
slave is quite a bit of what you are.

HELEN
Oh you go on so long,
and you're so wrong.
I'm not a slave—
I'm just well-behaved.
I live in a nice glass house
with glass bells—
I've been a cherished, petted child—
lucky person, lucky life—

AMAZON CHORUS
Helen, your horses,
what are they?
Can you ride them
or do you hide them?
Are they broken?
Do you deny them,
can you even find them?
Helen—your horses,
do they lead you,
or follow?
Are you keeping them,
in what meadow?

PEN
My memory is a long one,
it gives me no rest.
Though you recoil from me now
dressed in my blood and dirt,
and with my wounded breast—
is my sack of being
too leaky for your good taste?
Still, I'll give you advice
and of what I have—the best…
You say you stand
on the wall, apart, yet
everywhere there's a war
there you are, beautiful, desired
and right in the middle of it.
So I know you're a player,
whether or not you admit it.
This is what I know, Helen,
of the nature of war,
if you stay in battle long enough
you'll find you carry every arm,
do every harm
in every heart

of every storm.
No horse you own remains unridden,
no hand you hold remains unplayed.

HELEN
And what of love in all this talk of death?
And what of my high hopes?
And my force? What is it? Is it politics?
Is it science?
What is it really can rise from dust?

AMAZONS
Helen, your forces
are in the beauty of your memory,
do you remember?
Can you ride them like horses?

HELEN
What is my science?

AMAZONS
Your science is in the memory of your beauty.

HELEN
How can I re-form from simple dust
to remember myself, how can I ever understand
the nature of my beauty?

AMAZON CHORUS
Under the mask of Helen smiling
lies the Foe,
under the mask of the Foe
lies a dead Amazon,
under the mask of the fallen Amazon
lies Helen, sleeping.
Under the mask of Helen sleeping
lies the lady of the underworld
birthing fury,
and under the fury
stands the bull god,
wild-eyed, waiting
for his sacrifice.

HELEN
I remember, I remember, I remember—
the sky *is* a sheet of crystal on a day like this—
and I remember the whole war now,
and later my own crashing fall
and loss of power.

What a splash I made!
Golden light went everywhere,
a sparkling cloud of dust.
No wonder they call it Fairy dust!
What powers I had! What sciences!
Healing—predicting, even controlling weather.
Yet after that war
I was no longer one superior
focal point of light, like Venus.
I was scattered everywhere, wind-torn,
my villages burned to underground,
the old folks going down
on the forced marches,
after the teachers and the intellectuals
spewed their own blood along the fences,
while the women huddled in whore camps
with their brains stripped out of their skulls,
and everyone ate napalm rations,
our young men being clubbed to death in
the police stations, our children turned to strangers
in the boarding schools of force-fed reculturation,
after he sent the smallpox-saturated blankets,
after he marched my babies to the jailing baby school,
after the bombs, after the secret warehouse torture,
after the famine and the relocation,
after the war…

PEN
I became your fallen warrior eating dust,
my lips flattened in it,
while dogs pissed
on my torn coat the way a man, a soldier
might rape my
corpse between the legs, and call it
love or lust or even by its better name,
conquest, trying to do the sorcery of
soul-theft.

HELEN
I became a cloud, forgetful,
fearful and unpredictable.
Now how can I ever gather myself together again?
Are you one of my forces?
And you—who are *you?*
You're more blown apart
than I am. I expected a glorious
Amazon, not a blood-dripping corpse.

PEN [*kneeling*]
Oh I know I offend you
with my leaking chest
and bitter mouth,
my messages of hard reality,
but Helen, reach to touch me,
touch my fingers—dust we always have
to turn to;
touch is all we have to give
each other, while we're here.

Tangle fingers with me now
so you can remember who you are,
and I can live on earth again.

[*They touch fingers;* HELEN *wipes hers on her shirt.*]

HELEN [*thoughtfully*]
Now another woman's blood is on my hands.

[PEN *suddenly laughs, though not derisively and not at* HELEN, *pulling off her mask to reveal herself as* ERESHKIGAL. *She stamps her foot, and all the* AMAZONS *become* CROWS *who stamp their feet, too, and howl and whoop.* HELEN *recoils.*]

SCENE TWO: ABOVEWORLD

Her Shadow Falls Across Me

The basement of a large industrial building, preferably a steam plant, with lots of pipes, clouds of white steam, and some rubber plants. ENKI *is alone, dressed as an engineer, humming to himself, making adjustments. He addresses the audience in his first speech.*

ENKI [*in greasy overalls and with wrench in hand*]
Thoughts are public things,
ever think such a quaint idea?
(You got it from me, naturally.)

Have you thought about thoughts?
Do you have some?
Where do you think they come from?

Thoughts are points of sound/light
sheathing
stratospheres.
From up there
I have watched human beings

thinking they think.
Really, they hear.
Tuned in to radio bands
of collective understandings,
flashes of insight
going inside from outside.
Once in a while
a group magnetizes
a thought form, called
"a new idea," a sound mote—
and blaring it out
gets it caught up there in the sheath
with a new specific ionic band
all its own.
From above, this event appears
as a point of lighter air
rising into the biosphere.
Caught up there, it's available
to anyone else who wishes to share,
and to think they thought
by shifting their inner ears
to the exact note, and tuning in.
Interesting idea, this
that I thought I heard
while I was there.

Now I'm here, below below,
doing weekend duty
and fix-'em-ups.

NIN [*entering*]
I've been to the Father gods of Destiny,
War, and Economic Effort, talked to Proud Thomas
with his new girlfriend—the faithless husband!—
to see if any would help fair Helen.
To a man they were against it.
"We told her so! We told her so!"
they cry as though to add prediction
to their list of skills in lying.
I'm the only one who's caring for her person.
"Don't let her priceless, magnificent being
be broken in the underworld,"
I call to them, "don't let your forest be
a slag heap, or your river run with photographic fluid.
Don't let the daughter of beauty walk the streets
with rotten teeth and broken face."
I begged, I railed.

"What if she were your daughter, would
you leave her to disease and pimps and beggars,
drunkards and thieves and junkies,
and the irresponsible greed
of international companies?"
To no avail, they turn away.
"She wanted everything, to be a wife and mother
and a woman of the world. Let her see the price
she has to pay," they say. Their jealousy is evident.
Now I have come to make one final appeal to Enki,
last god on my list, the wisdom of nature,
a god whose peculiarities are entirely his. ⸸

ENKI
Who calls my name?

NIN
I looked everywhere for you †
and couldn't find you
in your usual haunts where I would expect
the god of natural things to be.
You weren't at Brighton-by-the Sea,
or the Black Forest, the Amazon River, or at Grand Teton.
I cabled Tibet, even spoke to the folk
who know the Glacier Elk,
tried all the deserts and the water tables,
checked out your favorite mountain peaks.
Your whereabouts were a mystery to monks,
physicists, the Audubon Society,
the Sierra Club, *and* Greenpeace.
Finally I consulted my Tarot
and was sent here—to below
this great metropolis of human activity.
What is it you are doing here, down under a city? ⸸

ENKI
Oh I have to be the one to help it go.
See that sign above my office door:
"GE," that's me—Grand Engineer. †
You know, they think they move
in opposition to me—
they're so much closer to me
than they know.
If I don't show up
on weekends at least
they blow up all the circuits
on their circuit boards, the bakers

can't control the yeast,
the airwaves jam, chemical combinations
simply don't combust,
and the sewage backs up the sluice
to swamp them. I just make sure the electric juice
remembers which way it needs to flow
so the city has its power, perhaps also
a little golden beauty and a bit of grace.
It's my way of keeping faith
between the human beings and me.

NIN
Speaking of things golden and beautiful,
I don't come for myself but rather to appeal
to you for Helen's sake.
Her grace and beauty strip away in an underground
cave of rare adventure. It's all very well
for her to learn some new and rougher ways of being,
but to stay forever—
where the rats dwell—
that's hell.
To stay forever in some gross industrial cave, that's
a kind of narcosis from which, to keep her beauty
active in our lives—we all must wake—

ENKI
Why do you make such effort for another woman,
for Helen? For someone fallen—
are you in love with her?

NIN
I don't know my motive or my gain,
I know her shadow falls across me
where I lay.

I know we must have been close
since now she's gone
I walk my life a ghost.

I don't know our middle or our end.
I know in our beginning
we were friends.

I don't understand her motive or her gain,
I don't know where she's been
or where she'll be again.

I know my life is not the same
without her flamboyance, or her flame,
I know her shadow falls across me where I lay.

I know I must be feeling bad
since now when I sleep
it's underneath my bed.

I never undertook to know her mind,
I'll never know her motive
or her plan.

I know her shadow falls across me
where I stand—

ENKI
Good gracious, don't go on.
I can see this has you very down,
though I think you know more about her future
than you're letting on,
and yes of course I'll help,
what else does nature do but try to help.
I'm amiable, mostly, both for building up and
tearing down. You want apples, ask the apple tree:
rounder, redder, more juice. She'll comply
as best she can. You want bombs that bomb the living substance
out of all Bombay and any other place you
care to name—well, you've got them.
We try harder, faster, longer,
here in nature land. I'll do what I can.
Besides, I certainly could use some assistance
teaching natural principles to the humans,
they're so certain of their own unnaturalness
they've made a cult of being ugly.

NIN
Ugly is incomplete beauty in my view.
Beauty caught short before it can complete
the act to some full end.

ENKI
No, ugly's a thing of its own,
a use of pain and alienation
toward some slavish end.
Those who believe they are ugly
objectify the rest of us.

NIN
But is it natural then?

ENKI
Oh it's natural enough,
but you don't have to live your days

in the very gut of Nature—you can, in your life,
choose qualities…

NIN
What is it you suppose our Helen needs
to get her freed?

ENKI
Someone like you, I think, a friend!
Someone to stand beside
without judgment, and to follow through.
We can't send you, you have to stay above,
and do your mourning of her loss.
I'll have to make some friends to see her through.
Marvelous objects come from dirt.
I've plenty underneath my fingernails; don't look
if creative process makes you squeamish.
Where do jelly doughnuts come from, if not dirt?
Just let me give them some interesting body shape
to walk around in for a lifetime…
These androgynous beings, genderless
and all-engendered, fairies of light
and liveliness. I call them into being purposefully,
to help restore the god of beauty
to our daily lives.

> [KUR *and* GAL *appear, stretching and waking; they are a young dike and a young faggot,*[20] *dressed in self-conscious country clothes such as clean new overalls, and with the appearance of health and innocence.*]

ENKI
May the fairies be vegetarian! †
May they be pure of heart as the earth is
in her shirt of dirt.
Let them be pure as air on Mount Olympus,
air inside an Atlantic blowfish, air pumped
into a rubber tire in 1932 in Nevada
before the explosions, before Reno, before traffic
smogged up Tahoe.
Let them be pure of body, let them
be vegetarian! Fruitarian! Breatharian! Let them
eat only bean sprouts, and then
only by inhaling the delicate breath of
someone else who has eaten bean sprouts!
Let them eat only thoughts!
Let them tell only pristine lies.
Let them be pure of brain, let them read everything
and watch thousands of movies. Let them seldom

have contact of a dangerous sexual nature,
let them have lots of love but
let them do much of their mating
on the telephone. Let them not be lonely, and
if they have to be alone,
let them be alone together; let them care for each other.
And let them get past the gatekeeper of the deadly
underworld, cleverly disguised
as a clean lean cloud of lean clean flies!
Let them carry the water of life and the tree of life,
to keep the apple of love and beauty growing in their hearts. ⸸

NIN
Enki, I'm so glad I came to you,
a woman is rich whose friends are true.
Helen will be back among us soon,
spreading her good cheer
and healing our wounds.

ENKI
I have some bottled, bubbly, crisp
imported water here
for them to take down to her
for her reconstitution,
and a gorgeous Payless Nursery
rubber plant.
And now we've got to figure out
how to trick the Vixen of the Great Below
before she reaches out to grab
these pristine creatures and then hangs them up
to roil and rot
before they get Queen Helen out.

[ENKI *pulls* NIN *and the two fairies into a circle of conspiracy, drawing on the floor with his wrench as they continue making plans.*]

GATE FIVE: BELOWWORLD

A Woman among Motorcycles

ERESHKIGAL'*s Crow Bar. The decor is greatly improved. It is Halloween, so there are black cats and pumpkins here and there. Most of the* CROW DIKES *are tattooed and dressed in black leather, carrying staffs or swords, with eyepatches and the like. Some are costumed as bees or nurses. The crossed swords at the back of the bar have been taken down and one is on the bar.* HELEN *has tied the other to her broom and is hacking at one of the roof support poles, or perhaps a large standing coatrack, then spears it through as though it were a bull and she a matador. Between thrusts she drinks liquor from a glass; there are several shot glasses near her and it is obvious she has drunk quite a bit. She is looking disheveled and as though she is not taking very good care of herself.* ERESHKIGAL *is counting money out of the register or taking inventory.* NOTHING *is tending bar.*

HELEN [*grunting and growling with effort, teeth clenched, ramming the pole with the sword or spear*]
Now I've got you where I want you.
You'll never escape my fury.

CROW
What is Venus doing I wonder?

CROW
She's doing some swordplay.

CROW
She's handling a big pricking stick.

CROW
That's cutting.

CROW
It's CAW stick.

CROW
She's practicing being a matador.

CROW
She's spearing Taurus.

CROW
She's trying to cut through all that bull.

[HELEN *whirls with the spear, knocking a glass off the table. It shatters, which infuriates her.*]

ERESHKIGAL
I hope *we* manage to escape your fury.
What is it you are doing? Is that your costume?
What are you dressed up as, Ernest Hemingway?[21]

HELEN [*insulted*]
I'm trying to learn to be a warrior;
I thought that was what you wanted.

ERESHKIGAL [*coming out from behind the bar*]
You don't have to learn to be a warrior.
You have to remember having been one.

[HELEN *tries to speak.*]

ERESHKIGAL
Silence, Inanna.
When you have a memory, you shall speak.

[*She holds a full-sized hand mirror in front of* HELEN*'s face;* HELEN *takes it and gapes into it, trying to smooth her hair and making tough faces.* [22]]

Look, Helen, look into your mind!
If yours is sodden, look into mine!
Women were warriors in Caesar's time!
Have you never remembered the warrior queens
who resisted conquest on Europe's greens?
Have you never remembered the bulldike queen
who nearly unseated the Roman's claim
on England, during Nero's reign?[23]

[ERESHKIGAL *takes the mirror back, then goes to the pile of costumes, rummages through, and comes up with a red braided wig, a long spear, and a long robe or tunic, Celtic style, which she puts on. As she performs, the* CROW WARRIOR *dikes act out various parts while* HELEN *clumsily but persistently joins in.*]

I, Boudica, †

a queen am I,
a warrior and a shaman.
Shameless is my goddess and ferocious;
my god's foot cloven.

I am protectress of my horse-bound clansmen.
A red-haired, full-robed, bronze-belted swordswoman,
I am a queen of sacred groves and other old realms
where astronomers divine from droves of animals
or flocks of birds, and study the signs in palms;
a queen of times when men are lovers to the men
and the women to the women,
as is our honored pagan custom.
Ever and ever did we think to reign
in such an independent fashion,
until the day the foe came.

He came to my temple.
In ships he came to me.
Our possessions upon the prow of his ship he put.
He with hired soldiers came
to our self-ruled regions.
The foe, he with legions, entered my court.

He put his hands upon me, he filled me with fear.
My garments he tore away, and sent them to his wife.
The foe stripped off my jewels and put them on his son.
He seized my people's lands and gave them to his men.

He put his hands upon me, he filled me with rage.
I spoke to him in anger.
I told him of his danger.
So for me myself did he seek in the shrines.
In front of my folk he had me beat;
and this was not the worst I had to meet:
he seized my young daughters and had them raped.
He seized my daughters
and had them raped;
oh queen of heaven, queen
who shatters the mountains;
how long before you must my
face be cast in hate?

A queen am I, my cities have betrayed me.
A queen, Boudica, am I, my cities have betrayed me.
In that rebellious year
of sixty-one A.D. I rose up,
I, Boudica, over the countryside
from clan to clan and ear to ear,
I drove round in a chariot,
my daughters with me.

To every woman and every man
I spoke:

> "Now is the battle drawn
> which must be victory or death.
> For today I am more than your queen,
> and more than your mother deeply wronged,
> I am all the power of women brought down;
> one who will fight to reclaim her place.
> This is my resolve. Resolve is what I own.
> We women shall fight. The men can live,
> if they like, and be slaves."

And so we went to war.
Our men went with us.
And for centuries since, the foe has
searched for us in all our havens,
secret circles, rings and covens;
almost always we elude him,
we who remember who we are;
we who are never not at war.

On that day
didn't I, Boudica,
didn't I up rise,
didn't I slay,
didn't I hold fast
the ancient ways.

Wasn't I like a wall
wasn't I a great dike
against a giant spill,
that iron sea
of Roman pikes
that came to conquer Gaul.

Even if for one day
didn't the foe almost fall,
didn't his teeth gnash,
wasn't his bladder galled,
didn't the foe, even he,
know fear;
he feared me.

He feared me, then,
in his being
unable to fully win
unable to fully kill
the rebel things
my name means,
he fears still.

He fears me still,
for my shameless guise
and lesbian ways;
for undefeated eyes,
a warrior's spine
and all my memories
of women's time.

A queen am I, my city
needs to find me.
Meantime the foe arrives
unceasingly
from every steel-grey sea,
by every mountain road on earth
he enters all my cities
and for me myself he seeks
in my varied shrines,
in my temples he pursues me,

in my halls he terrifies me,
saying, "Cause her to go forth."
He goads. He burns, he murders.
He erodes.

A queen am I,
a warrior and a shaman.
Shameless is my goddess and ferocious;
my god's foot cloven.

A queen am I, a living memory
who knows her own worth
and who remembers that the future
is the past rehearsed,

> and *not should I go forth*
> unless it be for battle girthed.
> Unless it be for battle girthed,
> and belted, *not should I go forth*

until the foe is driven from the earth.[24] ⸸

> [*The* WARRIOR CROW DIKES *cheer wildly and toast their queen, pulling out bottles and parading around in their costumes.*]

ERESHKIGAL [*breathless from her effort*]
Who else has a memory, let her speak.

> [*A* CROW DIKE *steps forward, dressed like a Viking, with long blond braids and a sword; she is a large woman.*]

CROW DIKE
I am Ildreth remembering.[25] †

All in green I rode a tall horse
deep in the North woods, my hair
so yellow it was white and fine and
down to here.

Big as any conquering Viking man I tracked them
and by trickery caught one or maybe two.
Stepping noiseless behind I ran
one fellow through
before his ax could pop my skull.
Blood along my scabbard told the others
to steer clear.

Protecting other women and the children
and the older people was my task.
Proof is here on my face, in this new mark…
I studied in the mirror this morning
getting ready for work…

or was this from just last weekend
when I, racing nowhere in my car,
wrecked it, going head first
through the windshield and being
drunk when the cops came,
got out, of course, and blindly fought them
and was beat raw to the pulp
that left, from cheek to jaw,
this deep pink scar?

I swear I'm going to quit this life
of drinking whiskey, trying to keep
a girlfriend—spending all my money
in the bar.
I'm going up to the country to build a house
with my own hands,
find some ground—to love,
to leap, and land upon.

I'm going to the country to build a house,
maybe invite a few friends,
some strangers—people in my same bind,
no name for what they're doing in
their sacks of skin.
Going to go looking for my real mind,
the one I think I once had
before my memory got lost.
Going to sit at the back of my house
and gather my old thoughts
    like scattered birds,
and make images of mud,
and words and glass,
and gather my old gods
    like a flock of birds
from a soul-place,
and touch my fingers
gently to my own
and to my lover's face,
and study up.

ERESHKIGAL
Who else has a memory, let her speak.

[HELEN *steps into the semicircle. As she speaks, the* CROW DIKES *become men* MOTORCYCLE CROWS, *revving their engines as they circle her.* ERESHKIGAL *sits at the bar, watching.*]

HELEN
I remember a time, a night when the sky

was a sheet of crystal and the air was dry,
I became a Woman in the Middle of Motorcycles.

One night, a night of the full moon †
rising just as Venus lowered in the West,
I went out walking, miles
into the hills, alone,
not even my dog went with me.
It never occurred to me to carry a gun.
I crossed an abandoned parking lot
whose asphalt had begun to rot,
with grass and thistles already pushing
thinly through,
and the first roar of the motorcycle
only startled me,
then two more, then three,
I wasn't frightened until they were five
and circling me, their black boots
and jackets armor against the moonlight.
Dense with terror, I turned to see
they were ten, all single men, grinning
and grim and watching me.

I knew instinctively this was not the time to fall.
Begging, showing fear or pain would be my death.
I drew a great first breath
and throwing back my head, I called down the moon,
"Mother Moon," then
"Mother Venus," I called,
as the cycles crawled past, circling and waiting,
and roaring and watching me.
And then I said my mother's name
and hers and hers and hers and hers

Grandmother Mabel I said,
Grandmother Kate I said,
Grandmother Clementine I said,
Grandmother Mary I said,
then I called my aunts to me,
Margaret, who baked bread when grandpa died, Helen I know nothing
of at all, Agnes spanked me till I cried, Sybil helped build her
own cinderblock house by the shores of Lake Michigan,
Gertrude who wasn't mechanical drove her
very first car
straight up a telephone pole,
Betty worked forty years in a grocery store, and Blanche
wore a high-topped dress,
black stockings, and a brilliant smile

in the only photo I have seen,
when she was seventeen, in 1917.

When I had finished with my aunts,
I called the gods and mothers of the gods, Mary,
Anna, Isis, Ishtar, Artemis, Aphrodite, Hecate, Oyá, Demeter,
Freya, Kali, Kwan Yin, Pele, Yemanya, Maya, Diana, Hera, Oshun,
and after that some saints, Barbara, Joan, and Brigit;
as my memory ran out I made up some more saints,
canonized them on the spot.

And finally I called my friends including from high school,
Francine who has ESP and never leaves me,
Karen who wore black and was a warrior, Betty who is able to
live her dreams, Karen who wears pink sweaters and has a face of
sunshine, Alice of the little furry paws and dedicated life,
Carol piercingly faithful to her own axis, Pat whose heart is
always hanging in my hallway, careful careful careful Eloise,
Willyce with her singingvoice, all the rest, then each woman I
have ever worked with, then some heroines, Eleanor, Gwen,
Gertrude, Margaret, Amelia, Hilda, till I had chanted every
woman's name I knew.

When I was through I said them all over again,
turning in my own circle with my face up and the moon
shining in, it must have been an hour or more I whirled
and chanted, filling my ears with my woman-naming roar.

When I opened my eyes
the angry men were gone;
Venus had set, the moon was down,
I stood in the asphalt field
alone—
and not at all alone.[26]

[*As the above proceeds, the* MOTORCYCLE CROWS *one by one spin out of the circle and freeze in positions of goddess statues: sitting palms up on their knees, standing growling like shamanic Kali, standing gracefully with palms lifted like Kwan Yin or the Cretan snake goddess, standing with hands in Marian prayer attitude, standing aiming a bow and arrow like the warriors Diana or Oyá, arms clasping each other like the reunited Demeter and Persephone.*]

ERESHKIGAL
I can see that you already see, Helen,
there is more to standing
than simply having standing, and more
to understanding than simply falling down;

there is standing your own ground.

[*The* CROW WARRIORS *break their statue postures and begin dancing a ring dance, with* HELEN *and* ERESHKIGAL *dancing too,* HELEN *so drunk she is staggering in and out of sync. Stage rear* NOTHING *also dances, alone and spinning in the opposite direction.*]

GATE SIX: BELOWWORLD

Judgment of Helen

ERESHKIGAL*'s Crow Bar, with* ERESHKIGAL, HELEN, NOTHING, *and* CROW DIKE JUDGES. *The bar is now completely spruced up, looking colorful and light, with candles and green decorations. There is a lot of crystal in evidence, as well as* ERESHKIGAL*'s wind chimes. But* HELEN *is looking terrible, haggard and doped up, dirty and disheveled, with dark circles under her eyes. She is drinking at the upstage center table, and there are pill bottles and other paraphernalia of drug addiction on the table also, or any other contemporary signs of deterioration. She is laughing and talking very closely, perhaps dancing with* NOTHING *her voice noticeably high-pitched and tense. The* CROWS, *who are* JUDGES *in black gowns in this Gate, are playing pool.*

CROWS [*singing*]
Green, green, green is the color
of my true love's hair,
and of her teeth, and of her toes,
and of her face so fair.

ERESHKIGAL [*striking the wind chimes*]
Deny, deny, deny, deny.
Seven venial virtues
cloud the crystal of her eye.

She's keeping counsel with Nothing;
I keep the counsel of the carrion crow.

As hour by hour, I go on growing older †
I like the carrion crow
as my advisor.
Not many are more wicked, not many are wiser.

For advisor I'll take the carrion crow
to stand upon my shoulder
with his caw-caw-coffin chatter
keeping me self-conscious.

Keeping me so super conscious
that my flesh, however pretty
and however dear to me

belongs to someone else tomorrow
(or to no one)
and is only borrowed clay.

Is only modeled clay, my loves,
to animate the fray
and we'll slough it off to burrow
in a lighter cloth of sky.

In a lighter coat of sky, my bird,
to lay out the next play,
we'll cough it off to burrow
in the beauty of the sky.

As for beauty of the being,
it isn't fixed in time
longer than the ching ching ching
of a wind chime.

It's an animating play, my crow,
of light on surfaces.
Like the carrion bird I carry
on my shoulder, beauty strips away
the dross, so we can fly—

in a lighter coat of sky, my friend,
in a wind chime's clime—
and we'll laugh it off to burrow
in a lighter cloth of time. ⸸

HELEN [*her voice heavy with cynicism and disillusion*]
If the mother of life is death
who is the mother of death?

CROW CHORUS OF JUDGES [*rapid exchange*]

CROWS
There's no crow like an old crow. †

CROWS
CAW CAW CAW

CROW
What has a crusty shell
and turns red when it is boiling mad?

CROW
A crow dad!

CROWS
CAW CAW CAW

CROW
What gets all decked out
and then hangs from a peg
in order to frighten people like us?

CROW
A scarecrow![27]

CROWS
CAW CAW CAW

CROW
Darken up, you crows!
We're here to seriously, or is it cereally, or is it
surlily, or is it surely or is it sorely or is it
scornfully or is it scorefilly—

CROW
We're here to CAWnsider—

CROWS
CAW CAW CAW

CROW
Here to CAWnsider the CAWS of death—

CROW
And to try the goddess of life and beauty—

CROW
Try life!

CROW
Give life a trial!

CROW
CAWL life to the stand!

CROW
Bring out the evidence—

CROW
The evidence is here in the form of this lovely lady.

HELEN [*self-mockingly*]
I am the planet Venus, traveling toward the dawn—

CROW
Who thinks she is Venus incarnate—

CROW
Evidently—

CROW
The evidence is evident—

CROW
Die, you Helen—

CROW
The first CAWS of death is this:
first, it was alive,
then, it died;
therefore my CAWnsidered opinion is:

CROWS
CAW CAW CAW

CROW
The CAWS of death is life—

CROW
A scandalous revelation—

CROW
Yet imminently true—

CROW
And effectively false—

CROW
It is true
everything that is now dead
was formerly alive
and if *A* inevitably precedes *B*
we are obviously talking CAWsation—

CROW
And CAWruption.

CROW
And CAWnsternation.

CROW
Therefore, in retaliation
I CAWndemn life to death.

TWO CROWS
Brilliant! Charming! Correctly morbid!
Essential logic!

CROWS
CAW CAW CAW

CROW
Therefore I CAWndemn all life to death
on the grounds that life is the CAWS of dying.

CROWS
CAW CAW CAW

CROW
What grounds is this?

CROW
CAWfee grounds—

CROWS
CAW CAW CAW

CROW
Here it turns out that all this time
dirty old Life is the primary CAWS of death—

CROW
And must be punished—

CROWS
CAW CAW CAW

CROW
Ooh oooh oooooh PUNished—

CROW
How dreadful—

CROW
I *hate* puns—

CROW
How ungrateful—

CROW
The Gateful Dread—

CROW
A pun is the lowest form of twit—

CROW
All life is hereby condamned to death—

CROW
Condomed to which?

CROW
A condomnation of death to life—

CROW
I haven't felt so completely dead in a long time—

CROW
You always did make me feel so dead—

CROW
Let's go out on the town and die a little—

CROW
Die it up while you can—

CROW
It makes a person happy just to be so dead—

CROW
Just to be so dead and a player in death's little game—

CROW
Death's CAWn game—

CROWS
CAW CAW CAW

CROW
It makes a person happy
just to be so depressed
and playing in the CAWn game of death—

CROWS
CAW CAW CAW

ERESHKIGAL
Admit. Admit. Admit. Admit
when you see with the crystal eye of death
you'll see into the heart of it.
Here Helen, take this gift—a mirror
of memory.
This mirror is called,
"when this you see remember me."[28]
When your ordinary mind is cloudy,
look into this larger one.

HELEN [*taking the hand-mirror*]
Oh Ereshkigal,
I'm not sure I want to see what's in here.
Oh god, I'm wrinkled around my eyes,
my mouth is puckered and my nose is misshapen.

ERESHKIGAL
Is that my face or yours that you see in there?

How is she ever going to look into her mind
when she can't see past her face?

HELEN
Thomas was right.
Nothing ages a person like experience.

NOTHING
I do the best I can.

ERESHKIGAL
Well, you're on your way to being a goddess,
of sagacity, at least, if not of popularity.
There are four kinds of memory;
you've recollected three. First, your mythic memory
as a goddess; second, your past-life history,
both the outer and inner versions in your mind;
third, the collective, consciously connected
recollections of your kind.
The last is of your own person,
the carefully buried splinter memories of childhood.
It's time for you to see whatever you dare to see.

HELEN [*staring past the mirror*]
Mirror, mirror here I stand.
Help me remember who I am.

I was a cherished, petted child.

ERESHKIGAL [*rolling her eyes*]
Mirror, mirror in the sky.
Help her learn how not to lie.

Helen, your memory— †
what is it?
Is it your mother?
Is it what she doesn't say?
Are there relatives you love
but never want to see?
Is it an evil glitter
in your own eye?

Is it the First Word,
or a dancing bird? Is it Idea
or is it a girl named Ida?
Or is it "I did it"?
Is it a story with an end and a beginning,
or a spider spinning her web
in every direction?
Is it space-time as an abstraction,

or is she a person?
Helen, your memory,
is it convection
or simple conviction,
is it a movie
or is it moving?
Helen, your memory! Look into your mind!
If yours is cloudy, then look into mine!
You were not only a petted, cherished child!
You were a martyr in your childhood time!

[HELEN *looks into the mirror and slowly and carefully begins to recover her childhood memories; she does not act drunk during this scene. She sometimes stands still, sometimes walks around the stage, holding her face, or pulling her hair, falling on* ERESHKIGAL*'s shoulder to moan or cry.* ERESHKIGAL *is extremely tender and comforting.*]

HELEN [*shuddering*]
The mind is a sheet of crystal
when your memory is clear.
I remember my fear.
I remember the entire war.
I remember being there.

My father struck me with his hand
when I was five.
Lucky me, lucky me,
lucky to be alive.

My mother threw an iron at me
when I was four.
I lay unconscious on the
bathroom floor.

I don't know their motives
or their pain.
I know their shadows fell across me
where I lay.

My brother stabbed his sex in me
when I was three.
My anger dangles in my throat,
shamefully.

My sister pressed pillows on
my face at two.
Thick mush: To hush, to hush, I
struggle through.

I don't know the motives

of their rage.
I know their shadows fall across me
all my days.

My mother thrust a pin in me
when I was one.
Distrust. Distrust of
everyone.

I was a cherished,
petted child.
Lucky me, lucky me,
lucky to be alive.

ERESHKIGAL
Well done, you counted down to one.
But you aren't done.
Can you count down to zero
is the question.

HELEN [*after a long pause*]
At zero I begin to understand
murders repeated, in my hand.
At zero I begin to count again:
my mother and I are one,

my father and I are two,
my brother and I are three,
my sister and I are four,
and my daughter she is five.

Sometimes she is cherished,
sometimes she is a battered child.
Lucky her, lucky her,
lucky to be alive.[29] ⸸

ERESHKIGAL [*rocks* HELEN *in her arms for a few moments, then she disengages from* HELEN, *moving behind the bar*]
Admit. Admit. Admit. Admit. †
The eye of death
is at the heart of it,
and the clearest eye
is the eye of I-did-almost-die.
Admit. Admit. Admit. Admit. ⸸

HELEN
Offer me something, Nothing.

NOTHING
I've offered you everything I have †

left in my bag:
Have a depression, have two.
Have a serious bout with the six-month flu.
Have an addiction on repeated prescriptions,
and have a habit of drink, of course.
Have any addiction that devours
your resources and sours your friendships.
I'm really not particular;
have whatever hurts you more, more, more. ⸸

ERESHKIGAL [*to* HELEN]
I have to congratulate you †
for accepting everything Nothing
has had to offer, all the liquor
you could drink, every kind of drug
to hallucinate you into every phony mental state,
depression so steep your grave is half a kilometer deep,
annihilation in all its clever shapes,
alienation, nihilism, extreme materialism,
projection, violent subjugation—
repression, psychic and physical sterilization...
congratulations to you for accepting
all that was offered, including the most extreme
isolation of any creature on or underneath
this earth. It's not as simple as it may seem
to poison the apple of self-esteem.
Goody goody goody you,
you gobbled the entire apple down,[30]
and while you'll never be
as big a Nothing
as you think you are, still you've done it all
at Nothing's beck and call,
and I congratulate you
for being such a nice girl, for taking it
without too much complaint,
for eating absolutely everything you found on your plate. ⸸

[*During the following poem and chorus* HELEN *drinks, takes drugs, sobs in desolation, passes out on the table, then drops to the floor in a state like death.*]

HELEN
Is this what dying is really like? †
I have the sensation of needing to regulate
my every breath;
of my life being something I stand and watch,
a falling star against a falling sky—

reality I thought I had in hand
suddenly dropping down
a funnel of air—
I have the sensation
of the black hole of creation
squeezing me through its bloody gate,
to what's out there;
what's out there?

I wait. I cannot breathe. I shake.
What if I admit, admit, admit,
and still can't make sense
of any of it?
What if I'm crazy?
What if I never again act right?
What if everything—
even the mirror of sound and sight—
is a lie?
What if all I ever do is die?
What if I don't, and hate
every minute of staying alive?
Is this what being born is like? ⸸

CROW
The Queen of Swords will take you through †
the House of Horrors.

CROW
Where is Helen now?

CROW
She's gone to the House of Horse.

CROW
She's gone to the House of Horus.[31]

CROW
Horace took her to his house.

CROW
She's gone over to the Horace House.

CROW
Helen is a fallen woman.

CROW
Falling through a crack.

CROW
She's descending.

CROW
Down goes our Venus.

CROW
She's gone to Horrid Horace's Whorehouse.

CROW
As a customer (or consumer I mean)?

CROW
Not as a consumer, as one of the commodities.

CROW
How venial.

crow
Falling onto her back.

CROW
How funereal.

CROW
Falling onto her head.

CROW
How venerable.

CROW
Falling into her heart.

CROW
How vulnerable.

CROW
Falling into her vulgar vulva.

CROW
How venereal.

CROWS	CROW
How venereal	an episode
How venereal	an afternoon
How venereal	a painting
How venereal	two flowers
How venereal	lady day
How venereal	mashed potatoes
How venereal	my life story
How venereal	love is the answer
How venereal	without trying
How venereal	dear old Mom
How venereal	a funeral

How venereal someone's ambitions
How venereal as the world whirls
How venereal at a snail's pace
How venereal with Horace
How venereal and how responsible
How venereal and candied apples
How venereal a corporation
How venereal and how pig-headed ⸸

[*The* CROWS *lift* HELEN*'s limp body as they perform this last chant, carry her to the crossbeam upstage center, or to a large standing coatrack, or to a deeper chamber and hang her on the back of a door by the back of her dress or shirt. She hangs limp, facing the audience, nearly over* ERESHKIGAL*'s head.*]

ERESHKIGAL [*to* HELEN]
Helen, your memory! Look into your mind!
If yours is sleeping, then look into mine!

[*To audience.*]

The secret is, love is all †
we ever need to eat.
It's the vital golden flow
we get from wheat and meat and beets,
and art, and sex, and lovely conversation.

It's the glow that pours through doors
of any open-hearted person,
who if she doesn't know the secret,
doesn't keep it under lock and key,
leaks more for me, more for me.

I've taken all her offers,
to breach her coffers;
I've used her vitality
for my own young glow.

I have eaten her energy,
I have borrowed her beauty,
and I've gotten her to eat enough crow
to keep her forever here below.[32] ⸸

[ERESHKIGAL *holds her stomach and rocks in pain and obvious sorrow.*]

GATE SEVEN: BELOWWORLD

Reconstitution: Just Stand Her Up Again

ERESHKIGAL's *Crow Bar has not changed since Gate Six except that the dead* HELEN *has been laid out on the bar. She is covered with a sheet of clear plastic.*[33] *Three days and nights have passed; the* CROW DIKES *have been holding a wake for her. The* CROWS *become* DEMONS *near the end of this Gate, perhaps with widely banded black and yellow sweatshirts and pointed hats, long black fingernails, black and yellow stockings. At opening* ERESHKIGAL *is in pain, upstage left center, holding her stomach and chest, rocking back and forth. Mythically speaking, she is now giving birth to the new Inanna.*

ERESHKIGAL
For three days and three nights
she has looked like this.

She lives on a glass mountain. †
She sleeps in a fishbowl.
She's wrapped in Saranwrap.
She's silent under her bell jar.
She's locked in her tower of glass.

She's Queen of the Ice Queens.
She feels none of her feelings.
She acts none of her actions.
She speaks none of her insights.
She hears only the crash
of her own cold pulse,
and the words: it's getting worse
and worse
and worse. ⸸

CROW
She's inside Mount Venus.

CROW
She looks terrible.

CROW
She's dead.

CROW
She looks dead.

CROW
She smells dead.

CROW
Whatever it was she did she overdid it.

CROW
There's Nothing growing on her.

NOTHING
I'm not growing on her.
She doesn't care for me.
Leave me out of this.

[*Enter the* FAIRIES, KUR *and* GAL. *They are vivacious, dancing and chanting with tambourines. They commiserate with* ERESHKIGAL *in her mourning.*]

FAIRIES
Isis, Inanna, Artemis, Kali,
Ishtar, Gaia, Hera, Hecate.
Lady of many lives we love you.
Lady of deadly powers we need you.
Lady of shadow motives we respect you.
Lady of midnight skies we greet you.

Are you sad?
We're sad too.
Does your heart ache?
Our heart aches too.
Does your womb hurt?
Our womb hurts too.

ERESHKIGAL [*interrupting*]
Alright, alright, GodDAMMit
Now you've got me crying.
What is it you want?
I'll give it to you.
Just don't try to flatter me.
Offer them something, Nothing.

FAIRIES
OH NO, anything else, but
Nothing for us, no, Nothing for us.

CROW
They don't want Nothing.

FAIRIES
We're happy just as we are.[34]
We've come to reconstitute the Queen.

ERESHKIGAL [*pointing to* HELEN]
That ugly thing?
She's an Ice Queen.
Unresponsive and cold,
and growing old.

CROW
She's an Ice Queen Crone.

[*The* CROWS *examine the* FAIRIES]

CROW
They've come to reconstitute her.

CROW
To reconstitute her—

CROW
—just stand her up again.

CROW
To reconstitute her—
CROW
—just add water.

CROW
Stir a little—

CROW
—just add lettuce.

CROW
Just add vitamins.

CROW
Just add a little music.

CROWS
Just add Fairy dust!
Just add a little plasma!
Just add some rubber tubing!
Just plug something into her!

CROW
Just add some chloroform.

FAIRIES
Not chloroform—chlorophyll!

[*The* FAIRIES *reconstitute* HELEN *by changing her makeup and her clothes; meanwhile the* CROW DIKES *become* CROW DEMONS.]

ERESHKIGAL [*still mourning* HELEN]
Control, control, control, control. †
Seven venial virtues
cloud the crystal of her soul.

She came here believing she's something
and that though others are poor and downtrodden
she herself is wealthy and generous,
when Nothing is what she is related to.

She came here believing that nature loves her
and that mankind is a vicious brute.

She came here believing that while others rape
and batter and make war
she herself is innocent.

She came believing women are weak
and cannot defend themselves.

She came believing that she was a pampered,
petted child, never abused by her family.

Worst of all she came here believing her beauty
lives only in the vitality of her youth.
Since I have stolen her beauty,
she has no choice but to think she is ugly.

She came here believing—umm—oh crum—
I can't remember the seventh one— ⸸

> [KUR *and* GAL *hold* HELEN *in their arms, crooning to her, singing the Fairy chant, Isis, Inanna, Demeter, Kali, etc., giving her sips of water and nibbles of the plant, fanning her and petting her, and dressing her in a gorgeous gold and white, or perhaps salmon and deep blue, gown they have brought with them.*[35] *They help her off the bar, where she staggers center stage, wobbling. Exeunt* KUR *and* GAL, *gaily.* ERESHKIGAL *acts surprised to see her back on her feet.*]

HELEN
I fell through a hole †
in the eye of death;
I drew Zero's breath.

I went to where the wind lives—
I put my ear there.
I went down below.
Where the wind lives is chaos;
what the wind does is blow.

The center of the wind is paradox,
completely orderly and patterned,
a mathematical, coherent person
with a mind, even a soul.

The eye is a sheet of crystal

on the other side of time;
the sky is a paradigm.
I could see myself reflected
in my inner and my outer mind.

Deep in the eye of death
the light is never standing,
it's dancing, it's unfolding,
light is holding dark,
shy is holding bold,
everything is blowing hot
with cold;

and that glancing of
the light that is not standing,
that speculating,
is the partnership we have
with death that is not, is
not dying, is glowing,
is chancing.

I'm no longer lying
in my cave of glass, I'm rocking,
I'm shaking,
I'm expanding

knowing flesh with all its names
is just a lovely little screen,
a speckled net,
for keeping some particular thought
intact

while we do
such juggling in the light
as we can do,

the clumsy stancing
that we call our standing
and our falling
through the blowholes carefully provided
in the eye of death.

I went all the way to Zero,
leaned in Zero's door;
and you know what lives in there?
Absolutely everything—everything at all.

ERESHKIGAL
Speak, Helen. Speak into my ear.
Speak until you lose your fear.

[*As* HELEN *revives her strength she begins to revile* ERESHKIGAL. NOTHING *offers* HELEN *a glass of liquid or a glass pipe, which she flings to the floor where it shatters.*]

HELEN
I thought I needed you,
I've had enough of you,
you're trying to own me,
you wish you *were* me;
my beauty is real,
you can't take it,
You—who are you!
You stripped me—

[HELEN *walks around furiously, followed by* CROWS.]

CROWS
You stripped me;

CROWS
Stripped!

HELEN [*screaming at* ERESHKIGAL]
Like a chevrolet parked too long on a side street.

CROWS
Stripped!

HELEN
Like a chicken in a restaurant
specializing in chicken kebob.

CROWS
Stripped!

HELEN
Like a woman alone in a hotel
with a guilty-looking stranger.

CROWS
Stripped!

HELEN
Like a new recruit in the army.

CROWS
Stripped!

HELEN
Like a corpse thrown from a car at midnight.

CROWS
Stripped!

HELEN
Like a house before its next paint job.

CROWS
Stripped!

HELEN
Like a turkey on his way to the crap game run by foxes.

CROWS
Stripped!

HELEN
Like a fur seal in fur seal clubbing season.

ERESHKIGAL
I just remembered her seventh venial virtue.
She thought she needed another person
to guide her through her life.
Is anything more tawdry
than the end of a love affair between two people
who had entirely different expectations?
All right, all right, you're going!
I can see that!
I can't wait to get you out of here!
I'm going to give you everything of yours
and more than you bargained for.

Recall! Recall! Recall! Recall!
Heaven and earth are yours, Helen,

you'll be Queen of the May.[36]
Clarity of vision,
clarity of hearing, too, you'll be hearing voices.
You'll have such a memory, as
remembers the future,
try to explain to your friends how you know so
much about them! Measurement and number
belong to you, Helen, now
you'll have to be a teacher.
Curiosity and scholarship will be yours
and metaphor—
you'll be a scientist—and more—a seer—
looked up to by everyone,
pitied by none; half the population will blame
their troubles on you. You'll sometimes hate it.
Decision is yours, Helen, and forcefulness comes

with it; no more excuses. You'll be known as
a speaker of truth, and all your suffering
will be amusing since you'll know—
how absolutely it's for Nothing.
But you asked for it, so you're going to get it.
Consciousness especially will be yours,
and its sister conscience.
Use them to polish the apple of self-esteem.
Worst of all your beauty will increase
as you get older, even in your own eyes, along
with your stature. You'll never be able to retire.
Never to complain. Never to want, always to
have, to be a provider. You'll get tired.
Don't expect me to pity you.
All I ask in return is that you choose
another innocent one to take your place.
Someone who needs to count down to Zero!
Demons of guilt will go with you
to make sure you keep this pledge.
Don't expect me to call you.
We've met before; you know we'll meet again,
if not in this life, then in some other one.

[HELEN *leaves, leading a procession of seven* CROW DEMONS; *they climb up to the upper world.* ERESHKIGAL *sits in the chair upstage, with the little table, contemplative, facing the audience as the lights go down on her. She blows the candle out.* NOTHING *blows all the other candles out. Lights rise on the street outside the Crow Bar. There on the street the procession meets* NIN, *plainly dressed, anxiously waiting for* HELEN.]

CROW DEMONS [*beginning to grab* NIN]
Let's go, let's go.
Here's a likely one, let's take her.

HELEN [*shoving* CROWS *away*]
You can't take her,
she loves me.

When I bowed down so low,
she bowed down too.

Even when she couldn't find me
she stood beside me.

Even when she couldn't understand me
she stood by me.

Even when she couldn't stand me
she stood for me.

You can't take her,
I love her as a friend.

Because of her I know more
about being human;

more than "stand up for myself,"
I know "stand up for another woman."

[NIN *and* HELEN *embrace and begin talking excitedly to each other about recent events.* ENKI *comes in, with* KUR *and* GAL. *He is dressed in fire-fighting garb, with a crown of leaves around his head, and so are the* FAIRIES. ENKI *is carrying a fire hose. The* CROW DEMONS *grab* KUR *and* GAL.]

CROWS
Let's take these!

CROW
They seem perfectly good for Nothing!

CROW
Let's take these little easier-to-carry
fairy ones!

HELEN [*pushing the* CROWS *away*]
You can't take them,
they saved me.

ENKI
You can't take them,
I need them.

[*Explaining to* HELEN.]

I'm on my way to put out a forest fire.

NIN
How generous of you to take the time.

ENKI
Oh, you know, I feel responsible.
The god of lightning set it,
to win a bet we had he couldn't do it
in the rainy season, that he'd fizzle
like wet matches. Now we have to
take our hatchets and go help
put an end to Emerline.

HELEN
Emerline?

ENKI
The forest fire's name is Emerline.
Don't you name everything? I do.
Helps me remember who is who.

HELEN
I thought a forest fire is what.
Not who.

ENKI
Who is what, ever think of that?
Ever think you might be *what*
(you think you're not)
instead of *who*
(you think you are)?

Consider all the names based on
occupations—Baker, Walker,
Carpenter, Fisher, Swisher—
if who you are is what you do,
and no one in your family does it any more?
Or if what you are is a star—
you could be Venus, of the evening,
traveling toward the dawn,
or you could just be called
"traveling toward the dawn"
and would you be a what, then,
or a who—I mean, is a what
changeable or is it personable?
When people say you're not who you used to be,
what if what they mean is true?
What became of the rest of who is you?

Ever wish upon a star?
Imagine if you couldn't call it by its name.
Imagine if you only knew how far away it is,
and its specific gravity; what would you wish for?

Is a plant a what?
Is a ghost a who?
Imagine thinking that a made-up television character
is a real person but your dog is not.

Is who a house cat but not a laboratory rat?
Is what a rock—then what is Mr. Spock?
Is a street who if it has a name
and what if it has a number?
Try to remember

what you've been
and who you've been seen in the person of;
is a person the sum of its parts?
Try to count yourself in instead of out.

Some people personify, others quantify.

Measuring the mettle of a person
or measuring the person of a metal
or meddling in the meter of a motor
or metaling the measure of a mother,
would you lose some of the stars you see
if you could count them only by their names?
Is counting a way of praying?

If what you really are is a number, say,
of conscious blobs of luminous light,
incandescing through your coat of flesh,
filling the entire viewing lens,
for a while, before your time to set,
then is consciousness a what?
An ability to see from far enough away
to count yourself out instead of in?

And isn't it true
that tax collectors created names
so they'd know what to do with who?
Then why is who's who any more than what's what?
Can you tell me that?

HELEN
You're driving me crazy
with all your assumptions,
you're driving me nuts with your qualifications.
I'm leaving, I'm going to my own house,
my own possessions,
and my own point of view.

CROW DEMONS
Let's go, let's go,
let's go to Helen's own house!

[*All exeunt,* ENKI *and* KUR *and* GAL *in a different direction;* NIN *and* HELEN *arm in arm.*]

SCENE THREE: ABOVEWORLD

Venus Shrines Triumphant

Home of THOMAS *and* HELEN *Bull. It is near dawn.* THOMAS *is at home with his new girlfriend* GISHI, *who, if possible, looks like him. The place is a mess, things are oddly placed, and somehow gray or white instead of their real color—sterile, frozen, wrapped in cloth.* THOMAS *still has his telescope set up;* GISHI *sits in his lap while he makes notes. Enter* HELEN, *with* NIN *and the seven* CROW DEMONS; THOMAS *jumps up.*

THOMAS
Helen, where have you been?
You're disgraceful—leaving me here to fend
for myself, and to tend your home fires.

HELEN
You—who are you? †
You're the one who didn't notice I was missing,
never saw me
going down, never thought I might have crashed,
never wondered, never asked,
never missed me, never mourned.
You're the one who assumed my absence
meant you were in charge of the whole bash;
yours is the head
swelling up underneath my crown.
Yours is the big dead end
sweating upon my throne.
You never tried to find me,
you found a silly replacement.
You're the one who's disgraceful.
I'll tell you what's what, now that we know you
for who you are, you're the one of my choice;
you're next,
you're going to break, and risk;
you're going down, you're going for a spin,
you're the very very very next one! ⸸

CROWS
Let's go, let's go! You're going with us!

CROW
Grab him, grab him by the horns.
Grab him, grab him, grab him by the tail.

THOMAS
I haven't got a tail!

CROW [*flirtatious*]
Honey, everybody has a tail.

THOMAS [*avoiding the* DEMONS]
You can't take me, I'm married to a goddess! †
I'm married to a princess,
I'm married to Venus.
I live in a castle.
Can't you see what a successful man
I am?

You can't take me—
I'm a scientist,
I don't believe in demons—
I see you as illogical, irrational
figments of a savage
imagination—aaaeeee—
take your icy fingers off my arm! ǂ

GISHI [*clinging to* THOMAS]
You can't take him!
He can't take it!
He's too tender—
I'll go with him,
I'll go for him,
I'll go mend him.
He can't take it! I'll go
with him—
you might break him.
I'm not fragile,
I'm not worth it—

HELEN
Take her too—she's driving me crazy,
she's making me nervous,
she's making me violent!

[CROW DEMONS *lead* THOMAS *and* GISHI *off; they are clinging together.* HELEN, *her anger abating, is visibly upset by* THOMAS *going, although it is clear she will not change her mind.*]

CROW [*to* THOMAS]
You're going to be King.

THOMAS
King—really?

CROW
Crow-King!

CROWS
CAW CAW CAW

GISHI
Where are we going?

CROWS
Nowhere special, Nothing to worry about.

NIN
Don't they look just like Hansel and Gretel?[37]
Are you sending Thomas to a Lesbian bar?

HELEN
Our lady of the Underground †
is a very shape-shifting old crone,
she's related to Mercury, or a wishing stone.
You could call her a storm and not be wrong;
you could call her a dirt god with a dirt god's
habits, and be right on target.
You could call her a song of living time,
or death's wind chime.
By the time anyone gets down there
to be her student,
she's likely to be a boxing trainer
for the CIA, with a Theosophist bent,
or a Zen Buddhist with a PhD
in the physical sciences. Everyone's
shadows are custom-made
by their own needs. ⸸

[NIN *gathers a stack of books and begins reading to* HELEN.]

NIN
Venus is the morning star now.
She ought to be visible from where we are.
She spent two months turning over.
Now she'll be morning star for six months
before disappearing again.

HELEN
Sounds like me. I was gone two months
though it seemed
I went for seven years…as though time
is a series of events that mark us
like tree rings.

NIN [*reading*]
Venus rules Taurus the Bull.

HELEN
I'm not so sure I want to rule bull.

NIN
Are you serious?

HELEN
No, I'm only Venus. You can be Sirius.

NIN [*reading*]
Venus rules Libra, the balancing scale.

HELEN [*looking into the hand mirror*]
To hang in the balance and remember what we've been; †
to hang at the corner of the ceiling
and recall what we have dreamed;
not to be a maid—to be Joan of Arc—
the Maid, a warrior Maid,
to lead armies, nations,
pilgrimages, scientific expeditions
into the starry landscapes of the brain—
and the heart's brain.
To seek with all our intelligence and then
to find! to find!
to define, to map—
and to do more than understand,
to stand in the center of my own mind.
To combine
the inner, with the outer, whole...
now that's a science worth working for. ⸸

NIN
Beauty without truth is only wishful,
a fantasy, the false posturing of a fool.

HELEN [*looking through telescope*]
The sky is a sheet of crystal
and time is what we are.
Venus shines triumphant in the morning sky.
Oh—I didn't know she looked like that, so near.
So beautiful, so forceful and so bright.
My eyes can hardly bear
to look at her.

NIN
Truth without beauty is ugly
and unbearably cruel.

HELEN
The telescope's mirrors catch the light
and bring the image, not the object, near.
Everything we see we see in symbols—
what Thomas ever was to me
and I to him…was our metaphor for marriage.

NIN
Venus is luminous
but veiled. We never completely
see her. We never see her bare.

HELEN [*training the telescope on the audience; at times she stops looking through it to address* NIN *directly*]
She's veiled, but I believe I know †
what's under there.
The dark side of the mirror
is what is real.
To be completely in the dark
is to seek reality—the as-yet-unformed.
All else is metaphor—or worse,
is Thomas fantasizing Venus,
loving to measure himself against her parameters—
the image is a reflection of the shadow of the real.
We all use mirrors to trap the light,
the drawing of the light into an image,
the sorting of the images into a symbol,
the weaving of the symbols into a metaphor,
the gathering of the metaphors into a group of metaphors—
a metaform, a myth,
a play of light on surfaces,
to which we bring our suffering, joy, anger—
terror.

[HELEN *shrieks playfully as she plays the telescope around on the audience.*]

Oh what's out there, what's out there?

[*There is a knock on the door.* NIN *goes to answer while* HELEN *continues with telescope.*]

I too know how to use mirrors,
how to weave with lights and sound.
How to see from at least two points of view,
a parallax of measurement.
And I know how to recognize my own being
in the dark side of the wind… ‡

[NIN *comes back with a gift box.* HELEN *unwraps it.*]

NIN
Something for you.
From Thomas?

HELEN
No, he always sends flowers. Daisies.
This is from Ereshkigal, with a note of thanks.
He arrived in her domain. And safely.
I'm so glad.

[*Wiping tears from her eyes.*]

I was more worried about him
than I was letting on.

NIN [*seeing the present—a large black stone horse*]
Now that's substantial.

[*There is the distant sound of brass wind chimes.*]

HELEN
An onyx horse.
I wonder if I know what to do with it.

NIN
Of course you do.

HELEN
Of course I do.
"It isn't as simple as it may seem
to poison the apple of self-esteem."

[*She gives the horse a central position among the smaller glass horses, on a table, center stage, pauses thoughtfully, then addresses it.*]

HELEN
O Lady, Lady of the changing shapes, †
help me remember
how to dance in place;
when to witness,
when to harness,
when to charge with all my forces.

I don't know the reaches of my fate.
I know your shadow falls across my face.

O Lady, Lady of the Great Below.
Hard are your lessons,
many-fanged your harshness;
irresistible are your passions
and sweet, sweet are your praises.

I don't know the mazes of your soul.
I know your shadow falls beside me
everywhere I go. ⸸

[*The dawn continues brightening as* NIN *reads from factual "hard science" books on mathematics and new physics while* HELEN *dusts, unwraps, and straightens, her motions drawing attention to the presence of large treelike plants, an enormous globe, models of cities and other things that suggest that her house is the universe itself, rather than a simple house. Slow curtain.*]

Appendix: Background Notes on Characters in ***The Queen of Swords***

INANNA: Sumerian Queen of Heaven and Earth. She is also Venus, which she indicates by saying "I am Inanna, traveling toward the dawn." This can be interpreted astronomically as the "descent of Venus" in the planet's periodic change from evening to morning star. Inanna is also associated with the sun, the greatest power of the daytime sky, and with the moon, the greatest power of the nighttime sky. Enheduanna, the earliest known individual poet, exalted Inanna at length in about 2300 B.C., and was a priestess of the moon temple.

Inanna's cycle of stories, of which the descent myth is only one, constitutes a great psychological drama with profound meanings for modern people, as well as being an invaluable sacred text revolving centrally around female characters whose attributes have figured prominently in the literatures of many cultures. Goddesses related to her in other contexts include Demeter, who turns the earth completely barren as she seeks help in getting her daughter Persephone out of the underworld; Freya, a Nordic goddess for whom Friday, Venus's day, was named; and the Egyptian goddess Isis, whose Dumuzi is named Osiris. Other goddesses with similar attributes are Ama-terasu, sun goddess of Japan; Iyeticu, corn goddess of certain American Pueblo Indians; and Oshun, a West African goddess of beauty and love.

ERESHKIGAL: Lady of the Great Below. As queen of the spirits of the dead in her palace of Ganzir (the desert), she is naked, shamanic, and ruthless, a counterpart of Kali, the Celtic Morrigan, Ceridwen, Hel, and other destroyers of the merely physical. She does not have an elegant metal and jeweled throne but a plain wooden one. With her *shem* drum, long fingernails, and tangled hair she is one with the truly ancient shaman figures such as Baubo, who bawdily confronted Demeter, or Uzume, who enticed the Japanese sun goddess Ama-terasu from her dark cave. In later stories Ereshkigal was villified, and her human counterparts were burned at the stake, tortured, and driven underground; she remained in variants of the Inanna stories as "the wicked queen," the "dark Morgan, Queen of Fairy" (Morgana Le Fay), "the evil stepmother," and so on. The black and red of anarchy and birth/death are her colors, as is purple, the color of transformation.

ENKI: His name means literally "God of the Earth." He is variously god of wisdom and sweet waters. I decided a jovial, generous-hearted nature god with a touch of eccentric physicist fit him best in *The Queen of Swords.* He appears in more than one of the related Inanna myths. In his male aspect his "sweet waters" have been interpreted as fertilizing semen that permits the growth of plants in the arid Sumerian landscape around the Tigris and Euphrates rivers. Enki's city Eridu is located where these two rivers meet the Persian Gulf. He is a magician and master of ritual and incantation; he has a marvelous nurturing and drunkenly generous side. In his female aspect he is described as "pregnant" and perhaps at some earlier time he was completely female.

In the story called "Inanna and the God of Wisdom," a drunk and effusively generous Enki gives the young Inanna the gift of *me* (pronounced *may*). *Me* are groups of special god-powers. She decides to keep them, loading them into her great "boat of heaven" (an extended metaphor for her vulva). A sobered and more possessive Enki schemes to have them returned, but all his attempts are foiled by Inanna and her *sukkal* (powerful servant) Ninshubur. Inanna gives up her *me* to make her descent, and as a result of her gamble acquires additional powers of the underworld.

NINSHUBUR: Queen of the East. Wolkstein and Kramer, in *Inanna, Queen of Heaven and Earth,* read Ninshubur's role as servant to Inanna as representing "the inner spiritual resources of Inanna, which are intended for the greater good of Sumer" (p. 149). This is one interpretation I have tried to follow in *The Queen of Swords,* of Nin (Ninshubur) as Helen's "higher mind," the ultimate good sense that will stop her short of total destruction or enslavement and make possible her ascent. In addition, Nin's role as friend seems to me particularly important for women at this time/space in our story.

NETI: The gatekeeper of Ereshkigal's domain of Ganzir greets Inanna, then is instructed by the Lady of the Great Below to let her pass through one gate at a time, stripping her, silencing her, and bending her low at each one. The word *neti* means "nothing" in Sanskrit. In numerology zero is the source of everything. This is particularly intriguing to me since Neti is the "higher mind" of Ereshkigal. (Or is it "lower mind"?) I conceive of Nothing in *The Queen of Swords* as genderless, a dealer in whatever brings us face to face with our own essential nothingness. More broadly, Nothing is the creative power of zero, the limitless possibility that yawns wide each time our circumstances or our inner attitudes change.

KURGARRA and GALATURRA: These two creations of the dirt under Enki's nails embody the profound principle of reducing everything to the truth of dirt, to the understanding of oneself as "nailed fast to the fat earth" (to quote a line from "Descent to the Butch of the Realm"), of needing always to return to Mater Materia for the basic knowledge from which wisdom grows. That they disguise themselves as flies or demons is particularly appropriate to their role of calling attention to elements despised (at our peril) that are actually sacred, vital, and sustaining of life.

The "trick" they use on Ereshkigal is empathy, commiseration. Many a con game has succeeded using the same trick. On the other hand empathy is a primary tool in healing of all kinds, especially in psychological therapy as well as in groups that commiserate about common oppressions, traumas, and addictions. In the throes of a gripping depression sometimes a single understanding sentence will trigger release, allowing our ascent to ordinary life on earth, with the usual accompanying heightened zeal of newly coming into a fresh understanding from a "below" place.

DUMUZI: The bull god consort and lover of Inanna is a character of great fascination to me; he has an extensive history which is not even hinted at in my play, where he takes a minor part. The last quarter at least of the text of "The Descent of Inanna to the Underworld" tells of Dumuzi's pursuit by the underworld demons, his prophetic dream of his own capture, his hiding at his sister's house, and her decision to spend half the time in the underworld in his stead. Both Inanna and Dumuzi's sister Geshtinanna have sympathy and love for him. His "error" in the descent myth is his self-aggrandizement; he does not wear poor clothing and mourn the fallen goddess. It is clearly his overweening arrogance and insensitivity to her trials that cause Inanna unhesitatingly to fix on him the "Eye of Death" that she has won so dearly in the underground.

Some of the derivatives of Dumuzi's name are Damu, Adam, Tammuz, Adonis, Tammerlane, Tam Lin, Tannis, and Thomas. Even this short list, including as it does Sumerian, Babylonian, Scots, Irish, German, Hebrew, Greek, and English heroes, suggests the tremendous dissemination of his story in European folk culture.

As the male god of sacrifice he is in the company of Osiris, Jesus, and others. As the "shepherd king" he is an early version of Paris. In the Sumerian text he has a reed flute; I have substituted a telescope in *The Queen of Swords.* On his steppe grows the apple tree of eternal life.

GESHTINANNA: Although at least one source interprets Geshtinanna's volunteering to go down in her brother's stead as the heroic act of a mature woman who has finally learned how to truly and unselfishly love a man, my own experience and study of contemporary therapeutic theory tells me that Geshtinanna is a classic co-alcoholic who cannot let her brother bear his own burdens and the consequences of his actions and attitudes. That she is associated with the fermentation of grain for beer and he is associated with the fermentation of grapes for wine only strengthens my decision to cast her as someone as much in need of Ereshkigal's ministrations as is the arrogant and terrified Dumuzi. Because there is no easy way in our fragmented culture to identify with a brother-sister team, I cast her in *The Queen of Swords* as Thomas's new girlfriend. Nin suggests their original brother-sister relationship in her remark about Hansel and Gretel.

ANNUNAKI and GALLA: The seven judges of Ereshkigal's dominion as well as the seven demons who accompany Inanna to the world above seeking her replacement easily suggested to me the crows that accompany European death-goddesses. That they are also "bar dikes" is simply an addition of modern urban underworld reality and influence. As dissemblers of thought they are a good accompaniment for Ereshkigal's surprisingly sensible approach to teaching Helen/Inanna.

Notes

The following are Judy Grahn's notes on the text which appeared in the original publication of *The Queen of Swords.*

Scene One

[1] Although Inanna's priestesses, notably the great "first poet" Enheduanna and perhaps also the biblical Sarah, were moon-temple officiates, she is so strongly associated with Venus that in later times the goddess of heaven and earth, of life, beauty, and love, came to be called Venus (Roman) and Venus Aphrodite (Roman-Greek). The planet Venus disappears from view for a time as she "descends" to be the morning star or "ascends" to be the evening star again.

Gate One

[2] The name of Ereshkigal's domain of underworld, or desert, in the Sumerian myth was Ganzir. Here it is represented as a Lesbian bar, the secret meeting place for the underground Gay culture for centuries. The culture owes a great deal to the brave bar owners who provided us with our only means of public expression before the advent of Gay/Lesbian political movements.

[3] Ereshkigal's instrument is a "shem drum" in the Sumerian text. I prefer "wind chimes" because of the connection of the wind to the Queen of Swords in the Tarot.

[4] Nothing: Neti, the gatekeeper's name in Ereshkigal's domain of Ganzir, translates as "nothing" in Sanskrit.

[5] Crows and ravens often accompany the goddess of death in mythology, and represent the world of spirits from the land of the dead. A crow is one of three birds who visited Snow White (a latter-day Inanna) as she lay in her glass casket on the mountain. On the American continent Raven is a trickster figure, especially among Native American tribes of the Northwest.

[6] Portrayals of the Queen of Death in later stories associated her with black and red, also the colors of the devouring goddess Kali. Snow White and other derivatives of the Sumerian myth also use the colors red and black. White, of course, is associated with Inanna.

[7] Clytemnestra was Helen's sister in the *Iliad.* Clytemnestra murdered her husband on his return from the siege, and was in turn killed by her own son and daughter in a major reversal for the older matriarchal culture; Helen was also killed by the brother and sister, but did not "really" die. Instead she rose into a cloud, her scarf trailing behind her.

[8] Priestesses of the temples of Inanna, Ishtar, Astarte, and others had sacred offices whose vestigial characteristics may be found in modern subcultures such as "prostitute" or "dike," "lesbian."

[9] "Inner ear" can be translated as "ear wisdom," according to Wolkstein and Kramer in *Inanna, Queen of Heaven and Earth.* Betty De Shong Meador, a Jungian analyst, considers it a reference to intuition or psychic skills: "listen to your inner self."

[10] At every gate Inanna starts to question why she is being stripped and is told, "Silence, Inanna. Sacred customs must be obeyed." I suppose this is one reason she does not talk very much in the first half of my play.

[11] The wise man Simon Magus and Helen were considered gods and were rivals of Jesus during his lifetime. Peter Fortunato, a poet who played Paris in a staged version of "The Queen of Wands," suggested to me that Simon may have lent his name to Simon Peter. There is a story that Simon Magus attempted to fly in Rome in order to outdo Peter's god.

What I love Simon Magus for is calling Helen she "who stands, has stood, will always stand."

[12] The apple of eternal life hung originally on Dumuzi's tree; the goddesses of life and love bestowed it on mortals to guarantee they could safely return to earthly form from the spirit realm. According to Barbara Walker, under Christianity the apple became poisoned, as in the Snow White version of the story, where it is used by the wicked queen to kill Snow White.

Gate Two

[13] "Nature doesn't give a damn" was a fortunate piece of recovery. I had completely forgotten the poem in the tumult of my life. One day while stopping over in Denver I felt compelled to call my friend Francine Kady Butler. We became best friends in 1954 when we were both fourteen, but by 1985 I had been out of touch with her for about ten years. She answered the phone, "Oh, I see you got my ESP." A month before, being unable to find me, she had "put out a message" into the stratosphere, for me to call her. She then sent me a small bundle of my letters and poems from 1960-1962, among them "Nature doesn't give a damn." I was in my early twenties then, probably twenty-one when I wrote it.

[14] One tradition says that Helen's mother was "Memory"; the other tradition says she was born in the form of an egg from Leda, who had mated with a swan. A later Greek version said Zeus assumed the form of a swan and raped Leda.

[15] In the Sumerian myth "Inanna and the God of Wisdom," Enki is portrayed as an expansive, generous drunk, who confounds himself by giving her all his powers. In still earlier stories Enki "gives birth" and very possibly was a female god at an earlier time.

Gate Three

Note on the title: *Butch* is a Gay cultural word, stemming from a root word meaning *goat,* and related to sacrificial rites of the great horned god (a version of Dumuzi as the wild bull) of the European Old Religion. Butch and femme are roles in Gay culture that may be played by either gender, with either gender switching at will in all but the most rigid parts of the culture. In ancient ceremonial terms, Butch is the leather-wearing goat-god priest/priestess, either the sacrifice itself or the sacrificer. In some ancient rites the future was read, in a "butcherly" fashion, from the entrails of slain animals sacrificed in the place of the king. Although the sacrifice of a king is considered a male-only office in our historic times, the myth of Inanna's descent makes it clear that the older version of the story began with the idea of female sacrifice—by another female. In more recent times, Joan of Arc has been considered a ceremonial sacrifice, part of an underground pagan culture.

[16] *Dike* seemed a more than appropriate title for the Ereshkigal of this story. *Dike* is a Lesbian cultural and lower-class slang word with two distinct roots—one from the lower class and one from the upper. In the former case, *dike* or *dyke* is a shortened version of the name of a queen who fought the Romans, Boudica, whose name was driven underground. Dike as remembered by the literate, upper class was a goddess of Greece. She had both warrior and underworld shamanic qualities. Her name means "natural justice" and her companion was named "Truth." She is portrayed with the wheel of fate, hence the tattoo "Destiny" in the poem. In a latter-day Greek version of the Inanna myth, Dike was softened into Eurydike, or Eurydice, who was held captive against her will in the underworld. Her lover Orpheus (a shepherd-musician like Dumuzi), who went to the underworld to rescue her, looked back at her after having been forbidden to do so, and thus lost her. He then waited for her for seven years on the banks of the Styx before being murdered by maidens.

[17] In Gertrude Stein's rendering of the Helen story, "Dr. Faustus Lights the Lights," she characterizes the goddess as "not possibly fooled"—or more exactly, "no one can deceive me."

[18] The poem "Descent to the Butch of the Realm" is constructed with three different rhythms. The first I call "Idiomatic Narrative." It consists of loosely rhythmed and rhymed common American speech pattern lines such as "You won't find me sitting home in front of TV / drinking beer, not me, I'm outdoors..." The second rhythm is a "Tightening Couplet" worked into the fabric of the Idiomatic Narrative. This form is an incomplete sentence, and consists of a couplet in four trochaic or occasionally iambic feet, that rhymes the first two syllables of the first line with the last two syllables of the last line, and contains at least one instance of alliteration, and preferably more. For example: "little yellow egg of being / broken on my greasy griddle." There are nine such tightening couplets in the poem. Their purpose is to pull the looser narrative into a firmer structure so the poem has more tension and "breathes." The third rhythmic form I call "Translation Tablet Chant," based in translations of Sumerian poetry originally written on clay tablets: "Oh descend to me / and my desiring."

Gate Four

[19] H.D.'s *Helen in Egypt* is based in a variant of the Helen story, according to which only her dream-self, her illusion-shadow, appeared at Troy. Her real self remained in Egypt.

Scene Two

[20] Like *dike*, *faggot* is a ceremonial Gay word, referring to a history with wands of divination, and then of persecution by burning during the Inquisition. See my book *Another Mother Tongue* (Boston: Beacon Press, 1984) and Arthur Evans, *Witchcraft and the Gay Counterculture* (Boston: Fag Rag Books, 1978).

Gate Five

[21] Ernest Hemingway, a protégé of Gertrude Stein's for a time, wrote grippingly of bull fighting.

[22] The "eye of death" that Ereshkigal fixes on Inanna and that Inanna later fixes on Dumuzi became, in later stories based on it, a mirror of divination, a crystal ball, the surface of a pond—all for the purpose of "seeing with the inner mind," of having psychic or higher-minded knowledge.

[23] There is more about warrior queens and Queen Boudica, in particular, in my own book, *Another Mother Tongue.* I based the poem "Queen Boudica" on research I did for that Gay history book.

[24] Because of the length and complexity of this poem, for staged production purposes I think it can be heavily trimmed.

[25] Crow Dike actresses with physiques different from Ildreth's flaxen North European one may want to substitute for the first stanza one of the following:

All in fur I rode a small horse
deep in the Asian steppe, my hair
so shiny it was black and fine and
down to here.

All in beads I rode, my tall legs
deep in the African grass, my hair
so nappy it was dense and fine and
out to here.

The words *Viking* in the second stanza and *pink* in the third stanza should be changed appropriately.

[26] In a staged production the actress may want to substitute her own personal names in the listing of female friends and relatives in order to give the poem a strong subjective dimension.

Gate Six

[27] According to Barbara Walker, the scarecrow is a remnant of rural memory of the Old Religion and the practice of sacrificing the king or substitute king. Perhaps to hang a scarecrow on a peg in the grain fields is to reenact a little bit of the Dumuzi/Inanna myth.

[28] This line is a direct quotation from Gertrude Stein.

[29] Helen's history in the Greek stories is extremely violent. She was kidnapped by Theseus at the age of nine, and raped. When her twin brothers retrieved her from him, she bore a daughter. This girl, Iphigenia, was given to her older sister Clytemnestra to raise. Later when Helen went to Troy, Clytemnestra's husband Agamemnon could not sail his ships of

war out of port because the goddess Artemis had stopped the wind. He sacrificed Iphigenia, who was then about nine herself. In some versions Artemis snatched the girl from death and made her a priestess in her own province.

Helen had a second daughter, Hermione. Inanna appears to have had two sons, each of whom is seized by the Annunaki; Inanna refuses to let them be substituted for herself in the underworld.

[30] "Little Snow White," in Grimm's fairy tales, is an incarnation of Helen/Inanna, who swallows a poisoned apple, given to her by an old crone who is actually the "wicked queen," or Ereshkigal. This causes her "death" trance.

[31] The House of Horus, the falcon-headed god of Egypt, is also the House of Isis, his mother and a goddess of heaven and earth, similar to Inanna, Ishtar, Astarte, and Demeter. Nephthys, the sister of Isis, ruled the underworld; both goddesses visited the land of the dead in rites for Osiris, the Egyptian god of green plants and sacrifice.

[32] The phrase "eating crow" is a euphemism for "eating shit," a reference to the old Native American stories of Raven the Trickster, who keeps people captive by getting them to "eat shit," that is, to endure humiliation and to capitulate to the demands of a more authoritative person. The only escape is to trick Raven into "eating shit" him/herself.

Gate Seven

Note on the title: "To reconstitute her, just add water." From *constitute,* to set up, from *status, state,* p.p. of *stare,* to stand. To stand her up again.

This is a very different sense from *resurrection,* from *resurrectus,* from *surge,* to go straight up, to rise, related also to *regere,* to lead straight and *rectus,* right, and *erection.* All of which apply very well to a male god and not, it seems to me, quite so well to a female one.

[33] Snow White was put in a glass coffin.

[34] The prohibition against eating fruits from the land of the dead, lest one be consigned there forever, is widespread, from the apple of knowledge in Genesis to dozens of folk tales and ballads that warn the hero not to eat what the lady offers.

[35] According to Betty Meador, Inanna's colors were carnelian and lapis blue. Gold and white seem always associated with later descriptions, while salmon and blue belong to Mary, who is another version of the queen of heaven and earth.

[36] The *me* are powers of godship in ancient Sumer. Inanna acquired them in a mythic text entitled "Inanna and the God of Wisdom" (see Wolkstein and Kramer, *Inanna, Queen of Heaven and Earth*). The word is pronounced *may,* hence the pun "Queen of the May." There were dozens of these powers, from specific priestly rites to such abstractions as "truth," "decision," and "compassion." These qualities stood alongside the power to sack cities, spread discord, use flattering speech, and other characteristics that our culture has separated from the concept of "goodness" and consigned to Ereshkigal rather than to Inanna. Inanna, however, had all of them.

Scene Three

[37] They are Hansel and Gretel. The story of the two children abandoned in the Ganzir of the woods by their evil mother picks up the Sumerian story at the point where Dumuzi and his sister Geshtinanna descend to the domain of death. Ereshkigal, in this medieval folk tale, is represented by both the selfish mother and the boy-eating witch of the woods. Hansel's wits and Gretel's faithful love get them through most of their ordeal, until the moment Gretel kills the witch by tricking her into the oven.

Their names are highly suggestive of their original names, since the suffix el is a diminutive meaning "little" or "child." Gret retains three out of four letters from Geshtinanna, and Hans bears auditory resemblance to Thomas, Tam, Tannis, and Tammuz, later versions of Dumuzi's name.

In addition to the most obvious, "Snow White and the Seven Dwarves," other stories from the Grimms' early nineteenth-century collection echo parts of the Inanna/Ereshkigal/Dumuzi saga.

NONFICTION

Preface to *Another Mother Tongue*

In 1961, when I was twenty-one, I went to a library in Washington, D.C., to read about homosexuals and Lesbians, to investigate, explore, compare opinions, learn who I might be, what others thought of me, who my peers were and had been. The books on such a subject, I was told by indignant, terrified librarians unable to say aloud the word *homosexual,* were locked away. They showed me a wire cage where the "special" books were kept in a jail for books. Only professors, doctors, psychiatrists, and lawyers for the criminally insane could see them, check them out, hold them in their hands. The books I wanted to check out were by "experts" on the subject of homosexuality as it was understood at the time. The severe reaction of the women librarians, who by all rights should have been my allies, plus the censorship of the official, professional written material of which my own person was the subject, constituted some of the serious jolts I experienced in my early twenties concerning the position of Gay people in American society.

These jolts, which included being given a less-than-honorable discharge from the armed services with its attendant demoralizing treatment, having my parents and friends notified of my "crime" of Lesbianism, being denied jobs and housing, being beaten in public for looking like a dike—these taught me everything I would ever need to know about the nature of the oppression of Gay people. And made me angry and determined enough to use my life to reverse a perilous situation.

In 1963 I picketed the White House with the Gay rights group Mattachine Society, one of a little band of fifteen Gay people, three of us women. In 1964 I published an article in *Sexology Magazine* under a pseudonym, stating that most Lesbians were "not sick" but were normal, ordinary people. Since my letters and notes had been seized and used against my friends in the service, I was afraid even in civilian life of having my writing notes grabbed; I burned some cards I had been keeping about Lesbian couples in Washington, D.C. Then in 1965 I wrote an angry satire, "The Psychoanalysis of Edward the Dyke," storing it away because of the impossibility of getting it published. I did publish a few short poems, also under a pseudonym, in the Lesbian magazine *The Ladder.*

In 1970, tired of waiting for a publisher radical enough to handle my material, I printed poems myself on a mimeograph machine, which grew into a complete, productive press. As the wave of Gay Liberation, Lesbian, and feminist groups became the huge groundswell of organized transition that characterized the seventies (on the heels of the civil rights and Black power movements and the peace and hippie movements of the sixties), I became a poet and a voice of Lesbian/feminism and "the common woman," among other things. In 1974, after writing "A Woman Is Talking to Death," I began to work on long prose pieces. I decided to investigate women's history and Gay history.

In finding and recording some of the Gay cultural histories, I have drawn upon my own life history as a Lesbian and as a Gay activist during the last third of the twentieth century in America. I have recalled my utter isolation at sixteen, when I looked up *Lesbian* in the dictionary, having no one to ask about such things, terrified, elated, painfully self-aware, grateful it was there at all. Feeling the full weight of the social silence surrounding it, me, my unfolding life. I have gone over and over in my mind the careful teaching my first lover Von gave me, as she recited in strictest secrecy the litany of words and phrases related to the forbidden subject of our way of being: *Gay, faggot, tribadism, round, straight, in drag, coming out,* and a mysterious word she had no definition for: *catafoil.* In addition, I have remembered words and phrases used about Gay people by heterosexual culture. The list I made to research consisted originally of twelve words: *dyke, queer, butch, femme, Gay, camp, fairy, faggot, purple, pansy, bulldike, Lesbian.* I have used both *dyke* and its alternate spelling *dike,* because I love both words; they are still in an oral tradition, not yet standardized into one spelling. *Catafoil,* I now believe, came from a Gay book Von read while standing in a drugstore—a habit she had, especially with Gay books since it was socially embarrassing if not dangerous to buy them. This book was *Quatrefoil,* a Gay novel by James Barr first published in 1950.[1]

My methods for gathering information can be called eclectic. I used dictionaries and history, anthropology and sociology, poetry and the occult. I used a lot of common sense and an uncommon amount of perseverance. I spent more than one evening in complete frustration sitting banging a dictionary against my knees screaming, "I know you're in there!" after months of chasing the word *bulldike.* I read and read, filled boxes with notebooks of notes, thought and thought, wept, cried out to the phantoms of history, muttered to myself. I am a poet and a Gay cultural theorist, not an etymologist. Word derivations find their way into dictionaries after etymologists have gathered information based on the contexts in which the words may have been used. There has been no acceptance and exploration of the Gay context that would allow our subterranean slang words to enter the world of dictionaries. It is as a Gay person, using Gay cultural contexts and meanings, that I have explored words such as *faggot, fairy, bulldike,* and so on. These words have a far different meaning for Gay people than they have for straight people in general, including etymologists. This is because heterosexual people have a different mindset from Gay people just as Anglos, for example, have a different mindset from Navajos. Even when Anglos study Navajo culture, therefore, they do not ascribe the same meaning a Navajo does to what they see. Nor does the Navajo tell everything to the Anglo, as some things in Indian culture are kept secret for protection. Gay culture too keeps secrets for its own protection.

Gradually I formulated theories that Gay culture is ancient and has been suppressed into an underground state of being, that everything has meaning, that slang is not necessarily a transitory language form, that old traditions transform, they do not really perish. If Sappho's fragments were preserved, why not other elements also? Once I had gathered a few clues, people began to bring me information, from other countries, from specialized fields of study, from their lives as bar dikes and faggots; and I was beginning to know what questions to ask. Years passed. I began to see that my own life fit into a pattern of Gay culture too, and I undertook to use stories from my own experience as examples of a dike's life. And now that I knew what kinds of questions to ask I did some interviews of other Gay people or people with expertise that was pertinent to my subject. The worlds that began unfolding were exciting beyond my imagining, as my little list of taboo words turned out to be keys to knowledge.

The Culture Is Everything

What gives any group of people distinction and dignity is its culture. This includes a remembrance of the past and a setting of itself in a world context whereby the group can see *who it is* relative to everyone else.

I have always been bothered by the definition of homosexuality as a *behavior.* Scratching is a behavior. Homosexuality is a way of being, one that can completely influence a person's life and shape its meaning and direction.

In *Another Mother Tongue: Gay Words and Gay Worlds* I am suggesting parameters and characteristics of homosexual culture as I have experienced it and as others have spoken or written about it. In doing this I have often used stereotypes, even derogatory ones, very deliberately, as points of entry into the history, for *something* about stereotypes is usually true and therefore open to study.

The Gay culture I have set about to describe is old, extremely old, and it is continuous. The continuity is a result of characteristics that members teach each other so that the characteristics repeat era after era. I have found that Gay culture has its traditionalists, its core group, that it is worldwide, and that it has tribal and spiritual roots. Gay culture is sometimes underground, sometimes aboveground, and often both.

Another Mother Tongue: Gay Words and Gay Worlds traces Gay cultural attributes, words, and phrases—both those used *within* the Gay underground and those used by outsiders about it. Chapter One deals with the antiquity of lavender as the Gay color, taking us back in time to tribal traditions. Having described some tribal holdovers in our modern industrial culture in Chapter Two, "The Original Underground," Chapter Three establishes the high public positions frequently held by Gay people in American Indian tribes in the recent past, while Chapter Five, "We Go Around the World," extends these positions to references from cultures around the globe. Chapter Four, "Fairies and Fairy Queens," applies the same Gay attributes to the tribal vestiges underlying European societies, an important connection since the slang phrases of the Gay underground in America virtually all stem from European languages, particularly English of course. I next examine the French terms *butch* and *femme* as well as the English *bulldike,* with an eye toward establishing modern Gay offices that have some similarity to their counterparts in the more openly Gay-tolerant European pagan cultures of centuries ago. Chapters Seven, "Riding with the Amazons," and Eight, "Flaming, Flaming Faggot Kings," also examine offices (very unofficial) that Gay people hold in society. The last two chapters concern more generalized functions of Gay culture in our society, such as the importance of women bonding and the effect Gay leadership has had on our society. The last chapter considers whether there is a special Gay philosophical attitude that can help us in today's crisis-oriented mass universe.

My own life story weaves in and out of the other Gay stories, and the book is addressed to my first lover Von, whose memory kept me company throughout.

To this work I bring my understanding that "women's history" parallels, crisscrosses, and influences Gay cultural history. I also have come to understand while working on the book that "women's history" and "tribal history" have certain things in common.

Some of the names of modern Gay people in the book have been changed or the surname has been omitted for protection, the persons preferring anonymity to the threat of losing a job or family love. Yet the number of people who are able to live as openly Gay is astounding compared to the case in former decades and speaks of a growing place Gay people occupy in the arena of public life. I hope this book clarifies and intensifies that influence.

Notes

[1] James Barr, *Quartrefoil* (Boston: Alyson Publications, 1982).

Butches, Bulldags, and the Queen of Bulldikery*

I am the wall at the lip of the water
I am the rock that refused to be battered
I am the dyke in the matter, the other
I am the wall with the womanly swagger
I am the dragon, the dangerous dagger
I am the bulldyke, the bulldagger

and I have been many a wicked grandmother
and I shall be many a wicked daughter.

From "She Who,"[1] Judy Grahn

When I first went to live with you, Von, my first lover, we certainly didn't know a great deal about what Lesbians were supposed to be. Lesbians were warriors, that much we understood, and we affirmed the bravest, dikiest qualities in each other quite consciously. As you prepared to become a physical education teacher, everything about you made perfect sense to me—your muscles, your athletic ability, your physical courage all told me that you were acting out being a warrior. Somehow to me then in those early years, when you were in college and I was a renegade hiding out in your room, everything you did was a "dyke" thing. After all, I had no comparison, and you were utterly everything to me—husband, lover, friend, teacher.

I thought that your short hair, your square, muscled hands, your craft of leather tooling, even your habit of wearing electric-blue sweaters, were all "dyke" things. You had worked all through high school carving leather belts and purses to sell, so your hands were beautifully shaped: square, strong, precisely skilled. (And a Lesbian's hands are so important. We knew that, then, too.)

You were a warrior to me, and you knew it. You signed all your notes to me, "Your hero." You were completely cocky about this, and prideful. I loved those qualities about you; I hated it when you knuckled under to fear and to the Gay-baiting that was a constant factor in our lives, especially out on the street, where hostile boys would often follow us for blocks, taunting and threatening. I pressed you to be brave, and then I could be braver, too.

We both knew we were warriors, not that anyone else knew this. We were called "dikes," you said, raising your thick black brows and shrugging, for this word was a real mystery. And when we overheard boys calling us "bulldikes," it hurt our feelings. It made us afraid. The word "bull" sounded as though we were being compared to men, and we did not like that.

Being Called a Bulldike

After I entered the underground Gay bar culture, at the tender age of twenty-one, I could never forget the characters I met there, some of whom were me. The drag queens and faggots, the dikes and the bulldikes, the couples who

*[*Author's Note*] The words in the title of this chapter apply to women in Gay culture. *Bulldag* is short for *bulldagger,* a synonym for *bulldike.* While these three terms are used to describe a Lesbian and never to describe a Gay man, *butch,* especially as a complementary adjective, is in the vocabulary of Gay men and is discussed further in Chapter Eight.

called themselves butch and femme became a part of my definition of myself as a Gay person. I learned that a dyke was one way of being a Lesbian, and a bulldike was even more so.

Bulldike is the kind of word most women hope to avoid all their lives, for few things are more horrifying to be called, especially if a woman is walking alone in an anti-Gay and masculine-dominated street, surrounded by hostile bulks. Few words are as guaranteed to set off an explosion of fear in her belly as the word *bulldike* when it is used on a woman like a whip. Usually, heterosexual men wield this particular verbal lash. I remember being so jeered once by an entire four-story building-full of construction workers, at seven o'clock in the morning in New York City, which I had never before visited. A woman so confronted will either slink into a defensive posture, deny everything, and flee—or she will get mad, she will raise her head and swing her arms in a sudden, hell-with-you, butchy swagger. And the minute she takes this last action, she may feel from the name-callers something more than their utmost derision, their contempt, and threat to her person. She may feel also a grudgingly granted hint of respect not present in the other anti-Lesbian or down-with-women words she may ever hear used against her.

For many years the mystery of this strange word *bulldike* has burbled and thickened in my mind, along with the milder *dike*. I called my first book of poetry *Edward the Dyke* in order to begin to defuse the terror people have of the word, for it is considered as bad a word as *cunt* and more taboo to say out loud than *lesbian* or *queer*. And I used it to tie it to me, so I could never deny it; everywhere I go as a writer and performer, the word *dyke* goes with me. It is a lower-class word, not written into literature or the dictionary. It did not appear even in slang dictionaries until the 1940s, although a wonderful reference is made to it in the song "B-D Women Blues," recorded by Bessie Jackson in 1935.[2] The *Oxford English Dictionary* lists *bulldike*,[3] having taken it from an American Gay writer, John Rechy, who used it in *City of Night* in 1963. Only truly, obstinately honest and tough dikes use the word *bulldike* about themselves. Really nice girls of any sexual persuasion have never heard of it, and your nicer sort of boy thinks it means "prostitute" or "shady lady."

Bulldike (also spelled *bulldyke*), *bulldiker*, and *bulldagger* are also used somewhat interchangeably, and all of them are loaded, taboo words. They are used, especially by lower-class, "straight" people, to describe a tough, brave, bold Lesbian who is considered "mannish" or "butchy" in her characteristics and mannerisms. The word does not apply as much to her Lesbianism, although this is always part of the definition, as it does to her toughness—her muscular physicality and aggressiveness, her free-striding manner. In the 1950s, underground bar dykes and fairies took the word and updated it from *bulldike* to *dieseldike*, applying it to women who seemed to them particularly butchy, the *most* butchy a woman could be and still not be passing as a man. This suggested to me that the word dates from a time when bulls were as everyday a part of the culture as trucks were to America in the fifties.

These particular Gay slang words sounded as though they stemmed from Old English, so I began searching English history for a historical people who once worshiped or otherwise valued bulls. I soon came across references to the Celtic people of ancient Europe and Britain, tribal people who had horned gods and goddesses and whose Druidic priesthood sacrificed bulls in sacred rituals. The Celts depicted cows and bulls more than any other animals in their art. I also noticed that in two Celtic dialects, *cow* was spelled *bo* (Irish) and *buwch* (Welsh).

At the same time I listened closely to my friend Sharon Isabell, to the special way she had of speaking. She has been a Lesbian all her life and has had plenty of experience in the Gay bar culture, where she was a bulldike with a leather jacket, motorcycle, everything.[4] She still retained a particular Euro-American dialect. When she said "boa constrictor," she pronounced it "*bull* constrictor." Then I noticed two other people who are descendants of settlers from the British Isles and who still speak in the older manner. They each said "*bua*dike" instead of "*bull*dike," making a soft "h" sound instead of an "l" sound. I asked them to repeat the word until they gave me funny looks; I was amazed and excited, realizing I was hearing remnants of older English dialects and being given an important clue in my search for the meaning of *bulldike.*

Freshly inspired, I went looking for a word that could have the *bull* part spelled *boa* or *bua* and that would be likely as the source of *bulldike.* What I found was a historical personage, a woman listed as Boadicea, Queen of the Iceni, a tribe of Celtic people living in what is now Norfolk, England. They called themselves Hicca, "people of the horse." Like tribal people everywhere, they had Gay customs. Their queen is remembered through twenty centuries as the leader of a major Celtic revolt in A.D. 61 against the Roman conquest of the tribal people of Britain. A statue of Boadicea and her two daughters stands under Big Ben in the city of London, which she burnt to the ground.

Some mention of this queen, however brief or caustic, for she produces a mixed reaction in people's minds, now appears in most books of Celtic history. She appears, as "Boadaceia," on a plate of Judy Chicago's *Dinner Party* art piece—in deep crimson with a shapely spear in the center of Stonehenge-shaped dolmens. Her real name, however, was never Boadaceia or Boadicea. I believe those are modern attempts to soften her character and hide her ferocious history. Her name was Boudica and came to be pronounced "Boo-uh-*dike*-ay."[5] Or, as we would say (those of us who say such things) in modem American English: *bulldike,* or *bulldiker.*

Gay Customs Among the Celts

The Celts were not the first people to occupy the land that became Great Britain; they were preceded by the Fairy folk, whose spirit-worshiping, woman-oriented ways they assimilated into their own, which were originally more nomadic and warlike. Beginning around 1500 B.C., Celtic tribes spread in waves from Turkey to the British Isles, emerging with a culture considered to be midway between the ancient matriarchal and newer patriarchal. Women still wielded tremendous authority, owned much of the property in common, dispensed most of the values, and had rights over their houses and their bodies.

> Many types of marriage existed, including marriage for a specific length of time; marriage between one wife and one husband; between one husband and many wives; and between one wife and many husbands. If a woman had greater wealth, she and not her husband was considered head of the family.[6]

Elaborate marriage laws recorded in the eighth century provided for the property that was due a woman if her husband left her for a young man. Older women taught younger men the arts of love, which undoubtedly included methods of birth control and tenderness toward women's bodies. Older women also taught the men to fight with arms, for novice Celtic warriors of ancient times went to school under experienced warrior women, who were at the same time sorcerers.[7] The martial arts teachers of the best-known legendary Celtic hero, Cu Chulain, were two powerful women, Buannan ("The Lasting One") and Scathach ("The Shadowy One").[8] The men usually went to battle naked, having put all their wealth into the decorations for their horses; displaying proper courage was the purpose of the battle, not total conquest of other people. Groups of women warriors (ceremonial Lesbians with institutional power) called *gwiddonot* are recorded in a medieval saga, *Kulwch and Olwen;* these women fought in battles, lived together, and uttered prophecies for the tribe.[9]

A prominent and typical goddess of Boudica's old Celtic people crouched in stone over the doorways of her temples, legs angled steeply apart, to welcome her people. A number of chiseled rays radiated out from her pudenda in a stone visualization of the *aura clitoridis,* the self-sustained, generative power of the female residing in and coming from her clitoris.[10] I like using the word *pudenda.* I like it so much better than *genitals* or *crotch,* certainly, or *pussy;* better than *mons veneris* (Mound of Venus), *labia majora* or *minora,* or any of the other Latin euphemisms; and most certainly I like it better than my mother's shamefaced "down there." Even though in Latin it means "something shameful," the word *pudenda* sounds so officiously welcoming and so religiously businesslike: a cross somewhere between *agenda* and *pagoda.* Boudica was a barbarian and a Celt and her pudenda would have been active, unashamed, and radiating with female power all her life.

As for the Celtic men, the main god with whom they identified was an amiable-looking bearded man with antlers. He was the Horned One: "The horned god was especially linked with male sexuality and often appears with an erect cock Moreover, when erect, he is sometimes portrayed in the company of men, not women."[11] Horny was his name, giving us our slang word for sexual desire, *horniness.*[12]

Writing just eighty years before the A.D. 61 rebellion of Queen Boudica against Roman occupation of her tribal lands, the Greek historian Diodorus Siculus had this to say about the homosexuality of Celtic men:

> Although they have good-looking women, they pay very little attention to them, but are really crazy about having sex with men. They are accustomed to sleep on the ground on animal skins and roll around with male bedmates on both sides. Heedless of their own dignity, they abandon without a qualm the bloom of their bodies to others. And the most

> incredible thing is that they don't think this is shameful. But when they proposition someone, they consider it dishonorable if he doesn't accept the offer![13]

Considering Celtic customs, it would have been utterly unnatural of Queen Boudica not to be a Lesbian. She was, after all, a queen and a military leader of her people. The Celtic tribesfolk would have certain expectations that her behavior would not differ markedly from their own. They would have expected too that a woman who roused and led them into battle against the Roman state would herself be a fighter. A Roman, writing three hundred years after Queen Boudica's time (and referring to the Celts as "Gauls"), described with Roman astonishment the reality of Celtic women:

> Nearly all the Gauls are of a lofty stature, fair, and of ruddy complexion; terrible from the sternness of their eyes, very quarrelsome, and of great pride and insolence. A whole troop of foreigners would not be able to withstand a single Gaul if he called his wife to his assistance, who is usually very strong, and with blue eyes; especially when, swelling her neck, gnashing her teeth, and brandishing her sallow arms of enormous size, she begins to strike blows mingled with kicks, as if they were so many missiles sent from the string of a catapult.[14]

Boudica's Electrifying Name(s)

Queen Boudica's name could very well have been a title rather than an individual queen's name: *bulldike* and *bulldagger* may mean bull-slayer-priestess. As high priestess of her people, perhaps the queen performed the ceremonial killing of the bull (who was also the god) on the sacred altar-embankment, or dyke. As bull-slayer she may also be related to another Lesbian/Gay word: *butch,* a word that comes originally from *goat* and may have referred to the slayer as well as to the goat-as-god.[15] If Boudica is in fact a title, meaning sacred Bull- or Cow-slayer, or sacred Bull-slaying-altar, she would have been vested with the power of the people transferred through her from the dying bull. The bull, stag, goat, cow, and pig killing of pagan tribal religion was sacrificial, after the animal had been pacified in a dance or other hypnotic rite, for the purpose of transferring its life-blood power to the people and of divining their collective future from its internal organs.

In Boudica's territory, the sacrifice was carried out on the flat tops of large mounds of earth, special sacred embankments, "dykes," used by the Celtic priesthood and the wisewomen for bull sacrifices. Centuries later, "over the dyke with it" was an expression reported to have been used by some English witches during coven ceremonies.[16]

The modern bullfight is a secular version of the old pagan bull sacrifice practiced in ancient Crete, for instance, and carried on now in a less covertly religious fashion in Spain and Mexico. Instead of the innards used to divine the fate of the people, the ears and tails are cut off as prizes to the matador and the meat is given to the poor. Women sometimes still perform as the bullfighter, although most matadors are men. In her pretty and very ceremonial black and silver and red pants and vest and white silk shirt, carrying a black and red cape, the female matador looks not unlike many dykes I have known who love to dress in similar fashion.[17]

If *dyke* meant sacred "altar," "sacrificial mound," then the title Bull-dyke just possibly meant "altar of the people's power," as the people's power was vested in the god-spirit of the bull. Altar originally was the lap of the goddess, the Great Mother of the people.

Whether it was a formal title or not, Boudica's name has a large number of puns and associations surrounding it. For instance, soldiers in A.D. 61 made defensive embankments consisting of a long ditch with the earth from the ditch piled into a wall on one side; the soldiers stood in the ditch while they waited for the enemy to advance. These embankments are called *dikes,* and they abounded in Boudica's war. Her association with dikes as a military structure is amply evident; she stood on them, made speeches on them, her enemies built them, and she stormed them. So many women warriors fought in this war that the women constituted the line of defense, just as the line of earthen dykes did. Large, ancient, ruined dikes around London were long credited to Boudica's war by historians. Her most famous statue is called "Boadicea's on the Embankment." *Embankment* is a synonym for *dike.* Another version of her name is Bundaca;[18] *bund* was a word used in British colonial nineteenth-century military slang, and it meant "dike."

Bulldagger, which may be Boudica's name pronounced in a slightly different dialect, strongly suggests the sort of knife or short sword a priestess would use in sacrificing bulls for religious purposes, and in modern slang *bulldagger* strongly suggests "castrating woman," something Lesbians are often accused of being merely by our existence. The Gaelic word *biodag* means "short sword."

Boudica may also be the source of mild slang words that I realize I have heard and used for years without thinking much about them: *bodacious* and *bodacity,* meaning "bold and audacious," with the sense of *chutzpah* as well as true grit. That I know of, these words do not particularly apply to Lesbians more than anyone else, though we tend to use them rather often. I was reminded of the term after meeting a transsexual who was minutely imitating all things Lesbian and whose dog was named Bodacious. Lesbian comedian Kate Clinton told me she had overheard some Black male students in a class she taught in New York State calling each other "bodacious." She asked what they meant by the word but they wouldn't tell her. Finally one of the boys stayed after class and said, "Do you really want to know? It means *'bodacious faggot.'*" So it certainly has some kind of Gay connection in slang language.

Without the common folks' habit of retaining old words in slang, Boudica's name could never have survived so many centuries, especially during the aftermath of her rebellion, when the Romans heavily suppressed her tribe. Then it would have been suicidal to say "Boudica" in front of people of authority, "nice" people. But she has become a lady of many names, after all.[19]

Boudica's War

Rome colonized in a classic manner, flooding a territory with highly trained soldiers who had been promised pieces of colonial land for their retirement. The

Roman-established provinces, guarded from their own populations by military posts, were headed by governors-general who levied taxes on all the resources of the provinces. From these they were expected to make personal fortunes and build major political and military careers.

After the military colonization of the British Isles came Roman money lenders and merchants, who promised economic "progress" to all who became indebted to them. They loaned back to the native peoples, at high interest, some of the riches that had already been stolen from them by the soldiers and governors. In this way the patrician Roman class acquired new labor and new fruits of the land. In addition, captured Celtic people were sent to Rome to become slaves. Some went to the houses of patricians as male and female prostitutes, artisans, musicians; some went to rapid deaths laboring in heavy industry; some went to be used for sport in the arena, as gladiators.

The Celtic tribal people were angrily divided between those who cooperated with the Romans, crowding into the colonial centers such as London, and those who stayed in the countryside with their own people and did not cooperate. In their dealings with the Hicca people, Boudica's "people of the horse," the Romans negotiated an arrangement with the king, Prasutagus, rather than the queen. The arrangement turned half of all Celtic goods over to Nero, Emperor of Rome at the time. Then in A.D. 60 the Hicca king died, leaving the rulership clearly in the hands of redheaded Queen Boudica. Refusing to acknowledge a female head of state, Roman army veterans gleefully and roughly seized land and property from Hicca noblemen and relatives of the king. They increased their persecution and massacre of the Druid priesthood.

Outraged, Queen Boudica protested their behavior, whereupon the Romans had her hauled into a public place and flogged. Then they raped her two daughters, to discredit her queenship and her female powers.

There is no reason to believe Boudica had ever agreed to the original treaty with Nero, since it turned the Celtic people over to the Romans without a fight. Now, seeing the bitter results of the treaty and feeling them so personally, Queen Boudica rose up in a terrible rage. Secretly, and biding her time, she met with the other Celtic leaders, who were equally outraged by the Roman use of force. In a few months she united the greatest number of tribes and raised the largest army that had ever been seen in Britain—120,000 people turned out for the war, according to Cassius Dio, who described how the Romans saw Boudica.

> In stature she was very tall, in appearance most terrifying, in the glance of her eye most fierce, and her voice was harsh; a great mass of the tawniest hair fell to her hips; around her neck was a large golden necklace; and she wore a tunic of divers colours over which a thick mantle was fastened with a brooch. This was her invariable attire. She...grasped a spear to aid her in terrifying all beholders.[20]

Waiting until the governor-general, the Roman Paulinus Suetonius, was occupied miles away (where he had trapped priests and priestesses of the Celtic religion along with other refugees and was slaughtering them), the Celts under the fierce leadership of Queen Boudica gathered and took the town of Colechester, then London and one other town; they dealt fiercely with the people they found there, Roman and Celt alike. "Beautifully timed and vigorously pressed, the sudden outbreak of the rebellion brought immediate success to the Britons," according to one account.[21]

Suetonius rushed to London in a panic when he heard that half of Britain had risen against him, and then he fled London, leaving it to the fury of the rebels. Boudica and company took London to the ground, undoubtedly dealing especially harshly with the Romanized Celts, for Dio reports that they bloodily sacrificed large numbers of prisoners in a sacred grove.[22]

One last, tremendous, grinding battle between the two forces decided the outcome of the rebellion, which hinged entirely on differences in the way the two peoples fought. On the Roman side, Suetonius came to the battlefield with a small, mobile, well-armed army of professional soldiers. He told his men not to be afraid of the Celts as they were mostly women anyhow, and badly armed. Boudica arrived with, it must have seemed, the whole countryside, for it was customary for the whole tribe to turn out for a Celtic battle, even the children hanging on the wagons shouting encouragement to their relatives. Dio claimed that 230,000 people participated in the battle.

Tacitus described Boudica on this day and paraphrased the speech she made to her army of united, furious peoples:

> Boudica drove round in a chariot, her daughters with her. As they reached each tribal contingent, she proclaimed that the Britons were well used to the leadership of women in battle. But she did not come among them now as a descendant of mighty ancestors, eager to avenge her lost wealth and kingdom. Rather was she an ordinary woman, fighting for her lost freedom, her bruised body, and the outraged virginity of her daughters. Roman greed no longer spared their bodies, old people were killed, virgins raped. But the gods would grant a just vengeance: the legion that had dared to fight had perished: the others were skulking in their camps and looking for a means of escape. They would never face the roar and din of the British thousands, much less their charges and their grappling hand-to-hand. Let them consider how many they had under arms, and why! Then they would know that on that day it was victory or death. That was her resolve, as a woman; the men could live, if they liked, and be slaves.[23]

It was altogether a remarkable speech for Boudica to make, the warrior queen who was leading women as well as men to war, to protect the ancient female and tribal powers. The tight Roman lines, all modern iron and leather, moved in close at a slow trot, using their short swords like bayonets against the British mix of women warriors, naked men warriors, children, dogs, and oxen. Some of Boudica's vast number escaped that day; the rest were penned against their own overturned wagons, and 80,000, warrior and civilian alike, were slaughtered, as Tacitus boasts.

The tribal resistance against Roman rule did not stop, however, nor did the vengeance that Suetonius extracted throughout the countryside, especially concentrating his hatred on Boudica's own people. He submitted the Hicca villages to so much genocidal "fire and the sword" that the spareness of the archeological remains in those areas is attributed by historians to his extreme harshness against them.[24]

The Romans were told that Boudica took poison after the last battle, and they particularly hunted for her grave, "for they would not allow any memorial of Boudicca to survive."[25] Suetonius was so vicious that he finally had to be removed and a man with a less murderous colonial policy installed before Roman government could be reestablished in the area.

At this time Boudica's name would have gone underground, become a loaded, emotion-filled word meaning suicide if pronounced in front of the wrong people in the wrong tone of voice. *Bulldike* is the kind of name to come very early to America—perhaps directly from the slang of rebellious descendants of her tribal people. These were also exactly the people who would be most likely to remember, metaphorically and through common slang, that their ancestors practiced homosexualism as a matter of choice and as a matter of social rite and tradition. They would remember that their great, rebellious, loud-voiced queen—who came from a female warrior tradition, carried a spear and a sword, and took her people to war against the mightiest patriarchal military state ever seen to that time—that she and warriors like her were to be called bulldikes.

Perhaps Boudica and some of the other Hicca women in that war were ceremonial Lesbians; perhaps like other tribal folk they also had special homosexual gods of their own and special rites concerning their social functions. In any case, through their slang, her descendants and others like them gave to Lesbians—the most rebellious, armed, "masculine," warriorlike, dangerous, and deserving—and give them still the ancient, proud, frightening, street-talk title: *bulldiker, bulldagger, Boudica.*[26]

> And so we went to war.
> Our men went with us.
> And for centuries since, the foe has
> searched for us in all our havens,
> secret circles, rings and covens;
> almost always we elude him,
> we who remember who we are;
> we who are never not at war.[27]

Butches and Femmes

Butch is another Gay slang word that makes reference to a particular office or life-role—like *dike*—that a Lesbian may take on for herself early in her life. Unlike *bulldike,* which is usually spoken by a straight person, *butch* and *femme* are words from inside Gay culture, part of the working vocabulary of most American Lesbians.

The "role-playing of butch/femme," as it came to be called (rather negatively) during the Lesbian/Feminist movement of the 1970s, was in full swing in the Gay bar cultures of the fifties and sixties and of course remained in many of them during the next decade as well. It is easy enough to tell from old photographs of

Lesbian couples that the women early in the century used the designations too. You can often tell the butch from the femme in the pictures of well-known Lesbian couples: Gertrude Stein is certainly butch while Alice B. Toklas is femme; Bryher is butch and H.D. femme; Vita Sackville-West is butch and Virginia Woolf femme; Rosa Bonheur is clearly butch in every regard; Radclyffe "John" Hall was so butch she wore men's underwear, while her lover Una Lady Troubridge was extremely femme. With other couples it is not so easy to make the designation. The very butch Amy Lowell, for instance, called her lover, Ada Russell, "Peter."[28]

Perhaps Ada and Amy were more like you and I together, Vonnie dear, for while you were always butch and I was always femme, anyone had to look close to tell the difference.

Butch and *femme* are French words. *Femme* derives from *femina,* "woman," more literally "who gives suck" or "who nourishes."[29] If the taking on of butch/femme roles were merely the imitation of male/female roles, we could expect the partner of a femme to be an "homme," which is French for "man." Gay characteristics, as we have seen with the drag queen and the bulldike, are far more original to the Gay underground culture than they are imitative of the aboveground heterosexual culture. The word *butch* does not derive from *man,* but more likely (and even if it is also short for "butcher," the French *boucher*) it is from the French for goat, *bouc.*[30] This in turn is related to *bucca,* "buck," the male stag, hare, or goat; *buck* is also a slang word used in a derogatory manner in the United States to designate Negro or Indian males and to refer covertly to their recent tribal connections. The stag and the goat, like the bull, were sacred to European tribal people, especially on the continent. Tribes in what is now the nation of France valued the goat in particular. All these animals were part of special festivals and ceremonies, were impersonated as gods, and were sacrificed on certain holy days. The goat-god (a version of the Horned God) and his impersonators were sometimes titled "Puck." Puck, or *puca* (Irish for "elf"), appears in Shakespeare's play *A Midsummer Night's Dream* as a Fairy character who can be played by either a male or a female.

If the ancient ceremonial role of bulldike was fulfilled by the Warrior Queen, the ancient ceremonial role of butch for women was probably a priestess taking the part of Puck—the Fairy goat-god who was sometimes also sacrificed ("bouchered") to keep the people prosperous. This ceremonial office of impersonating the goat-god (in butch drag) was last acted out in the grand public manner by Joan of Arc.

Certainly Joan was the quintessential ceremonial dyke, the warrior maid who listened to Fairy spirit voices under a sacred beech tree, who cropped her hair at the age of sixteen and put on men's clothing and armor because her own spirit voices told her she must do so for the sake of her people and her dauphin, the as yet uncrowned King Charles VII. Joan the Maid ("La Pucelle"), or Maid of God as she would be titled after her death in 1431, perhaps had a beloved female companion, as she preferred to sleep with young girls,[31] but her reputation for innocence and chastity is pervasive and it is doubtful that physical desire troubled her; she had other things to do. Nevertheless Joan is every inch a Gay figure and a ceremonial butch.

After her successful military battles against the English who had invaded her

French homeland, she was arrested, accused of paganism, of consorting with fairies, and of cross-dressing. Anthropologist Margaret Murray believed that no hand of her own people was raised to save her because she was a self-chosen sacrifice, a stand-in for the dauphin whose battles she had fought and won.[32]

Joan could have saved her own life during her trial by agreeing, as the court suggested, to put aside her men's clothing and to put on a woman's dress, *but she refused,* and this refusal was taken as a signal of tremendous significance by everyone concerned.[33]

Her cross-dressing was apparently a ceremonial decision, a signal to the populace with their still-potent pagan beliefs that she would not give up her special office of Warrior Maid and that she was truly a stand-in sacrifice for the dauphin. As such, she would of course have worn men's clothing. She was burned only after her refusal to give up her men's clothes.

Margaret Murray was convinced that Joan was part of the still-existent Old Religion of Europe and was standing in for the dauphin with the full backing of pagan elements in the army, the royal government, and the populace. Joan not only led and inspired the dauphin's army, she went on to be sacrificed in his place in order to pass on to the people the traditional sacred strength of the office of kingship. In pagan terms, the dauphin was the horned god of the people, the goat-god power, and Joan was the scape-goat, the substitute sacrifice. According to Murray, Joan volunteered, took it upon herself to go to the dauphin as a warrior and save his crown from the foreign invasion because, as she said, her spirit voices instructed her to do so.

Murray thought that Joan was a member of a secret coven whose members helped direct her actions and decisions. Certainly the common people understood her ceremonial nature, and they followed her, a sixteen-year-old girl, into battle and virtually worshiped her person before and after her death. People brought sick children to her for her blessing and asked her advice as though she were already a saint in her lifetime. They valued her butch characteristics of physical courage, short hair, men's clothing, disarming forthrightness, honesty, quiet but intense intelligence, and contact with the Fairy or spirit world. And of course, people valued her piety.

She cross-dressed with great significance, like many another shamanic Gay person fulfilling a particular office in her or his society. She had self-containment and the kind of integrity that takes its value from within or from natural or spiritual elements rather than from the worldly marketplace of ideas. She was a model dyke of high degree, a warrior-maid, the female Puck, a ceremonial butch, Maid of God, and a woman with whom many Lesbians have identified.

Baby Butch in the Modern World

I certainly identified with Joan of Arc. And I was a tomboy, of course. It is no exaggeration to say that in general women who become dykes were known as tomboys when they were children. Of course, many aggressive, athletic, rambunctious tomboys never become Lesbians, and many Lesbians were never tomboys. Nevertheless, having once been a tomboy is a major theme in the life stories of a great majority of Gay women, especially those designated in Gay culture as dikes, and especially those dikes who are particularly butch. In England, a slang word for Lesbian is *tom.*[34] *Tomboy* is also an old and perhaps spirit-based word, for one of the witches persecuted in England during the thirteenth century was accused by the authorities of having an imp, or spirit, in the form of a grey cat whose name was Tomboy.[35]

My mother tells me that at the age of three or four I invented or perceived an imaginary imp or playmate who went everywhere with me; no street could be crossed unless I first held his hand to make certain he was safe; no goodnight passed but that he must get a kiss too. And this little character, my innocent and unworldly mother has told me I told her, was named Butchie. I fought to wear pants at the age of five, and the snapshots my mother took of a curly-haired, pink-dressed person were all contrived, family lies. For at heart and at every opportunity I was a tomboy—out on a limb, up on a ledge, down a chimney, adrift on a raft, playing mumblety-peg barefoot with toes spread, daring some other child to throw the knife. I identified myself not only as Jo in *Little Women,* but as a pirate, cowboy, soldier, doctor, lumberjack, and, finally, adventurous writer in all my games and stories. Alone all day, I chose to play with my father's sparse property: knives, a handsaw, pistols, rifles, a machete, a bandana, bull's horns. Stomping around our tiny apartment in my brother's enormous engineering boots, sneaking a shotglass from the top kitchen shelf and repeatedly filling it with double shots of Pepsi Cola, I practiced becoming a tough-talking frontier drunkard while engaging in terse cowboy dialogues with the spirits who surround isolated eleven-year-old tomboys. That was the year I made myself a Roman breastplate out of beer-can tops. Later I would memorize Shakespeare's speeches by Marc Antony and Julius Caesar, having already become completely familiar with the metal and the leather, the postures and the play-acting of a man's world.

As a brazen twelve-year-old I sexually courted an unsuspecting married woman until her husband's astute suspicions interfered: "Are you sure she's supposed to lay her head on your breast like that?" he would ask worriedly. "But like *that?*" I loved her big firm breasts, and her big-boned body, and her thick blond hair. For the next two years I courted Pamela, a girl one year younger than I, going with her everywhere she would dare to go with me, pedaling madly on our bicycles, showing off to get attention, putting my arm around her shoulder in the movie house, overstaying my welcome at her large, well-kept house, writing her passionate philosophical poems. Her mother did not allow her to go to my house, for we were poor and in disgrace, I suppose. Their maid had as much social standing as my family did, perhaps more. They had a piano that Pamela played with much sneering and reluctance, while I hung over her, panting for a chance to get my hands on the keyboard. Pamela was outwardly a very boring person with little in the way of personality showing, self-control being her major attribute; consequently, I could imagine anything about her and it *might* be true. I imagined her as a brave, adventurous person who was completely crazy about me.

At night I would sneak out a window and go to her house and throw pebbles against her window, as I had read in romantic boys' stories, especially Mark Twain. She would crawl out her window and we would ride for miles in the moonlight on our bicycles. During these episodes I called her Tom Sawyer, and I called myself the more renegade and lower-class Huck Finn, my version of early butch/femme based on class difference. One night my mother caught me sneaking back in and was terribly angry. I explained, stuttering, that I had heard a noise and, thinking it was a prowler, had gone to investigate. She praised my courage. I felt very heroic.

Romeo and Juliet Replayed

> Good-night, good-night! parting is such sweet sorrow
> That I shall say good-night till it be morrow.
> Sleep dwell upon thine eyes, peace in thy breast!
> Would I were sleep and peace, so sweet to rest![36]

In 1954 a peculiar, small, Levi-clad figure strode boldly along the silent streets of a small class-bound southwestern town, reciting Shakespeare in a loud voice and plainly ready for any mischief. At fourteen I was ready to move on to more exciting body contact than holding sweating hands, hoping Pamela felt more than some girlish crush. I wanted to kiss Pamela, who had by her actions, or rather her lack of negative actions, led me to believe she liked me a lot, and I thought I had found a foolproof method of bringing up the subject of kissing in a nonthreatening manner. Shakespeare! Literature! Shakespeare was going to help me kiss Pamela. Oh good for you, Shakespeare. It happened that both Pamela and I were invited to a timely sleepover party at the house of her best friend, Jo Ellen. Riding merrily to Jo Ellen's house on my trusty blue bicycle, with a hard-earned copy of *Romeo and Juliet* in my back pocket, I was very disappointed to arrive and learn that Pamela's mother had not allowed her to come. And no one else had been invited. Oh no. All my scheming and rehearsals would be for nothing unless—did I dare? Did I dare to try to kiss Jo Ellen? Did I even *want* to kiss Jo Ellen? She was so crazy. You could never tell what she would do. But so what? I would try it.

Jo Ellen was a strange person, extremely thin and anemic to the point of translucence. She did not exactly move, she flitted in a sideways direction and then abruptly came to rest. She had boyish bushy hair and was very nervous. Both she and Pamela were under increasing pressure to be respectable, to be on display at the country club, to prepare to take a highly regulated place among the elite of the town. What was a horsey crooked-toothed character like me doing at her house? I didn't know. She had invited me. Now she lay stiffly beside me in a sleeping bag stretched out on the floor of her parents' garage. I was reading *Romeo and Juliet* to her by flashlight and asking if she wanted to read a scene with me. She did, and I had it carefully prepared and marked, a scene in which Romeo kisses Juliet. First we just read the lines out loud, and that went fine. Then I suggested we do it again, only this time, I said, "We could act out the actions."

"OK," she said.

"And when we get to the part where Romeo kisses Juliet, Romeo will kiss Juliet," I said.

"OK," she said.

"OK," I said, "I'll be Romeo."

"OK," she said. She lay perfectly still on her back. This made me terribly uneasy because of its similarity to the joke in *Romeo and Juliet* about Juliet spending a lot of her time on her back once she was married, a joke I hated. Why did being married involve lying on the back, I wondered in horror. It sounded slavish to me.

Nevertheless, my fourteen-year-old heart thumped and whacked as we read the romantic lines of the play, and when I got to the kissing place I leaned over and kissed Jo Ellen's warm though will-less mouth like a passionate grown-up lover. Her green eyes widened and she seemed a little amazed, but she did not respond or twitch or say anything, and as the silence deepened and I said, "Well," and she said, "Well." I got nervous myself, feeling I had slid into water way over my head. What if Jo Ellen spread the news at school or among the adults that I had taken it into my head to kiss her and left out the part about Shakespeare? And about its only being a play? I decided nothing would help except to get her to be committed and as far in over her head as I was, and the way to do that was to induce her to make an aggressive sexual move.

"Well," I said as firmly as I could manage in the breathy atmosphere, "now it is your turn to be Romeo, and I'll be Juliet." I laid out flat and stiff on my back in imitation of her and waited. This time the pause was as deep as a well and as wide as a barn door.

Then her voice came. "OK," and she raised up on one elbow to read by the gleam of the flashlight on the floor by my ear. We got to the vital part, and then she stopped. "Well, come on," I said, impatient with sudden social terror. "Romeo kisses Juliet. It's in the play." And to my intense relief she leaned over to kiss me. Then just before her lips arrived a massive earth-rattling, thundering-end-of-the-world banging began in one side of my head that drove me into an instant frenzy and sent me hollering and pounding my poor skull on the cement floor. Had lightning struck, or psychosomatic illness? No. Drawn by the flashlight, a simple-minded moth had bumbled into my ear and was thrashing its great wings against my eardrum. The result was similar to being in a load of cement inside a cement mixer.

Humiliation followed, Jo Ellen's mother having to be called to warm some oil and pour it into my ear canal to drown the idiot, and when everything settled back into place with the moth blissfully dead and washed away, Jo Ellen had retreated into a deep, complete, nervous silence.

I saw both her and Pamela a few more times, and something volcanic must have built up in our tense relationships. Both of them were under increasing pressure from their parents to voluntarily drop me as a friend, particularly as they were beginning to attend Rainbow Star dinners and Cotillion dances where their formal gowns billowed awkwardly around their skinny, undeveloped bodies, and the fact that the children of cooks and clerks were excluded was what gave the event half its meaning. Jo Ellen and Pamela were cultivating the closed, artificially smiling faces and tight nasal voices of women expected to direct servants. I was of the altogether wrong class to follow them along their narrow and difficult path. However winsome and appealing, my pirate Huck Finn ways could no longer be tolerated; soon I would be banished from Pamela's life. Never again would she say a word to me, even in the hallway at school, let alone be Tom Sawyer to my Huck Finn.

The last summer afternoon before my banishment from the kingdom of the

Cotillion, we were all three together when something strange happened with the flitty Jo Ellen. Perhaps her thirteen-year-old mind just went berserk. That afternoon as I got to Jo Ellen's front door, Pamela met me. "Go upstairs," she ordered anxiously. "Jo Ellen is acting funny."

As I leaped up the stairs to the rescue, Jo Ellen charged out of her parents' bedroom holding a loaded derringer. Rushing down the first step and then steadying the blunt-nosed pistol with both hands, she aimed at the center of my astonished forehead just six inches away and pulled the trigger two or three times. Enraged when the derringer failed to fire, she continued down the steps aiming at Pamela, chasing her out of the house and across a field. The wispy and outwardly passive Jo Ellen had out-butched everyone and had gotten the plot all screwed up and was trying to murder Romeo, Juliet, everybody! We never mentioned the incident; it wasn't a terribly unusual occurrence, given the number of pistols, rifles, and unexploded bombs in any household in our little town. Well, goodnight, Jo Ellen; goodnight, Pamela and Huck and moonlit rides; goodnight! goodnight! Romeo and Juliet, goodnight!

Butch to Femme in One Easy Step

The only day in my life I voluntarily wore a dress was the day I went to my first lover. Unsophisticated and untraveled, unmoneyed and extremely optimistic, I put on a red quilt jumper and a white blouse from Penney's Dry Goods to ride the Greyhound bus seven hundred meandering southwestern miles for my "elopement" to a love so secret no one from my high school would guess for years what I was really doing.

Feeling certain that my dress would win her heart, I arrived in my lover's life like some bright-red, short-haired, self-created pagan bride. Yvonne came to meet me in her black cowboy hat and black boots, clean-pressed Levis and the Future Farmers of America jacket she had worn when she was rodeo queen of her diminutive town. With a dazzling open-hearted smile illuminating her handsome brown face and shiny eyes, with her expressive voice kept in the soft lower ranges, her well-kept muscles and strong square hands, she was the perfect dyke. Moreover, she was smart, proud, ambitious, and she had a strongly developed social conscience. Though I never again wore a dress except for the direct necessity of keeping a job, and not always then, we began our life together clearly organized as butch and femme. Our first two lovers' squabbles were about her needing to be more publicly daring and my not knowing how to cook well enough to cook for her. Yet in spite of our pretense I was as butch as she, and I hated having to play the femme, especially when she used it to get out of doing household chores.

We dykes of the fifties and sixties were not like the other women around us; our gestures, our manner of dressing, our expectations of life, our bodies and carriage, our philosophy were all different. We would be spinsters, we knew, and self-supporting, and sometimes painfully socially isolated. We would learn to defend ourselves and each other. We were also sexually active as our mothers and even our sisters were not, but we never said this openly. The fact that our kind were so completely misunderstood made us skeptical of authoritative ideas and the complacent acceptance of surface appearances. We would be quick to notice other forms of social injustice. We lived in two worlds at once, neither of them comfortable or safe. Unlike the women around us who schemed to capture husbands by putting out signals of helplessness, we kept our bodies physically active, and though we didn't dare show them to anyone except each other, we had a big bad butchy secret—we had muscles.

Yvonne was especially proud of her sturdy, athletic body, which was beautiful and solid and skilled. She concentrated on difficult acrobatic accomplishments. At nineteen she was one of only two athletes in the state who could do a triple back flip on the trampoline. Leaping and leaping until she was high on a column of thin air, suddenly her head would snap, her legs would pull up to her chest and over and over she would go, backward, like a rolling rock, to land balanced, graceful, and triumphant with her big grin, and then duck her head modestly and give out an "Aw-shucks-twarn't-nothin" remark when she was praised.

"There's no such thing as a 'boy's way' of throwing a ball and a 'girl's way,'" she told me, greatly excited by this information. "There's just knowing the *way* to throw it, and then there's *not* knowing. Boys teach it to each other. Girls throw in that awful dishrag way because no one teaches them differently."

Years later I went to bed with a woman, a feminist, who had the muscleless blobby flesh most women at the time claimed was "natural," or at least "appealing to men." She was amazed at my flesh. "Oh—you have a *hard* body," she exclaimed. "Most women are crippled," she said. My Lesbian lovers and my own dyke identification had never allowed my muscles and sinews to atrophy as hers had, for I have always expected physical tenacity and butchness in my lovers and they have expected the same in me. Even Von, who also wanted me to be femme. But not *that* femme. Of course, there have always been aphysical Lesbians and plenty of heterosexual women on ball teams—especially now in the eighties when the country is under so much Gay influence and crisscrossing of traditional sex roles.

Once, in the old days when I was living in a situation where I was isolated from other Lesbians, I made a painting of a woman. In an era when few women wore pants, she wore pants that hung a little below her waist, just tight enough to show off the shape of her narrow hips and muscled thighs. Shirtless, she had medium-sized round breasts with erect nipples, broad shoulders, and muscled arms. She faced forward, fisted hands balanced on her hips, meeting your eyes directly when you looked at her face, which had a serious expression. She had very short hair and delicate features. My heterosexual roommate was very upset by the painting, spending two hours impatiently lecturing to me that women did not look like this and that what was wrong with me and my painting was that I had no idea what women look like. Because I was already in a great deal of trouble for being Gay, I could not explain to her that most of the women I had been to bed with looked precisely like my painting; in fact, if I myself gained ten pounds and stood up straight I would have looked precisely like my painting. I certainly couldn't tell her that the title of my painting was *The Butch.*

Establishing the Lesbian Bond

Within any era, the external appearances of the bond between two women vary according to what the society expects, tolerates and defines as a bond. When our society stressed the man-wife bond, many Lesbians formed the extreme butch-femme bond so evident in the 1950s. When the Lakota Indians stressed maternity as a prerogative for being truly a tribeswoman, *koskalaka* "Lesbians" bonded "in the spirit of Doublewoman" and ceremonially forged a "rope baby" between them to seal the bond and make it public. When class relations are most rigidly adhered to, the roles of lady/maidservant or mistress/handmaiden or author/secretary prevail as the models for two women together. When property rights are most at stake, the women formally marry each other and adopt each other's children, one of them taking on "father-owner" status.[37] When shamanism, sorcery, and access to the spirit world are a major part of social relations, two Lesbians or two Gay men together may be shaman/apprentice or priest/novice. Among movement Lesbians during the 1970s in America, butch/femme was criticized and suppressed in favor of partnerships (often business partnerships) that stressed an equality of dikeness distributed between both partners.

Probably no matter what society is examined, same-sex bonds will be found that formalize along social lines using roles recognizable to society, yet across cultural lines the *bond* is essentially the same and for the same purposes—to strengthen the position of women in the society, for instance, to model alternatives to existing forms, and to retain older traditional forms in danger of being lost.

Butch and femme, the two extreme social roles of modern underground Lesbians in industrialized societies, seem on the surface to be simple-minded imitations of man/wife roles developed by heterosexual culture. And some Lesbians do act them out to an extreme, with one woman in short hair and men's clothing, the other in a dress and high heels. This is especially true of the proud working-class Lesbians, both Black and white, among whom the butch and her lady will dress to the teeth for a weekend date and have a hell of a good time. However, unlike "man and wife," the participants in butch and femme are often interchangeable, or actually much more similar than their Saturday-night garb indicates. The following excerpt from "My Lady Ain't No Lady" by Pat Parker illustrates the point:

my lady ain't no lady—

she has been known
    to speak in a loud voice
    to pick her nose,
    stumble on a sidewalk,
    swear at her cats,
    swear at me,
    scream obscenities at men,
    paint rooms,
    repair houses,
    tote garbage,
    play basketball,

& numerous other
un lady like things.
my lady is definitely no lady
which is fine with me,

cause i ain't no gentleman.[38]

When I was a young dike trying to stay alive in the ghetto of the city of Washington, D.C., I found my place in a scroungy downtown low-life bar. There we young dikes tried out the different aspects of butch and femme as though our entire future depended on the outcome.

One small woman, Tonie, went to the wildest extremes. A dental assistant who had been evicted from the marines for being a Lesbian, she would arrive at ten o'clock, with much ado, as Tonie the Butch. Decked out in a man's black tuxedo with black, polished shoes, a man's handkerchief, cuff links, her short red hair plastered to her head with Vitalis, she would ask all the femmes to dance. The next night she would appear, with the same amount of drama, totally transformed and nearly unrecognizable as Tonie the Femme, with a flaming red dress, mascara and lipstick, high heels, hair fluffed out and piled on her head, a little brown beauty mark decorating one cheek. She was trying out the extremes of how to be "in the life," as we sometimes called being Gay.

Most of us tried out the roles in moderation, using a slight modification of hair style. (Is it behind her ears? She must be butch. Does it resemble bangs? She must be femme.) Or we used the difference between a "blouse" and a "shirt." We would lead with one dancing partner, follow with another. Since the butch was the one who requested the dance, it took much nerve to learn to be aggressive toward another woman and to risk being rejected out loud in front of your buddies. On the other hand, the femme role seemed boring and even more nerve-wracking since it involved waiting for another, perhaps equally shy woman to hurry up and get aggressive toward you. Few of us novices wanted to be femmes or knew much about the art of being femmes, so we tried hard to be accepted by each other as butches.

The heterosexual male model is by no means the only factor involved in the mannerisms of butch women. There is a tradition, for instance, of short-cropped hair for Western women that is not connected to the short haircuts of men. (The male military haircut, the crewcut, was developed for the purpose of detecting and preventing lice in the close quarters of barracks life.)

Ancient Greek vases show short-haired women together, including some who were clearly Lesbians. One of Sappho's poems describes how young women cut their hair in mourning when one of their number, Timas, died unexpectedly and, "unmarried, went to Persephone's dark bedroom."[39] Cutting the hair was evidently a purification rite, or a sacrifice to a special power. Both Persephone and her striking mother Demeter are often shown as short-haired, dikish-looking women, as are numerous other goddesses, especially the arrow-bearing Artemis and the three intriguing friends Leto, Themis, and Hera, shown lounging over each other's laps in warm attitudes of sexual friendship. In Rome, the vestal virgins whose task was to tend the eternal flame, which once represented the interior power of the female, were required by their office to be short-haired, as were Roman Catholic nuns until recently.

Though I had believed for years that American dikes wore short hair in direct imitation of men and as an aggressive rejection of the perception of "femaleness" as a form of slavery, I saw for myself how waves of extreme hair-cropping took place in the Lesbian feminist movement at a time when the styles for men's hair had been long for years. The women were cutting their hair to become dikes, not to imitate men.

But however well I imitated the butches in that particular competitive underground bar scene, I soon learned I was not going to make it as a butch, at least not all of the time, and not even after I had screwed up all my courage to buy a pair of men's loafers. The shoes were so well made, they had so much more leather in them than women's shoes, I still treasure the memory of the weight of them. And I had found some friendly male barbers who thought nothing of cutting a young dike's hair any way she wanted it, no small feat in those harshly role-bound times. All day at work I combed my hair one way, then at night I put on pants and a boy's jacket, combed my hair another ("opposite") way, and went to my other life at the bar. Still, I could not sustain a relationship with another woman unless I modified my clothes and undertook to be the femme.

Once, more recently, a friend of mine took an informal head count in a Lesbian bar in "liberated" San Francisco. She found that few women wanted to say they were femme; one table of eight responded with eight enthusiastic butches, though some were in couple relationships with each other. These women were all highly active feminists; they were also traditional American dikes.

The Butch Is a Magical Figure

For the purpose of attempting an explanation, admittedly simplistic, let me say that for Lesbians involved in the underground Gay culture, the butch is, ceremonially speaking, Puck. Cross-dressing is a magical function, and the butch is the equivalent of the traditional cross-dresser who may also become a magical/shaman of the tribe. She is the one who cross-dresses, becomes a hunter or a sooth-sayer or a prophet or the first woman in a formerly all-male occupation. She keeps the idea of biological destiny untenable. She usually takes on butchness as a lifelong destiny, irrespective of whether she has a lover. As a single individual she may act out the role of spinster or of the hermit who prefers living alone in the mountains or consorting with animals to the company of humans.[40] Conversely, she may fit in perfectly with masculine company as "one of the boys."

As the butch of a European tribe, she would have taken on the garb and the persona of the Horned God, or "devil," during the witch coven meetings or other festive gatherings of pagan times. In her modern form she is still entitled to wear leather, to decorate her body with tattoos and heavy jewelry in the ancient tribal manner, to walk and carry her body in the old way of the cross-dressing female. She is a child of Oya, of Artemis, of Wila Numpa, of the Amazons, of the Valkeryes, and of Joan of Arc.

In the tribal societies, as the accounts have described the cross-dressing butch

Lesbian, she often married women who were not necessarily ceremonial dykes themselves, who were not butch in the same sense she was. These women, let us suppose, were "femmes" of the tribe or village, were regular women, were ceremonial femmes, were women with full female powers, being "wisewomen," "the Mother" (in the sense of creator), or "the High Priestess." No stigma attached to the femme when she married the butch, and apparently no special "Lesbian" status attached to her either. The femme's next lover was as likely as not to be a man.

In our society such public marriage between women is prohibited, and the status of womanhood is greatly reduced. There are no ceremonial femmes as there are no ceremonial butches, no daughters of Oshun or Aphrodite as there are no daughters of Oya or Diana, in any publicly acknowledged sense. The contemporary dike is almost always forbidden to openly court women and to marry. I could never have married Jo Ellen or Pamela, for instance.

There are examples in recent history of women "passing" as men and marrying women, simply by tricking everyone. And there are, of course, plenty of Lesbian couples who manage to slip by, with a "Boston marriage," as the secret Lesbian bond has been called in that city. There are many butch women who become lovers with femme women, even openly in their neighborhoods in some sectors. However, there is no social sanctioning for such unions, and there are no public ceremonies celebrating them in straight society. The tradition of the ceremonial butch, like that of her male tribal counterparts, the *Winkte* or *Mahu*, gave her a special place in the village or clan; she has been almost entirely displaced in modern society.

Modern Dykes Have Had to Marry Each Other

The dyke, or butch woman in our society, unlike many societies in the past, has been an outcast figure. Women who have sexual/love relations with a dyke are themselves placed in the special, outcast category of "Lesbian" and usually feel the need to vehemently deny Lesbianism in order to return to ordinary female status after having one or two relationships with butch Lesbians. As I know from my brief experience in the military service, even *knowing* or being seen in the company of an open Lesbian may be considered grounds for suspicion of being a Lesbian.

In the prohibitive society of the 1950s American women would not risk the losses such a stigma entailed. I have met dozens of women who wanted to have a sexual and emotional relationship with a woman during that period of time and did not dare. And so the ceremonial dykes of the day gathered in little enclaves both rural and urban and married each other; in the case of Von and myself, I had to give in and play the femme although I much preferred being seen as a butch. I am as much of a ceremonial dike as she was, and I resented giving up any of my hard-won subterranean status. Those parts of our society which are closer to the tribal traditions (including what is called "lower class" and the old aristocracy of Europe and England) are more likely to maintain the classic butch, a cross-dressing, assertive woman whose lovers are femmes. The femme of this kind is indistinguishable in any way from the other women of her group and is usually very assertively "feminine," wearing makeup, vulnerable pretty clothing, high heels, and in general displaying the full powers of the female.

Among middle-class American Lesbians, extreme butch-femme polarities are tempered. The dykes simply disguise both members of their relationship in a modified drag known as "Lesbian," with perhaps one haircut a little shorter, one voice thrown a little lower, or some other distinguishing butch mark. The couple probably makes a few jokes about it now and then, meanwhile following feminist movement rhetoric by maintaining that "roles" are "patriarchal" and beneath our advanced consciousness.

The reality is that we, who would formerly have been considered ceremonial dikes, are now mass-culture Lesbians who have been excluded from our own villages and towns by homophobia and antitribalism and are having to re-form in urban or semi-urban settings where the more overtly Gay people are partially ghettoized, while the rest are heavily closeted.

The new urban manner of being Gay has produced a "middle gender" (sometimes called in Gay jargon "the clone") that combines qualities considered masculine and feminine in the society at large. We cross-dress—a little. Maybe keys hang at the belt, or one earring is sported, something a little out of balance. In this mass-cultural Gay movement, there is less presence of the extreme butch woman, and of the drag queen as well. Everyone is a little butch, and a little femme at the same time. Because we can no longer easily live as the openly Gay members of our "village"—that is, our American hometown, neighborhood, ethnic group, or church—we are propelled into the world at large. We are forced to become Gay people, to act out our traditional functions in the national context of mass culture. In so doing we lead mass cultural movements, we press for more balance among human beings; we practice combining a greater number of diverse characteristics in one life. A more cosmopolitan person and a more cosmopolitan culture emerge from this combining of traits from different sexual sectors of the population.

This is a very interesting and good thing, this modern way of being Gay. We are forced to the cusp between psychological worlds, between the objective and subjective in an individual life. This gives us a particularly balanced position from which to view our society, to make social statements by our very way of being two women together, and two men together; and it enables us to make a balance between what is considered male and female. And if this is painful to accomplish, it's also ingenious in the insights it produces.

I think the word *butch* will remain with us in underground Gay culture, as a useful description of another way of being a female, and "butch-femme" relationships as another form of marriage besides male-female or man-wife. Butch, like bulldike, designates a Lesbian office, one with apparently quite a long history.

In the old times, Von, you scoundrel, you could have "married" one of the women you knew in northern New Mexico, or perhaps several of them, in succession. They would not have been Gay, particularly, just married to you for a while; you would have functioned like a man as well as a shaman—dike. But in our time you could not make such a marriage of course. Lesbianism was anathema to all the people you knew. So you secretly married me, another dike who was willing to take the social risks, since after all, being Gay is my life. To marry you I had to restrain some of my butch impulses and play the femme for you. Then the two of us together went out into the world (well it was more like lurching out into the world, but we got there). We acted out our Gay natures on a stage much larger than our hometowns could have provided. Like other Americans, we became national. We claimed several major cities as home; we thought of our people as all people. We sought out the company of other Gay people who had also been forced to seclude themselves away from the group of their birth.

Notes

[1] Judy Grahn, "I Am the Wall," from "She Who," in *The Work of a Common Woman* (New York: St. Martin's, 1978), p. 98.

[2] Allan Berube, *Lesbian Masquerade,* presentation notes from a public slide program. "B-D Women Blues," sung by Bessie Jackson, 1935, reissued on *AC/DC Blues: Gay Jazz Re-Issues, Vol. 1,* collected by Chris Albertson, Stash Records, ST-106, 1977.

[3] *The Compact Edition of the Oxford English Dictionary,* 2 vols. (Oxford: Oxford University Press, 1971).

[4] Sharon Isabell, *Yesterday's Lessons: An Autobiography* (Oakland: Women's Press Collective, 1974).

[5] Donald R. Dudley and Graham Webster, *The Rebellion of Boudicca* (London: Routledge and Kegan Paul, 1962), p. 143. The philologist K. H. Jackson says it was spelled *Boudica.* The Romans recorded the queen's name as Boudicca and Boudouica.

[6] Jean Markale, *Women of the Celts* (London: Gordon Cremonesi, 1975), pp. 36-37.

[7] Arthur Evans, *Witchcraft and the Gay Counterculture* (Boston: Fag Rag Books, 1978), p. 18, quoting Markale.

[8] Anne Ross, *Pagan Celtic Britain* (New York: Columbia University Press, 1967), p. 228.

[9] Evans, *Witchcraft,* pp. 18-19, quoting Markale.

[10] Lawrence Durdin-Robertson, *The Goddesses of India, Tibet, China and Japan* (Eire: Cesara Publications, 1976), under "Aura clitoridis."

[11] Evans, *Witchcraft,* p. 21.

[12] Eric Partridge, *The Macmillan Dictionary of Historical Slang,* abridged (New York: Macmillan, 1973), pp. 457-458. Also *hornification* (a priapism), *old horny* (the male member), *horns-to-sell* (a loose wife, also a cuckold), *horny, horney, hornie* (Scottish colloquial for the devil—*auld Hornie*), *horny* (disposed for a carnal woman), *at the sign of the horn* (in cuckoldom).

[13] Evans, *Witchcraft,* p. 19, quoting Diodorus Siculus.

[14] C. D. Yonge, trans., *The Roman History of Ammianus Marcellinus,* XV, xii (London: Henry G. Bohn, 1862), p. 80.

[15] *The Random House Dictionary of the English Language* (New York: Random House, 1966). The entry for *butch* as the partner in a Lesbian relationship who "takes the part of the man" suggests, with a question mark, "short-haired one" as the possible derivation. I believe there is far more reason to look to the Horned goat-god and the Gay tribal sacraments surrounding him.

[16] Margaret Murray, *The God of the Witches* (London: Oxford University Press, 1952), p. 109, and *The Witch-Cult in Western Europe* (London: Oxford University Press, 1921), p. 133. An English witch, Isobel Gowdie, testified that the Maid of her Coven, Jean Marein, was nicknamed "Over the dyke with it" because the Coven god-figure always takes the maiden's hand when the dance was Gillatrypes, and they leap while both chanting "Over the dyke with it."

[17] Among some Mexican villagers and Southwest Indians, the bull-killing rite is accompanied by Mattachino dancers who form lines to make a corridor that leads to the bull. They are dressed in special conical hats, ribbons, glass decorations, and flowered scarves. They each hold a tree of life in one hand and rattles in the other. The American Gay rights group Mattachine Society (whose founder, Harry Hay, spent years living among southwestern Indians) is named for French Mattachines, who were jesters or wisemen in the medieval court.

[18] Minna M. Schmidt, *400 Outstanding Women of the World and Their Costumology* (Chicago: Minna Moscherosch Schmidt, 1933), p. 129. Dudley and Webster, *Rebellion of Boudicca,* also list "Bunduica." Interestingly, American frontiersman reporting on "Berdache women," that is, cross-dressing Indian "bulldikes," wrote the French word *berdache* variously as *bowdash* and even *bundash,* as though combining the French term with one they recognized from an Irish, Welsh, or English tradition: Bundaca/Boudica. Jonathon Katz, *Gay American History* (New York: Crowell, 1976).

[19] Perhaps it is because Boudica's name is so close to the slang word *bulldike,* which derived from her story, that it apparently unnerves people who want to deny a "strong" female name or any suggested connection to Gay terms. In recent centuries, writers have tried to soften and romanticize the original name. Of the Roman historians who

reported the queen's rebellion, Cassius Dio (writing in Greek) spelled the Celtic queen's name *Boudouika,* and Cornelius Tacitus (writing close to her time and in Latin) spelled it *Boudicca,* both of which clearly indicate a hard "c" sound. For ten centuries following the decline of the Roman Empire, these records were lost from discussion. When Roman writings were resurrected about four centuries ago, prominent English writers discarded Boudica's classical name and other remembered versions, such as Bunduca, in favor of Boadicea, Boadaceia, and the like, I suspect because they thought these sounded less threatening and more ladylike. And even though a few scholars have insisted that Boudica and Boudicca must be closer to her original name, many modern writers have been strangely reluctant to use it. T. C. Lethbridge, for instance, in *Witches* (New York: Citadel, 1968), said he used Boadicea because he "dislike[s] the correct name, Boudicca," p. 78. Another author, with credentials from the British Museum, explained his persistent misuse of the name and his personal preference for Boadicea: "The name is, I admit, indefensible, except on the grounds of euphony and popularity. But though I am prepared to champion most forlorn causes, I confess it seems hopeless now to substitute the appalling, yet more correct, Boudicca or Buddug," T. D. Kendrick, *The Druids: A Study in Keltic Prehistory* (London: Methuen and Company, 1927), p. 5. Even well-known writers have problems with the name and what it represents. Writing of the queen more than 1600 years following her infamous battles, John Milton flew into an unseemly rage over Boudica's story in his *History of Britain,* published in 1670. Interrupting a paraphrase of Boudica's rousing battle speech as it was interpreted by Cassius Dio, Milton raged, "a deal of other fondness they put into her mouth not worth recital: how she was lashed, how her daughters were handled, things worthier of silence, retirement, and a vail, than for a woman to repeat, as done to her own person, or to hear repeated before a host of men…And this they [the Classical historians] do out of vanity, hoping to embellish their history with the strangeness of our manners, not caring in the meanwhile to brand us with the rankest note of barbarism, as if in Britain *women were men, and men women*" (emphasis mine). The quote is from Dudley and Webster, *Rebellion of Boudicca,* p. 123. A present-day Celtic philologist, Prof. K. H. Jackson, has a different perspective. Interpreting the name through Welsh sources, he says: "The name is derivative of *bouda,* 'victory,' and is of course the Mod. Welsh *buddug,* 'Victoria.' But *buddug* is a secondary development, with vowel-harmony from (older) *buddug,* and this is from British 'Boudica,' which is the correct form of the lady's name," Dudley and Webster, *Rebellion of Boudicca,* p. 143.

[20] Cassius Dio, *Dio's Roman History,* VIII, bk. LXI-LXX, trans. E. Cary (Cambridge: Harvard University Press, 1925), p. 85.

[21] Dudley and Webster, *Rebellion of Boudicca,* p. 61.

[22] Dio, *Roman History,* pp. 85ff. He adds that they "cut off women's breasts and sewed them to their mouths." Dio's account is generally contemptuous of women, claiming, for instance, that Boudica was more intelligent than other women.

[23] Dudley and Webster, *Rebellion of Boudicca,* pp. 138ff.

[24] *The Encyclopaedia Brittanica,* 13th ed., s.v. "Boadicea."

[25] Dudley and Webster, *Rebellion of Boudicca,* pp. 76-77.

[26] Boudica's story has passed in a folk version through the Irish folk tradition, with her name pronounced BOO-duhca. I believe it was the British who put the long "i" sound into her name, as they have for so many other words: pronouncing "mike" and "tike" for *make* and *take,* the drink daiquiri as "dikery." Some American dialects reflect a similar phenomenon, changing "decked out" to "diked out."

[27] Judy Grahn, "Queen Boudica," based on the research I did for this chapter. The poem was first published in *Extended Outlooks,* ed. Jane Cooper, Gwen Head, Adalaide Morris, and Marcia Southwick (New York: Macmillan, 1982). "Queen Boudica" is part of my book *The Queen of Swords* (Trumansberg: Crossing Press, forthcoming).

[28] Jean Gould, *Amy: The World of Amy Lowell and the Imagist Movement* (New York: Dodd, Mead, 1975). Stein and Toklas have been seriously disclaimed for the public "man-wife" aspect of their relationship, although it served to camouflage them. Feminists both straight and Gay have been critical of the two women's "role-playing," in spite of their obvious working partnership, in spite of the completely female-defined writing it produced, and in spite of the tremendous credit Toklas received from Stein, appearing in most of the photographs and in the title of her autobiography (as a little joke they must both have had on the world). This is in contrast to the lack of credit or attention given to the wives of the famous male artists and writers of their day.

The very dykish Bryher took care of the poet H.D. (Hilda Doolittle), their partnership lasting several decades. I believe Woolf modeled her brilliant half-male, half-female character Orlando after Sackville-West. Bonheur's paintings of heavy horse flesh and early morning hunting gatherings of men and dogs could only have been accomplished by a woman if she dressed as a man, as Bonheur did.

[29] *An Etymological Dictionary of the English Language* (Oxford: Oxford University Press, 1978), p. 753.

[30] *The Random House Dictionary of the English Language,* unabridged (New York: Random House, 1966), s.v. "goat."

[31] Regine Pernoud, *Joan of Arc* (New York: Stein and Day, 1966), p. 63.

[32] Murray, *Witch-Cult,* pp. 270-276.
[33] Evans, *Witchcraft,* chap. 1, and Murray, *Witch-Cult,* both discuss the transvestite aspects of Joan's trial.
[34] H. Montgomery Hyde, *The Love That Dared Not Speak Its Name: A Candid History of Homosexuality in Britain* (Boston: Little, Brown, 1970), p. 22.
[35] Murray, *Witch-Cult,* p. 216. Deep into the 1600s English witches were still calling imps, spirits, familiars and "the Devil" by the name Tom, making it even more interesting that modern-day English Lesbians are called by that term (pp. 211, 213, 214, 225).
[36] *Romeo and Juliet,* act 2, sc. 11, lines 184-187.
[37] Denise O'Brien, "Female Husbands in Southern Bantu Societies," in *Sexual Stratification,* ed. Alice Schlegel (New York: Columbia University Press, 1977), pp. 109-126.
[38] Pat Parker, "My Lady Ain't No Lady," *in Movement in Black* (Trumansberg: Crossing Press, 1983), p. 113.
[39] Willis Barnstone, trans., *Sappho* (Garden City, N.Y.: Doubleday, 1965), p. 101.
[40] See, for example, Gina Covina, *The City of Hermits* (Berkeley: Barn Owl Books, 1983). The novel includes a well-drawn portrait of a Lesbian hermit, a lover of horses and desert life whose butch qualities are so extremely defined as to make her a ceremonial figure, an archetype of Lesbian literature.

Writing From A House Of Women

And Sappho said this: *Hither now, tender Graces and lovely-haired Muses.*[1] And this: *Stand (before me), if you love me, and spread abroad the grace that is on your eyes.*[2]

Sappho wrote from the base of Lesbianism, of bonded women in an intact culture, who had common understandings, a common mythological framework, a shared religion. She was central to her culture, and even in fragments has been central as a poet in Western culture as it has developed over twenty-five centuries.

Once an Alexandrian poet named Meleager referred to Sappho as "little—but all roses." The poet closest in quality to Sappho in the twentieth century, H.D., disagreed not only that she was "little," but also that "roses" was an apt description for the centrality of her position in her own world. In her essay, "The Wise Sappho," H.D. wrote of her as:

> Not roses, but an island, a country, a continent, a planet, a world of emotion, differing entirely from any present day imaginable world of emotion; a world of emotion that could only be imagined by the greatest of her own countrymen in the greatest period of that country's glamour, who themselves confessed her beyond their reach, beyond their song, not a woman, not a goddess even, but a song or the spirit of a song.
>
> A song, a spirit, a white star that moves across the heaven to mark the end of a world epoch or to presage some coming glory.[3]

Sappho wrote *from* the context of a women's community, or what could be termed a "House of Women," *into* the context of her society at large. As a poet of her whole society she wrote stories illustrative of the doings of the gods, both male and female; she wrote instructions for the appropriate behavior with respect to the gods and to human society; and she wrote wedding songs, as well as the overtly Lesbian love lyrics for which she is so famed and ill-famed, for which her work was burnt and partially submerged. In everything that remains of what she did, she maintained a female-based point of view, a female collective center from which to speak of life and death, of beauty and love in general. She used an internal, subjective voice in an objective, public manner.

Sappho used clear, precise description and example to illustrate her points, drawing from the religious mythology and stories which were well understood as metaphors, as instructions for ordering the universe by the people of her time. So to give example of her love for a certain woman, Anactoria, she drew on the story of Queen Helen:

> *Some say a host of cavalry, others of infantry, and others of ships, is the most beautiful thing on the black earth, but I say it is what-*

> *soever a person loves. It is perfectly easy to make this understood by everyone: for she who far surpassed mankind in beauty, Helen left her most noble husband and went sailing off to Troy with no thought at all for her child or dear parents, but (love) led her astray...lightly...(and she?) has reminded me now of Anactoria who is not here; I would rather see her lovely walk and the bright sparkle of her face than the Lydians' chariots and armed infantry...impossible to happen...mankind...but to pray to share... unexpectedly.*[4]

As Helen loved Paris, so do I love you, Anactoria, she said in a very socialized and external voice. She often used a subjective internal voice as well, and H.D. felt that voice is the one we love most about her:

> The gods, it is true,...are mentioned in these poems but at the end, it is for the strange almost petulant little phrases that we value this woman, this cry (against some simple unknown girl) of skirts and ankles we might think unnecessarily petty, yet are pleased in the thinking of it, or else the outbreak against her own intimate companions brings her nearer our own over-sophisticated, nerve-wracked era: "The people I help most are the most unkind," "O you forget me," or "You love someone better," "You are nothing to me," nervous, trivial tirades. Or we have in sweetened mood so simple a phrase "I sing"—not to please any god, goddess, creed or votary of religious rite—I sing not even in abstract contemplation, trance-like, remote from life, to please myself, but says this most delightful and friendly woman, "I sing and I sing beautifully like this, in order to please my friends—my girl friends."[5]

It is this wholeness of itself that has given Sappho's work such value, and so much power as to keep the little scattered phrases vibrant and meaningful. In spite of tremendous opposition, deliberate misinterpretation, branding of her person as a moral degenerate, and the tranformations of society over twenty five hundred years' time, the words speak strong and clear today. She spoke of and to the gods, in her own personal voice, undistanced from them. In so doing, she spoke into the most collective consciousness of her culture without omitting her own personal consciousness. She spoke from a whole way of being, not an alienated, fragmented one; she spoke not as an outcast, but as someone at the very heart and center of her culture and of her times.

Her place was on an island, from what can be imagined as a "House of Women" in the middle of her world. This is a place of far more power than any of the descriptive titles and names modern people have tried to put to what she did. She was, far more than a priestess in a religion of Aphrodite, teacher to daughters of a dying gynarchy, salon-hostess to a bevy of active artists or just a lyre-playing Lesbian with a lot of sexy friends. She wrote from such an integrated female place as we modem women have only begun to imagine.

Even in the sparse fragments that remain, the names of her lovers and cohorts in the group around her are many, and her usual attitude toward them is instructive and descriptive praise:

> *I bid you, Abanthis, take (your lyre?) and sing of Gongyla, while desire once again flies around you, the lovely one—for her dress excited you when you saw it; and I rejoice;...*[6]
>
> *...Sardis...often turning her thoughts in this direction...(she honoured) you as being like a goddess for all to see and took most delight in your song. Now she stands out among Lydian women like the rosy-fingered moon after sunset, surpassing all the stars, and its light spreads alike over the salt sea and the flowery fields; the dew is shed in beauty, and roses bloom and tender chervil and flowery melilot.*[7]

H.D. has given us her own succinct descriptions of these women who formed such a constant and vital matrix of presence in Sappho's work, in "The Wise Sappho":

> I love to think of Atthis and Andromeda curled on a sun-baked marble bench like the familiar Tanagra group, talking it over. What did they say? What did they think? Doubtless, they thought little or nothing and said much.
>
> There is another girl, a little girl. Her name is Cleis. It is reported that the mother of Sappho was named Cleis. It is said that Sappho had a daughter whom she called Cleis... I see her heaping shells, purple and rose-edged, stained here and there with saffron colours, shells from Adriatic waters heaped in her own little painted bowl and poured out again and gathered up only to be spilt once more across the sands. We have seen Atthis of yester-year; Andromeda of "fair requital," Mnasidika with provoking length of over-shapely limbs; Gyrinno, loved for some appealing gesture or strange resonance of voice or skill of finger-tips, though failing in the essential and more obvious qualities of beauty; Eranna with lips curved contemptuously over slightly irregular though white and perfect teeth; angry Eranna who refused everyone and bound white violets only for the straight hair she herself braided with precision and cruel self-torturing neatness about her own head. We know of Gorgo, over-riotous, too heavy, with special intoxicating sweetness, but exhausting, a girl to weary of, no companion, her over-soft curves presaging early development of heavy womanhood.

Among the living there are these and others. Timas, dead among the living, lying with lily wreath and funeral torch, a golden little bride, lives though sleeping more poignantly even than the famous Graeco-Egyptian beauty the poet's brother married at Naucratis. Rhodope, a name redolent (even though we may no longer read the tribute of the bridegroom's sister) of the heavy out-curling, over-lapping petals of the peerless flower.[8]

Obviously Sappho had a group around her; in fact, she would later be called a whore for having so many women lovers in her life. From all appearances, they constituted a "community" to themselves, for some period of their lives at least. She seems to have kept track of them even when they had left her company, and often it appears they left her company only to go to that of another woman, women known as "Sappho's rivals." This is an interpretation based on a belief that women's relationships consist of either/or competition. In the Lesbian community as it exists in modem times, a "rival" may also be one's best friend, ex-lover, or lover-to-be, and the operation of jealousy is not so simple as it seems. Jealousy and other strong emotions, as well as love and desire, have to do with maintaining a network of Lesbians who support each other long after, or prior to, or in spite of never having been, lovers with each other.

For though Lesbian communities have been reduced since Sappho's time to a public example of two lovers, as in Gertrude and Alice, or one lonely Emily Dickinson pining after her brother's wife, such isolation is only public. The matrix underlying all Lesbian love is extensive and involves a group effort, and some sort of network of support from other women, women who are not Lesbian.

With the decline of the gynarchic states that set the stage for a poet such as Sappho in the first place, the community of women as a public force declined. It cloistered, and it survived in informal networks. It surfaced for several decades in the South of France during the twelfth century in concert with the women troubadors and other Gay and woman-centered social elements. After the women troubadors lived there that area was a center of widespread heresy in the 13th century, heresy that encouraged female as well as Gay leadership, the worship of a two-sided deity, Gay and other libertarian sexual customs. The language of the troubadours is rich with imagery from the female domain, of roses and hearts, chalices, and utter devotion to ideals and to love. But this movement was warred upon and swept under by the heavy hand of the Inquisition. Vestiges of a public women's community went underground with the whores, witches, Lesbians and other fairy people.

In the nineteenth century, Emily Dickinson, isolated spinster *par excellence,* had the presence of other women in her life and their dedication saved her work from extinction. Her friendly editor Thomas Higginson treated her like an exotic pet, did not really like her work and discouraged her from publishing it, although that seems to have been what she wanted more than anything. After her death it was the women related to her who put her poems into print. They managed to do this despite their fear of disclosing the sheer overtness of Emily's Lesbian feelings, which almost caused sister-in-law Sue Dickinson to destroy the packets of handwritten manuscripts. The packets were literally saved by Emily's faithful younger sister Lavinia. In trying to edit the controversial material decades after it was written, Sue's daughter, Martha Dickinson Bianchi, censored the Lesbian references from Dickinson's letters and poems before publishing very bland renditions of the poet's actual sentiments. But in spite of their difficulties with the overtly Lesbian and more sharp-tongued parts, they retained her work and they made it public, even in the absence of a real women's community.

And then, astoundingly, as the twentieth century opened, it all began to re-form: a vocally growing feminism, the open expression and development of a Lesbian community, and a public expression of the centrality of women to themselves. With Amy Lowell and her lover Ada Russell, this expression took the form of a coterie of Lesbian friends who kept in contact with each other, visited each other, influenced each other. They also had tremendous impact on twentieth century ideas and literature. This network of friends included H.D. and the novelist Bryher, who had a covert Lesbian marriage and child-rearing arrangement together, though the image projected by and about H.D. is that she was ambivalent about Lesbianism. She continually idealized male lovers; she was uncertain enough about being taken seriously as the brilliant female intelligence that she was that she used as a pen name her initials, H.D., instead of her name Hilda Doolittle. But she spent the greater portion of her adult life—more than forty years—in relation to Bryher; Bryher was her island from which she wrote. The main body of her work is a deep, intense exploration of female powers, couched in metaphoric structures drawn from classical Greek mythology and the Egyptian occult tradition.

Other early twentieth-century Lesbian writers who followed on Dickinson's Victorian/Calvinist heels were able to be openly or at least semi-openly Lesbian in the company of other poets, could even form a social group with them. So the very dykish Lowell stayed influential with the Imagiste movement that included Ezra Pound, D.H. Lawrence and William Carlos Williams, as well as H.D. And the very dykely novelist, Bryher, though she apparently had a terrible reputation among the men as a termagant and other frighteningly "butch" things, was at least moderately acceptable to H.D.'s peer's in the literary society so vital to all of their work.

Gertrude Stein in her beautiful and outrageous Caesar haircut is most well known for her position among prominent male artists of the century, but she and Alice were also part of a network of Lesbian friends. Those dinner parties, of course, did not receive public attention, yet they happened; I dare say they were sustaining.

Networks of contemporary women sustain Lesbian writers; and the writers themselves look to their own heritage for food and drink and direction. Dickinson had certainly read Sappho, though she was most directly and deeply influenced by Elizabeth Barrett Browning. Amy Lowell expressed fierce loyalty to the women poets who had gone before her. Jean Gould, in her biography *Amy: The World of Amy Lowell and the Imagist Movement* wrote this description of Lowell's devotion to her sister writers:

> Her poem, "The Sisters," opening with a meditation on the "family" of women poets, was published in the *North American Review.* This was the poem in which she stated her views on the "queer lot" they were... In "The Sisters" she paid tribute

> to three poets she much admired. Of "Sapho" she said: "And she is Sapho—Sapho—not Miss or Mrs." But the next poet, "Mrs. Browning," of whom she is very fond, she would never dream of calling "Ba," and says bitterly, "…as if I didn't know / What those years felt like tied down to the sofa. / Confounded Victoria, and the slimy inhibitions she loosed on all us Anglo-Saxon creatures!" The third "sister," Emily Dickinson, she could not bring herself to address as "Miss Dickinson," or send a formal visiting card; in her fantasy meeting with Emily, she "climbed over the fence, and found her deep / Engrossed in the doing of a humming-bird / Among nasturtiums." She called Emily a "Frail little elf, / The lonely brain-child of a gaunt maturity," who "hung her womanhood upon a bough / And played ball with the stars—too long—too long long— / Until at last she lost even the desire / To take it down." Amy blamed not only Queen Victoria again, but also Martin Luther, "And behind him the long line of Church Fathers / Who draped their prurience like a dirty cloth / About the naked majesty of God."[9]

The connections of contemporary Lesbian poets to each other, though they may have developed late, are of vital importance to the growth of our ideas. Of the contemporary Lesbian poets under discussion, Adrienne Rich has written about H.D., Dickinson, Lowell, Stein, Lorde and myself. Olga Broumas has credited Sappho and Rich (along with Sylvia Plath, Anne Sexton, Virginia Woolf); Allen has written about my work and Lorde's; with this essay I have now written about, and do hereby credit as influences, all of them, beginning about 1977, except for Lorde, whose work I was beginning to know and utterly love by 1971.[10] I am saying all these names as a way of showing the lineage, and how conscious it has been. We have consciously drawn from a tradition leading back to Sappho and to a House of Women whether we have called it that or not.

Writing from a House of Women Out Into the World

The decision an artist makes, to speak for women and to speak as a woman (and likewise as a member of any group, a Lesbian, a Jewish, Black, working class person, etc.) is probably the most powerful decision she will make. For in making it, she chooses autonomy, she chooses to stand somewhere in particular to speak out to her society. Her work, in locating itself so specifically socially and historically takes on a power it cannot have if she chooses, instead, to speak anonymously, "universally." But having made this choice, she faces another danger, for if she addresses only members of her special groups, her work will have limited power, and limited integrity. It is the acknowledgement and then the inclusion of *all* our selves that leads us to the idea of life as consisting of many expanding, multicultural worlds in which everyone is ultimately included (as well as excluded).

This expansion happens after the artist plants herself in the midst of all her groups, and embraces the cultural separatism that enables autonomy, self-definition and community to develop. From this strong home-base, then, she can approach the world at large as somebody in particular, as Sappho did when she bragged that no one could out-sing the poets of Lesbos.

If the network, or base of women bonded as lovers and as friends, is home base for the Lesbian poets, it is not for its own sake only. It has not been for the purpose of aggrandizing Lesbianism, nor even of "making the world a safer place," for Lesbianism (though that is sometimes a necessary effect). Rather it has been a place from which to speak and a lens through which to view our society at large. It is paradoxically both a central and an "outsider" position from which to take a stance.

In finding an appropriate voice with which to speak from her own highly eccentric dykely life, Amy Lowell was drawn to and highly influential within what Ezra Pound named the "Imagist Movement" of poetry. Imagism is poetry in which romantic sludge and conventional metaphor, rhyme schemes and taken-for-granted ideas were stripped away, sheared off to leave a crisp emphasis on the image alone, the image itself to convey meaning. This left the mind's eye free to make new connections, free of nineteenth century values. The Imagists, and Amy Lowell in particular, looked to the literature of American Indians, especially Pueblo Indians, who she openly imitated in a series of poems. She also drew from early Chinese and Japanese forms to find a cleanness of line and thought, a spareness of obvious truth. In her very ambitious and productive way Lowell was so busy an organizer of the Imagist Movement and supporter of the other Imagist writers that Pound later, and in disgust, called it the "Amigist Movement."

Lowell concentrated her artistic energies on stripping the poem to a clean, spare image, on writing in almost terse, "Americanized" poetic sentences, though still keeping to schemes of rhyme and rhythm that were relatively tight (compared to Whitman, who had opened sentences to loquacious freedom forty years earlier). Lowell began using coarse, startling, formerly unacceptable phrases, descriptions and ideas. The Harvard society of her father and brothers found the lines in her poem "Grotesque" to be insulting: "Why do the lillies goggle their tongues at me / ... / Why do they shriek your name / And spit at me..."[11]

Not that she didn't wax beautifully lyrical much of the time, especially in her love poems to Ada. In "Song for a Viola d'Amore," she writes:

> The lady of my choice is bright
> As a clematis at the touch of night,
> As a white clematis with a purple heart
> When twilight cuts the earth and sun apart[12]

"Patterns" is virtually the only poem of Lowell's to have been so heavily anthologized as to keep her name alive today, when her work is out of print and difficult to find. In this poem she translated the social strictures and pressures she felt on her own Lesbian life into a poem about a woman who is buttoned into the whalebone and brocade of rigid social convention. The woman walks in a lush, promising and sensual garden with her male lover, unable to give herself over to her passion though she is able to fantasize a naked embrace with him. As the poem proceeds we see that she is reading a letter announcing that the lover has been killed in battle, and all their careful adherence to sexual strictures has been for nothing. The poem's ending line, "Christ! what are patterns for," combines a bitter curse, a naming of the responsible party, and a crying out to god, all at one time. The words still shock, and in 1915 they were considered extremely coarse language for a poet, let alone an upper class lady poet, to use.

The emotional substance of "Patterns" came from her own life with Ada Russell, and from the social restrictions they felt about being a queer couple. Jean Gould says in her biography that after writing "Patterns" the poet was "so buoyant over achieving exactly the effect she desired that she could hardly wait for Ada's opinion, and she met her at the door with it when her friend came home."[13]

In "Patterns," Amy was writing out from a base of Lesbian love, out from it into the world at large, translating her own experience into terms a wide and heterosexual audience could instantly identify with. In so doing, she spoke against all moral strictures, for all who wanted to break with Victorian morality, for all who understood that the sexual inhibitions had something to do with the "pattern called war."

"Imagism" set up a form of new lyricism that H.D. fully developed after her early "Imagist" years. She turned to an astonishing, breathtaking epic poetry, where she explored epic themes in tight, precise, lyric couplets. The pairing together of the two forms was essential for her task of writing modern mythic-occult-prophetic-historic-epics from *within* a female point of view. With her form she, like Sappho, is able to portray both the inside world and the outside world: both the narrative of what happened and the inner dialogue of what the experience felt, looked, tasted, smelled like. In her form, she married the female/lyric/Sapphic and the male/epic/narrative/Homeric. She reversed their effects: the usually "objective" narration of events is focused on an internal/occult landscape:

> Clytaemnestra gathered the red rose,
> Helen, the white,
> but they grew on one stem,
>
> one branch, one root in the dark;
> I have not answered his question,
> which was the veil?
>
> which was the dream?
> was the dream, Helen upon the ramparts?
> was the veil, Helen in Egypt?[14]

The usually cold external narrative is told in a warm, lyric, personal voice; yet the story being told is epic, is history:

> Be still, I say, strive not,
> yourself to annul the decree;
> you can not return to the past
>
> nor stay the sun in his course;
> be still, I say, why weep?
> you spoke of your happiness,

I was near you and heard you speak;
I heard you question Achilles
and Achilles answer you;

be still, O sister, O shadow;
your sister, your shadow was near,
lurking behind the pillars,

counting the fall of your feet,
as Achilles beneath the ramparts;
you spoke and I heard you speak;...[15]

Perhaps only a woman who loved both women and men in her life could have accomplished, would have attempted, such a wedding of forms, forms that have been considered oppositional.

Turning the Inside Outside: Gertrude Stein

A classic dyke in form and function, Gertrude Stein sat with the male artists and intellectuals who visited the home she and Alice Toklas kept in Paris. She did not sit with the wives of the artists; she was a woman who crossed over into a man's world of writing and innovating literature. "I will come back a lion," she said of her move to Europe, and she meant a literary lion, not a pussy cat. And perhaps Alice did not want her sitting with the wives, and be subject to their flirting. Alice, after all, was the wife of an artist too, an artist named Gertrude, though unlike those other wives, Toklas' name is remembered. Women were the main subject of Stein's art; she wrote of them in portraits and stories, myths and poems, using humor, sensitivity, sensuality, commentary, description. She wrote *as* a woman of her times, using an interior female landscape. Mundane female objects and scenes were her field of study: furniture, pictures, cows, poodles, people at dinner, people in love, people talking together. For Stein, the House of Women was her own house, and her own female perspective on the nature of the house, as she developed it in the close companionship she shared with Toklas.

Writing out from the base of a woman to woman relationship considered taboo in the world, and translating this everyday personal experience into a literature that no longer overtly contains the taboo experience yet covertly contains it in great detail was a lifelong preoccupation of Gertrude Stein. In gaining the ability to put into her work the love between herself and Alice Toklas, she not only stripped poetry to the spare image, she also stripped away image and entered the domain of language itself. Once into that world, she began perceiving and treating words as individual bricks that have a free-floating meaning of their own, unattached to the automatic clichéd meanings they have in sentence form.

By detaching verbs from nouns, by detaching linear plot from language, taking apart the old formula that noun acts upon object and verb is amplified by adverb, she opened up the nature of language itself, made spaces in it. Into these spaces of "free-floating" or unclichéd meaning, she dropped the substance and the everyday happenings of her life with Alice, including their erotic life, their pet names for each other and their highly personal ways of being together. She did this with such subtlety that only one poem was considered overtly homosexual enough to be included in the *Penguin Book of Homosexual Verse:*

> I love my love with a v
> Because it is like that
> I love my love with a b
> Because I am beside that
> A king.
> I love my love with an a
> Because she is a queen
> I love my love and a a is the best of them
> Think well and be a king,
> Think more and think again
> I love my love with a dress and a hat
> I love my love and not with this or with that
> I love my love with a y because she is my bride
> I love her with a d because she is my love beside
> Thank you for being there
> Nobody has to care
> Thank you for being here
> Because you are not there.
>   And with and without me which is and without she
>   can be late   she
> and then and how and all around we think and found that
>   it
> is time to cry
> she and I.[16]

Stein opened up language itself, the very bricks of it, the very of of it, the it of it, the the of of. Amy Lowell and the Imagists had stripped poetry free of the sultry, stultifying imagery of the Victorian age in order to allow for a more "modern" content—and in Lowell's case at least, a more Lesbian content. Gertrude Stein stripped the structure of the language itself. She collapsed into one voice the two supposedly oppositional extremes of perception—objective and subjective—collapsed them into one form, one technique, one mode of understanding. The result is a truer form of objectivity, a virtually value-free language, as well as a truer form of subjectivity, an almost ego-free and sentiment-free experience of the work.

By equalizing the value of each word, Stein was locating the commonness of language, the equality of value each word has with every other. She treated each word as a unit of meaning in and of itself, taking the meaning new each time from the context of the other words around it, and also from the multitude of associations we make in our inner brains, in our word-poetic minds of simple association.

In exploring this terrain she freed language from its linear plot. Not only did she free the image from the old romantic affiliations as Lowell and the Imagists did, but she also freed each sentence from its linear plot of grammar: subject is a noun acting with a verb upon a subject and is modified by adjectives. She made nouns out of articles and verbs out of nouns and subjects out of adverbs and conjunctions. And in so doing she took all the moral judgmentalness from language, all the expectation: hero saves heroine from evil landlord. She removed all the expectation: this is good, this is bad, this is indifferent. In her sentences each word is indifferent, is good and is bad. Each word is evil, is a landlord, a heroine, is saving. And so she was able to use the substance of her inner life, her home life, her personal life and those of *all* her friends, not merely the socially acceptable ones. And because she had freed the language of all possible judgment there is no way to read her work and to judge her life in any terms except her own. It takes a very wild and major lion to do this, to set the terms of value, to the art.

Consider this passage from "Lifting Belly":

Lifting belly with me.
You inquire.
What you do then.
Pushing.
Thank you so much.
And lend a hand.
What is lifting belly now.
My baby.
Always sincerely.
Lifting belly says it there.
Thank you for the cream.
Lifting belly tenderly.
A remarkable piece of intuition.
I have forgotten all about it.
Have you forgotten all about it.
Little nature which is mine.
Fairy ham
Is a clam.
Of chowder
Kiss him Louder.
Can you be especially proud of me.
Lifting belly a queen.
In that way I can think.
Thank you so much.
I have,
lifting belly for me.
I can not forget the name.
lifting belly for me.

Lifting belly again.
Can you be proud of me.
I am.
Then we say it.
In miracles.
Can we say it and then sing. You mean drive.
I mean drive.
We are full of pride.
Lifting belly is proud.
Lifting belly is my queen.
Lifting belly happy.
Lifting belly see.
lifting belly.
Lifting belly address.
Little washers.
Lifting belly how do you do.
Lifting belly is famous for recipes.
You mean Genevieve.
I mean I never ask for potatoes.
But you liked them then.
And now.
Now we know about water.
Lifting belly is a miracle.
And the Caesars.
The Caesars are docile.
Not more docile than is right.
No beautifully right.
And in relation to a cow.
And in relation to a cow.
Do believe me when I incline.
You mean obey.
I mean obey.
Obey me.
Husband obey your wife.
Lifting belly is so dear.
To me.
Lifting belly is smooth,
Tell lifting belly about matches.
Matches can be struck with the thumb.
Not by us.
No indeed.
What is it I say about letters.
Twenty six.
And counted.
And counted deliberately.
This is not as difficult as it seems.

Lifting belly is so strange.
And quick.
Lifting belly in a minute.
Lifting belly in a minute now.
In a minute.
Not to-day.
No not to-day.
Can you swim.
Lifting belly can perform aquatics.
Lifting belly is astonishing.
Lifting belly for me.
Come together.
Lifting belly near.
I credit you with repetition.
Believe me I will not say it.
And retirement.
I celebrate something.
Do you.[17]

Looking at the outside from the inside and at the inside from the outside, Stein fulfilled her function of Lesbian poet to the highest degree. She also achieved a singular objectivity with this method, especially about highly charged social stigmas. After shelving as unpublishable her first, and completely Lesbian, novel of a triangle of young women, she proceeded to write *Three Lives,* three portraits of women very different from herself and from each other. The first of these, "Melanctha" is virtually the only example in literature of a white author writing of Black characters simply for themselves, and, like the Lesbians in her first novel, portrayed solely in relation to each other rather than to the outside (and white) world. Language conventions for describing race change so rapidly from decade to decade, that "Melanctha" may appear inappropriate to us in ways that were certainly not true when it was written.

From her early and relatively concrete, linear works ("Melanctha" has a recognizable plot, for instance) she continued to experiment more and more with the nature of language, thought and communication itself. In *The Making of Americans* (of which it is joked that only Toklas, who typed it, has read the whole thing), and in her erotic poems such as "Lifting Belly," and even more in her later plays, she treated language as a real being, plastic rather than fixed. Her language creates context rather than being contextual. She was exploring the neurological impressions and connections words make inside our brains. Modern psychologists, also being, as Stein was earlier, students of the great psychologist William James, would do this themselves in developing behaviorism and neurolinguistics.

Concerning naming she said, very specifically:

> So then in Tender Buttons I was making poetry but and it seriously troubled me, dimly I knew that nouns made poetry but in prose I no longer needed the help of nouns and in poetry did I need the help of nouns. Was there not a way of naming

> things that would not invent names, but mean names without naming them.
>
> I had always been very impressed from the time that I was very young by having had it told me and then afterwards feeling it myself that Shakespeare in the forest of Arden had created a forest without mentioning the things that make a forest. You feel it all but he does not name its names…
>
> I commenced trying to do something in Tender Buttons about this thing. I went on and on trying to do this thing. I remember in writing An Acquaintance With Description looking at anything until something that was not the name of that thing but was in a way that actual thing would come to be written.
>
> Naturally, and one may say that is what made Walt Whitman naturally that made the change in the form of poetry, that we who had known the names so long did not get a thrill from just knowing them. We that is any human being living has inevitably to feel the thing anything being existing, but the name of that thing of that anything is no longer anything to thrill anyone except children. So as everybody has to be a poet, what was there to do. This that I have just described, the creating it without naming it, was what broke the rigid form of the noun the simple noun poetry which now was broken.[18]

In collapsing the external and the internal into one view, lining them up on one single plane of being she is using a technique similar to that used by tribal poetry, by American Indian poetry, for example. She reversed the belief that so much Western writing and Western science has had: that one must and can choose between the internal and the external vision, can split them. (They are usually split artificially along gender lines, racial lines, and class lines.) But if we deny the internal we cannot see the external very clearly either, and vice versa, although we can have the emotional illusion of clear perception. This is a culture trance, a mythic story all participants give as "reasons" for their feelings and behavior in any given situation.[19]

By unifying the internal and external viewpoints, and by assigning equal value to each component of her work, each letter of the word, each word of the sentence, each image being described, Stein enabled a nonlinear, democratic and powerfully female landscape of the mind; she literally dis-enchanted the mythic "sleep," the "culture trance" or previous myths of Western partriarchal literature, and she did this primarily through her approach to language.

Toward a Contemporary Lesbian House of Women

For contemporary Lesbian poets who have undertaken a definition of the word "Lesbian" and its many implications, and who deliberately have established as large as possible a "house" of women based on bonding in the most essential ways, three major areas have concerned us. These are self-determination, autonomy and community, the same concerns that preoccupy any group attempting to maintain its identity in a hostile environment.

All these qualities seem implicitly present in Sappho's work. Certainly she had a community of women around her, even whose names are known to us; she had vital importance to her culture, as her popularity attests; she had an intact ceremony, a mythos, from which to draw connection to the forces of the universe. Her definitions, like her gods, were her own.

"As for him who finds fault with us, may silliness and sorrow overtake him,"[20] goes one popular poster version of one of her fragments, but nothing indicates it was the female-bonded culture she represented that anyone in her day would find fault with. Her words and definitions were hers, for her teaching, praying, singing purposes, delivered outward to the world from her position of female centrality in her society. An ancient writer named Demetrius said of her, "This is why when Sappho sings of beauty her words are beautiful and sweet; so too when she sings of loves and spring and the halcyon: every type of beautiful word is woven into her poetry, and some of them are her own creation."[21]

The effort of establishing and re-confirming self-definition in the voices of the contemporary Lesbian poets has included reclaiming words with loaded, stereotypic content such as, Lesbian, dyke, whore, cunt, mother, daughter, birthing and the like—and extending as a matter of the course of our lives into the other groups to which we also variously belong: Black, feminist, working class, Jewish, fat, Indian, alcoholic, intellectual, literary, leftist, mystic, revolutionary, and immigrant American. The effort of reconstructing a female self-definition also has included filling in the silences first pointed out by working class and feminist writer Tillie Olsen, and taken up by Adrienne Rich in her essays and her book *On Lies, Secrets and Silence.*

The leadership exerted by Lesbian and feminist poets as the mass movements of women developed during the 1970's cannot be exaggerated. Even well into the 80's I can hardly walk into a women's center anywhere in the country without seeing lines from any of a dozen of my own poems posted on the wall as mottoes of strength and inspiration to all who pass through. We have all been recorded, reproduced in all manner of media and read by millions of women (and men). Audre Lorde's poetic political stances have become ethical guidelines in more than one sector and so have Adrienne Rich's.

Poets—both feminist and Lesbian—but especially Lesbian/feminist, have repeatedly surfaced with the key words and phrases that later became full-blown movement issues and obsessions. These have included many aspects of sexism and the belittling of women, details of homophobia and compulsory heterosexuality, rape, alcoholism and its debilitating effects on our lives, and racism between women, to use some more obvious examples. Sometimes the poets write out of group consciousness as it develops among active people around them; sometimes they speak from their own individual courage and integrity. Sometimes they have absorbed the ensuing attacks of doubt and hostility as the issue is argued into a public life of its own. Always they are operating as Sappho operated, as any true poet operates: defining the culture around her, giving it name, substance and rhythm so it can grow into a full life.

The development of genuine autonomy has been a second great work undertaken by modern Lesbian feminists and given much attention by the poets. This has included stressing the necessity for women to begin, and to continue, looking to each other and to ourselves for our value and sense of esteem, looking to sameness and commonality for strength and motivation. Pat Parker in the last stanza of a poem called "GROUP" names a major source of reclaimed self-love after it has been torn from us, in this case by racism as well as sexism and homophobia. After describing lessons she learned of hatred of herself for looking Black, and from being called bad, "I do have memory of teachers / you are heathens / why can't you be / like the white kids / you are bad—" she concluded:

now
there are new lessons
new teachers
each week I go to my group
see women
Black women
Beautiful Black Women
& I am in love
with each of them
& this is important
in the loving
in the act of loving
each woman
I have learned a new lesson
I have learned
to love myself [22]

The Rise of The Common Woman

With the appearance of *The Common Woman Poems,* which I published in 1969 in a basement mimeograph machine edition, the Lesbian and all manner of other "exotic" female experiences were placed—literarily speaking—in a framework of commonality and at the *center* of female experience. "The common woman is as common as good bread, and will rise," the poems ended and they were quoted and sloganized over a million times in media that ranged from television to T-shirts.

Adrienne Rich commented on them: "The 'Common Woman' is far more than a class description. What is 'common' in and to women is the intersection of oppression and strength, damage and beauty. It is, quite simply, the *ordinary* in women which will 'rise' in every sense of the word—spiritually and in activism. For us, to be 'extraordinary' or 'uncommon' is to fail. History has been embellished with 'extraordinary,' and 'exemplary,' 'uncommon,' and of course 'token' women whose lives have left the rest unchanged. The 'common woman' is in fact the embodiment of the extraordinary will-to-survive in millions of women, a life-force which transcends childbearing: unquenchable, chromosomatic reality. Only when we can count on this force in each other, everywhere, know absolutely that it is there for us, will we cease abandoning and being abandoned by 'all of our lovers.'"[23]

By placing one Lesbian portrait into a matrix of seven portraits of seven women, I was writing out of the Lesbian couple bond (influenced by the feminist movement) into a much larger world of women in general, who can be seen as and can act as a group based on their commonality, their common interest in improving their lives, and their common strengths of experience and heritage. The idea of common women passed on into Adrienne Rich's *The Dream of Language* where it was greatly broadened by new phrases. The "Common Dream" was a common dream of women together, of the social implications and possibilities of the bond of women, to each other and to their own strengths and powers. This, she suggested, could be articulated by a common language, a "whole new poetry," called for in "Transcendental Etude."[24] By 1976, Olga Broumas would be confident enough about the possibility of a female language to write:

> A woman-made
> language would
> have as many synonyms for pink
> light-filled
> holy as
> the Eskimo does
> for snow.[25]

Lesbian and feminist groups of all descriptions have used the word "common" in one capacity or another, to name stores, restaurants, health collectives, or newsletters and magazines, as Midwest Lesbians did with "Common Lives/Lesbian Lives." Lesbian poets have repeated the idea frequently: Broumas mentions "common protest" in her poem "Snow White," and entering "into the common, suspended disbelief of love."[26] Alice Bloch calls her life with her lover our "common life" in a bitter poem expressing lack of social acknowledgement and support for Lesbian relationships.[27]

One critic has pointed out the all-important difference between "universal" and "common" as it has been explored in my work and in Adrienne Rich's. "Common refers to that which is shared; that which no matter how incomplete, as life is incomplete, no matter how imperfect—essentially non-ideal—exists here, now, in its particularity as true." And again, "We do not lose ourselves to find ourselves, we *find* ourselves to find ourselves."[28] Universal, "one-world" implies everyone having to fit into one standard (and of course that one, that "uni," is going to turn out to be a white, male, heterosexual, young, educated, middle class, etc. model). For if there can only be one model, how can it be otherwise? *This* is the white man's burden, to have to be the center for everyone. Common means many-centered, many overlapping islands of groups each of which maintains its own center and each of which is central to society for what it gives to society.

Critic Mary Carruthers has called my "She Who" poems a virtual book of common prayer for women,[29] and that was what I intended when I wrote the bulk of them over a nine month period in 1972. At that time the vision of commonality was solidifying into something both larger and smaller, but certainly more concrete. We were busy establishing a base of female controlled institutions that would begin to answer to the expressed needs of all kinds of women. Women were dramatically shifting the focus of their lives, entering the work force, changing their family structures, bonding with different kinds of lovers than they had ever imagined for themselves, launching careers and starting businesses. Commonality gave way to community, the attempt to concretize the bonding of women into a group identity.

Not surprisingly, the "She Who" poems were written while I was living in a household consisting entirely of Lesbians—some forty of them living there during a five year period. The "She Who" series ends with a list of "every kind of woman I could think of"—and the imagery is not limited to the United States nor to women in the industrial state.

> . . .
> the woman who escaped from the jailhouse
> the woman who is walking across the desert
> the woman who buries the dead
> the woman who taught herself writing
> the woman who skins rabbits
> the woman who believes her own word
> the woman who chews bearskin
> the woman who eats cocaine
> the woman who thinks about everything
> the woman who has the tattoo of a bird
> the woman who puts things together
> the woman who squats on her haunches
> the woman whose children are all different   colors
>
> singing   I am the will of the woman
>   the woman
>   my will is unbending
> when She-Who-moves-the-earth will turn over
> when She Who moves, the earth will turn over[30]

In each case, I had a specific person in mind, someone I knew or had read about. For instance, "the woman whose children are all different colors" was in honor of Diane DiPrima, who I have always admired for her free-wheeling choice of fathers for her five children.

The kind of international connection present in the "She Who" series is vividly apparent in Audre Lorde's work. In the startling, physically charged love poem, "Meet," the lovers are not only united with women in all parts of history, including the old slave trading ports of Palmyra and Abomey-Calavi, but also with the earth's own substance and the animal world, especially the lion family:

> Woman when we met on the solstice
> high over halfway between your world and mine
> rimmed with full moon and no more excuses
> your red hair burned my fingers as I spread you
> tasting your ruff down to sweetness
> and I forgot to tell you
> I have heard you calling across this land
> in my blood before meeting
> and I greet you again
> on the beaches in mines lying on platforms
> in trees full of tail-tail birds flicking
> and deep in your caverns of decomposed granite
> even over my own laterite hills
> after a long journey
> licking your sons
> while you wrinkle your nose at the stench.
>
> Coming to rest
> in the open mirrors of your demanded body
> I will be black light as you lie against me
> I will be heavy as August over your hair
> our rivers flow from the same sea
> and I promise to leave you again
> full of amazement and our illuminations
> dealt through the short tongues of color
> or the taste of each other's skin as it hung
> from our childhood mouths…
> Taste my milk in the ditches of Chile and Ouagadougou
> in Tema's bright port while the priestess of Larteh
> protects us
> in the high meat stalls of Palmyra and Abomey-Calavi
> now you are my child and my mother
> we have always been sisters in pain.
>
> Come in the curve of the lion's bulging stomach
> lie for a season out of the judging rain
> we have mated we have cubbed
> we have high time for work and another meeting
> women exchanging blood

in the innermost rooms of moment
we must taste of each other's fruit
at least once
before we shall both be slain.[31]

Commonality means we get to belong to a number of overlapping groups, not just one. Audre Lorde's work speaks out of the experiences and urgent concerns of the Black community which she uses as a base from which to speak to the white community most critically of murderous, neglectful and defensive white racist behavior. From the base of Lesbian/feminism she has been able to speak critically of Black attitudes painful to her; and now from her newest base of Black and Third World women, including Lesbians, she is speaking critically of the treatment of Black women by Black men in poems such as "Need: A Choral for Black Women's Voices."[32] By standing in so many places, she is able to teach a philosophy of wholeness, of all our splintered selves that need to be brought together in love, in anger, in pain, in refusal to lie, in listening, in desire, in greatness of thought, in common understandings.

The movement of the modern Lesbian poet has been toward establishing a Woman's House of Power and Unity from which to speak as a healing and critiquing voice, directly into each community of which we are a part—and these are specific to each author and diverse from each other.

So we find Paula Gunn Allen working to create a body of literary criticism that will, first, define and clarify the emerging literature of American Indians as a whole, and more recently, concentrating on the women writers of that group. We find Adrienne Rich writing of her life in a half-Jewish family in the Lesbian anthology *Nice Jewish Girls.* Her latest poem, "Sources," ends with a declaration that she will claim her Jewish heritage and it will be from the perspective of women and the power of women. And my most recent poems, *The Queen of Wands,* are more related to my mother's life and the tradition of the heterosexual European folk-goddess Helen, than to my own personal life as a Lesbian. (Yet Helen is a large part of me, too.)

Common Likeness, Common Difference

A most interesting development of the idea of commonality has appeared in the term "common differences:" defining and retaining racial and ethnic identities without losing either our affinity as women and or as Lesbians. This means acknowledging that more than one island of centrality exists, more than one "House of Women" is operating. We can see this while still keeping the continual underlying capacity to learn from, listen to and love, protect and support each other. This involves listening with an open heart to *how* we differ, even inside a common structure. Knowing also, as Lorde has pointed out repeatedly, "other" is an aspect of ourselves projected.

"The Garden" from *Shadow Country* by Paula Gunn Allen is one of a number of poems that speaks directly into the idea of common differences:

scene i

sky still bright
we weed, companionable.
she on her side of the low wall
me on mine
"they leave their shells in the ground"
she says, "see these holes? I don't know
why, they have to be dug up and
thrown away." she holds up
a transparent thing,
tissue pattern for an insect dress.
her petunias, my corn, beans, squash and I
nod amiably.

in the hills last night
two more animals
dismembered:
rectum, lip, nostril, vagina
split.
bodies left bloodless
on the unmarked grass.
something out there.
something unknown.
I straighten, groaning
wipe sweat from my eyes.
mystic impulse all around
slicing holes in air
digging bad dreams
in daylight.
sun like a corpse over me.
sky blooming deep.
a shroud.

scene ii

unmannered.
soft as night.
air keening.
sky building.
what manners these?
fear lightly easing itself over
back wall, through trees.
starshine
beginning at the edge.
her dress moves with ease, eyes

glitter, hair
so soft in evening wind, she
recalls summer nights,
arms like branches singing, body
sinking graceful into dusk.
comfort of lounge chair
holds buttocks, back, pliant neck.
she dreams of Pentecost, tongues
of flame above her shining hair,
longs for beatitude, so suited
to this place.
a manner of speaking touches her lips
lightly, careful for her carelessness,
words slip cautiously toward formation,
birds settle in for the night, crying.

daylight evaporates as she swirls
her drink, sips cold with perfect ease
against her teeth, rests against cushions
soft as dissolving clouds
overhead.
trees by the back wall
begin to stir
ominous.
sky goes dark.
she doesn't see,
she doesn't make a sound.
Pentecost shimmers
flows from her hair
between her thighs.

scene iii

light angling
volunteer's face ashen
up two days and nights
starshine is not what
got in her eyes.
he used a knife
on her vagina she tells me,
and maybe the hatchet we found
beside the bed
the blood, my god, she tells me.
outside surgery we stand
uneasy, graceless, longing
for the carelessness of birds.

scene iv

haunted
tissue paper hulls
bad dreams in daylight
no sleep in dark
before my eye
a shadow
photograph of Brazilian Indian woman hung
by the ankles from a pole
long hair sweeping down
blowing in the laden breeze
white hunter standing next to her
spread legs. she is naked.
she is dead.[33]

"The Garden" is a particularly sharply drawn theme that is a familiar and unresolved one: the two women are placed in a garden, which is their commonality as females, with female traditions. But the reality of what is happening there is entirely different for one than it is for the other. For the shadow woman there is ever-present horror, which she can never lose sight of, for she is never safe and never has the illusion of safety. For the comfortable woman there is obliviousness of danger, of the real nature of her neighbors, of even the nature of the insects in her little garden or the attacks on animals in the hills behind her house. She has the frivolity that results from ignorance and over-shelter. She does not have any idea what the Indian woman sees; and in this poem she makes no attempt to find out. So she is shut out from knowing the other's view of life, but she is also cut off from her own life as well, for one cannot live on petunias and dreams of beatitude. Yet in spite of the denial of the oblivious woman and her inability to acknowledge the danger, let alone protect, they are nevertheless *in fact* united in horror, in blood and in rape.

Here is what I know:
Even the most golden
golden apple sometimes
rolls down the long wand limb
and lands in the lap of fire[34]

As Helen says in *The Queen of Wands.*

The fragmentation of the fabric of our myth, the myth connecting us all in a House of Women, a House of Muses, causes pain, anger and the adoption, among Lesbians, of the role of the outcast. Audre Lorde has called her book of political essays *Sister Outsider;* Olga Broumas clearly defines her place among women as "kissing against the light." And in all of our work it is clear we understand our role as that of the outsider. Sappho expressed the feeling: *Like the hyacinth which shepherds tread underfoot in the mountains, and on the ground the purple flower…*[35]

Yet "outsider" is only half the term for what we do and know about what we do. For in seeking wholeness, integrity and the utter transformation of our society, we have also been busy reconnecting to the various houses from which we come.

As "outsiders" to one culture, we increasingly become insiders to several others. In becoming outsiders to male-defined society we have certainly become insiders to female-defined society.

The Ideal Place of Wholeness Appears in All Our Work

An ideal place appears in much of the imagery of Lesbian poets: in a similar way that Rich has used Stonehenge, H.D. used the white island and the sacred orchard; Lowell used the garden and Dickinson used her own unique concept of "heaven"—not the patriarchal heaven, but the one where she would find her own name and could reunite with her lost female love. In a similar way, Lesbians think of Lesbos as an ideal place, home, where one is central to one's own life, and where the women are bonding, are sisters—and more than sisters. Where there is a House of Women, a myth, a place of centrality.

In each poet this ideal place of wholeness is expressed differently.[36] This place of home base is alternately longed for and defined by Lorde. It is a name she seeks to learn, a "tree under which she is lying," the lover's (that is, Woman's) body she would like to plant crops of the future on.[37]

In Allen's poetry this place is called "home" and home is idea—"an idea of ourselves is what we own."[38] In my work the place itself is found in each other, gained through "work"—by which I mean the yeast of creative effort, as "to work magic"— as well as decision, resolve. With Adrienne Rich, the home place is mind, and choice. From "Twenty-One Love Poems:"

> *XV*
>
> If I lay on that beach with you
> white, empty, pure green water warmed by the Gulf Stream
> and lying on that beach we could not stay
> because the wind drove fine sand against us
> as if it were against us
> if we tried to withstand it and we failed—
> if we drove to another place
> to sleep in each other's arms
> and the beds were narrow like prisoners' cots
> and we were tired and did not sleep together
> and this was what we found, so this is what we did—
> was the failure ours?
> If I cling to circumstances I could feel
> not responsible. Only she who says
> she did not choose, is the loser in the end.[39]

In "Twenty-One Love Poems," Rich locates a new place, a not-Stonehenge-simply, but the mind "casting back" to a shared solitude "chosen without loneliness." This place equals an end to the alienation that has been the price of forming any little piece of a House of Women bonded—when it has been secretive, as "two against the world." Rich walks into this new place, a place of both "heavy shadows and great light." "I choose to be a figure in that light," she says, "I choose to walk here. And to draw this circle."[40]

Building communities that can center in a House of Women has figured strongly in our work and in our lives also, since we believe our work, and act on it. Building communities means making cross connections and healing the torn places in the social fabric of myth we have all inherited, but that the outcast especially inherits. No trace of this ripped fabric of fragmented life is evident in Sappho's work, besides that the work is itself in fragments, and she herself has been shredded so often. But anti-Lesbianism and institutionalized misogyny developed centuries after she wrote as a highly esteemed citizen in what must have been a remarkably intact holistic society.

Paula Gunn Allen writes of the creatrix, the primary god (Spider Grandmother) of the Keres, an American Pueblo Indian culture:

> ...she was given the work of weaving the strands
> of her body, her pain, her vision,
> into creation, and the gift of having created,
> to disappear.
> ... After her I sit on my laddered rain-bearing rug
> and mend the tear with string.[41]

After Sappho the others of us who are doing this work sit mending tears in the fabrics of our myth also, mending the tears in the tales Sappho said Love weaves, mending the tapestries the old women storytellers once made of the substance of a wholistic life, its spider meanings.

We are mending the rips and tears, yes. And we are doing more, we are attempting, I believe, what Stein accomplished when she broke the culture trance between the objective and subjective worlds. We are, each in her own unique way, attempting to completely rearrange a particular way of thinking, to turn it inside out. We are taking on the forces within us and outside us, as Rich says:

> ...
> this we were, and this is how we tried to love,
> and these are the forces they had ranged against us,
> and these are the forces we had ranged within us,
> within us and against us, against us and within us.[42]

Rich writes into a female version of history and into a sense of the intellect that includes mystic elements to make her demanding critiques of modern civilization. She holds female qualities up as a model for behavior: let the men have the courage of women, she says, and meanwhile in her lover's small, strong hands she can trust the world.

For each of us, the points of contact differ, the Houses of Women have different origins and are woven of slightly different stuff. Broumas, for instance, waded into the common Western European myths of women. Simply by completely restructuring Leda and the Swan, eliminating the former rapist/Zeus/father she rearranged the relation of the female to what impregnates us. The Swan, she said, was another woman. In this outrageous act, she opened the world of Western mythology, so it became easy, even less radical, for me to walk into the myth of Helen in *The Queen of Wands* and interpret it according to my own intuitions, history and research.

I think that it is my ability to place the exotic, extreme and overlooked stereotypes of the female—not only of common women, but of queens and whores, wives and dykes—into a place of tradition and centrality, that gives my work its "re-membering" qualities. It restructures the usual patriarchal myth of female/male class structure. In my work the most hidden, taboo qualities of female life are pulled to the surface and seen not only as charged and magical, but as having integrated mythical reality—as reaching back and forth in time—as defining qualities central to all female-centered power.

Audre Lorde in the special mediumship of her work takes full force the racial as well as sexual stereotyping for the stuff of her exploration of the inside and the outside. The feared "other," she says in dozens of ways, is a projection of ourselves: "I think you / afraid I was mama as laser / seeking to eat out or change your substance" she wrote in "Letter for Jan."[43] She speaks of "all her faces." And in "Dream/ Songs From the Moon in Beulah Land," she specifies the special deafness of stereotyping: "If I were drum / you would beat me / listening for the echo / of your own touch."[44] And the functions of the female warrior in our society she defines succinctly and brilliantly:

I come like a woman
who I am
spreading out through nights
laughter and promise
and dark heat
warming whatever I touch
that is living
consuming
only
what is already dead.[45]

Paula Gunn Allen's work also seeks to unhook a culture trance that has racial definitions as a major basis for its terrible operations. This racial designation, "Indian," is also a metaphor for the whole half-buried tribal world, a world that held spiritual and intellectual understandings far different from those given to us since the downfall of the world of Sappho. In many of her poems, Allen places the material world and the spiritual world in a juxtaposition of idea, tugging and tugging at the Western definitions of what is alive, what is dead, what has meaning.

All of this is conscious effort to alter and break the "culture trance" of the belief system around us, so we can speak our own truths, from the basis of our own lives. We speak them out into a world at large, which then learns its own interpretations and makes its own uses of what we say.

Mythic Realism and a House of Women

Mythic realism is a phrase I have used for years to help myself understand what I am doing and what my contemporaries are doing in their art. I invented it (so far as I know); I was comparing my novel, *The Motherlords* with the artwork of Lesbian artists Wendy Cadden and Karen Sjöholm, and also the artwork of a Black woman who is not a Lesbian, Irmajean. All of them use female subjects portrayed realistically on one level, yet with deep connections to a communally held myth at the same time. Mythic realism means to me that when myth and reality are combined the result is art based on our collective consciousness and collective unconsciousness. Gay writer Robert Gluck, heavily influenced by Lesbian/feminism as well as his own Jewish and Gay cultures, speaks of taking into account both the local (the community and the individual) and the sublime (the unknown and unknowable). The village and the wilderness, as Paula Gunn Allen might say.

Mythic realism describes much of the work of all five contemporary Lesbian poets discussed here. Audre Lorde called *Zami* a "biomythography" from the same perspective.[46] *Zami* is partly a biography, based in physical fact, and partly it is mythic, drawing strong erotic/power essence from the great stream (the cultural dream stream) of Africa/Caribbean/American Black Orisha (gods). In *Zami* this myth is carried in the person of the ever intriguing lover character Kitty, who is really the old female poet-warrior-god Afrikete manifested in the flesh in the Gay culture of Harlem.

We do not take the sacred, the political, the social, the details of everyday, and carry them "away" or split them from each other. We place them all together in the real lives of real women in the present, in the raucous, dangerous, tumultuous marketplace/urban/warzone/suburb of modern life. As Sappho did. In this way we help to re-found a House of Women from which to approach all other worlds, a re-connection to the Roses of the Muses, the intact fabric of the female myth.

Notes

[1] Sappho, *Greek Lyric,* David A. Campbell, trans., Harvard University Press, Cambridge, MA, 1982, p. 147.

[2] Ibid., p. 155.

[3] H.D., "The Wise Sappho," *Notes on Thought and Vision,* City Lights Books, San Francisco, 1982, pp. 58-59.

[4] Sappho, 1982, op. cit., p. 67.

[5] H.D., 1982, op. cit., p. 60.

[6] Sappho, 1982, op. cit., p. 73.

[7] Ibid., p. 121.

[8] H. D., 1982, op. cit., pp. 65-66.

[9] Jean Gould, *Amy: The World of Amy Lowell and the Imagist Movement,* Dodd, Mead and Co., NY, 1975, p. 319.

[10] I learned the basics of my writing as a child, especially from Edgar Allan Poe, Alfred Lord Tennyson, Alfred Noyes and other balladeers, John Donne, ee cummings and Gertrude Stein.

[11] Gould, op. cit., p. 180.

[12] Amy Lowell, *The Complete Poetical Works of Amy Lowell,* Houghton Mifflin, Boston, 1925, p. 443.

[13] Gould, op. cit., pp. 180-181.

[14] H.D., *Helen in Egypt,* New Direcitons, NY, 1962, p. 85.

[15] Ibid., p. 103.

[16] *The Penguin Book of Homosexual Verse,* Stephen Coote, ed., Penguin Books, Suffolk, England, 1983, pp. 272-273.

[17] Gertrude Stein, "Lifting Belly," *The Yale Gertrude Stein,* Richard Kostelanetz, ed., Yale University Press, New Haven, 1980, pp. 45-47.

[18] Gertrude Stein, "Poetry and Grammar," *Lectures in America,* Beacon Hill, Boston, 1935, p. 236.
[19] Paula Gunn Allen tells me that she believes it was Timothy Leary who first coined the phrase "culture-trance." During the Sixties he taught that it could be broken through the carefully controlled use of mind-altering drugs, especially LSD.
[20] The poster was taken from Sappho, "Translation #2," *Sappho, A New Translation,* Mary Barnard, trans., University of California Press, Berkeley, 1958.
[21] Sappho, 1982, op. cit., p. 185.
[22] Pat Parker, "GROUP," *Movement in Black,* Crossing Press, Trumansburg, 1983, p. 136-138.
[23] Adrienne Rich, "Power and Danger: Works of a Common Woman," *The Work of a Common Woman,* The Crossing Press, Trumansburg, 1984, pp. 17-18.
[24] Adrienne Rich, *The Dream of a Common Language,* W.W. Norton, NY, 1978.
[25] Olga Broumas, "with the clear plastic speculum," *Lesbian Poetry,* Elly Bulkin and Joan Larkin, eds., The Gay Presses of N.Y., 1981, p. 211.
[26] Olga Broumas, *Beginning With O,* Yale University Press, New Haven, 1977, p. 70.
[27] Alice Bloch, "Six Years," *The Penguin Book of Homosexual Verse,* op. cit., pl 375.
[28] Arlene Stiebel, "The Common Woman's Common Language: Poems of Rich and Grahn," unpublished ms., pp. 2-3.
[29] Mary Carruthers, "The Re-Visioning of the Muse: Adrienne Rich, Audre Lorde, Olga Broumas," *The Hudson Revies,* Vol. XXXVI, Number 2, Summer 1983, pp. 293-322.
[30] Judy Grahn, "The woman whose head is on Fire," *The Work of a Common Woman,* op. cit., pp. 107-109.
[31] Audre Lorde, "Meet," *The Black Unicorn,* W.W. Norton, NY, 1978, pp. 33-34.
[32] Audre Lorde, *Chosen Poems, Old and New,* W.W. Norton, NY, 1982.
[33] Paula Gunn Allen, *Shadow Country,* University of California, Los Angeles, 1982, pp. 132-136.
[34] Judy Grahn, *The Queen of Wands,* Crossing Press, NY, 1982, pp. 22.
[35] Sappho, 1982, op. cit., p. 133.
[36] A "House of Women" who can call themselves "Africa" is described at length in Donna Allegra's poem "When People Ask," in *Lesbian Poetry,* op. cit., p. 257. "say you are Africa come calling…a house of sisters sat up telling each other…."
[37] Audre Lorde, "October," *Chosen Poems,* op. cit., pp. 108-109.
[38] Paula Gunn Allen, "Some Like Indians Endure," *Skins and Bones,* Passion Press, San Francisco, (forthcoming, 1985).
[39] Rich, 1978, op. cit., pp. 32-33.
[40] Ibid., p. 36.
[41] Paula Gunn Allen, "Grandmother," *Coyote's Daylight Trip,* La Confluencia, Albuquerque, 1978, p. 50.
[42] Rich, 1978, op. cit., p. 34.
[43] Lorde, 1078, op. cit., p. 88.
[44] Ibid., "Dream/Songs from the Moon of Beulah Land I-V," p. 75.
[45] Ibid., "The Women of Dan Dance With Swords In Their Hands To Mark The Time When They Were Warriors," p. 14.
[46] Audre Lorde, *Zami, A New Spelling of My Name,* Crossing Press, Trumansburg, 1983.

The There That Was And Was Not There

Essence, Value, Commonality and Play

Whenever a person, and especially a woman, calls herself great, or the greatest, of writers, that is of idea-formers, this is a signal to pay her some attention since either she is lying or she is telling the truth. And if she is lying we shall know it soon, as her work quickly fades and her effect never materializes. But if she is telling the truth her work will gradually expand its influence and power within our culture, and what on earth could be more exciting than to have a woman's philosophical work expand its influence and power within our culture after so many centuries of profound silence.

Gertrude Stein said that she was great, at least the writer of our century, and others have said that she is comparable to, say, Spinoza, and still others have belittled her and trivialized her work, and many people have heard of her and want to read her.

Yet she remains difficult to understand; some people try and soon give up. I have considered her my mentor for more than thirty years and I still cannot always read an entire book at a time. Every single person I know finds her difficult. At the same time I have gotten so much from her, more than from anyone, and I believe we need her philosophy more than ever.

Let's suppose you've heard so much of her, you think you ought to take her on, or perhaps you have tried in the past and now again you plow right into something long and tasty looking, something that looks like a regular novel, such as *The Making of Americans,* trying to read it in a dutiful, forthright, sincere manner.

At first, while you are perhaps puzzled at the odd frames of reference, the elliptical sentences that swirl back upon themselves, you are also delighted with the psychological insights. Then gradually the interest wanes as you feel annoyance with the enveloping loops of repetition, your readings become tedious, then you admit to a burrowing rage at the lack of resolution, the refusal of the stories to have orgasmic conclusion, the endless tickling of the brain's senses with no fusion of progression. Perhaps (as I have done a few times) you slam the book down resentfully, feeling exhausted and stupid, betrayed again by this intriguing-looking woman with the erratic though persistent reputation for greatness.

You are, I think, reacting typically to Gertrude Stein, and not differently than many a scholar and wise person. Is she merely making fun of us, as some people have believed? I don't think this, of course, but I butted my head against her work for years, and it was because my expectations were so different from her fulfillment.

Poet, novelist, playwright, essayist, philosopher and in her own definition of artists-as-modern-versions-of-saints—saint. By this she did not mean that artists are religious or belong in a Christian context. She meant that artists bear the same focus of leadership and shamanic interpretation of the cosmos to human perceptions, in our age, as saints did for their societies in the Middle Ages.

Completely self-centered in her work, she had the apparent audacity to define herself as the one great writer/thinker of our time. She placed herself well above the men she most immediately influenced during her lifetime: Ernest Hemingway, Thornton Wilder, Richard Wright, for instance. She placed herself, as a literary figure, in the company of the men who have most influenced Western literature, Marcel Proust, William Shakespeare, Walt Whitman; and finally she placed herself alone.

And there she sits as we approach her, finding again as always, no one to compare her to, no one to help us understand her in terms of...anyone else's mind. She is not "like" anyone, her writing is unique. We are left with her words, and ourselves, alone.

Since Gertrude Stein's death in 1946 increasing numbers of her books have been put into print, her plays are performed, her ideas are explored more seriously than during her lifetime, when her style was as often mocked as it was emulated and absorbed into the common language.

Suppose she was telling the truth when she said that she is the most important writer of our time, then the adage about Muhammed going to the mountain applies here. In going to her mountain, the mountain of work that she left us, we find that she is with some justification considered obscure for much of her work seems indirect, and its meaning veiled, and this even though her vocabulary is scrupulously "accessible."

For years I thought: "She is difficult," until one day it occurred to me to say it the other way: "She is easy. I am difficult. "

Suppose it is not that she is veiled and obscure but that we, her readers, are. We are veiled by our judgments. We come to writing prepared to compare it to other writing we have known. Since there is no one to compare her with, this method doesn't work for Gertrude Stein.

We have been taught by most of our writers to expect certain functions of writing: that it model emotion for us, as blues singing also does, allowing us to explore feeling; that it provide tension-relief in the form of solved mysteries, cliff-hanging adventures and will-she-won't-she romances; that it recreate foreign and exotic places, and fantasy landscapes; that we be reflected back to ourselves in sociological form or slice-of-life photographs. Stein's work does not perform any of these social functions nor did she ever intend that it would.

Stein spent much effort distinguishing for herself the difference between identity and essence. "Am I I because my little dog knows me?" she asked.

Or stated this way: Can I enter her or anyone's writing only if I already recognize myself and my own past experiences in it? Can I experience the writing as current event rather than reflection?

By suspending judgment about how a story, poem or play "should go" and by agreeing with myself to keep reading even when I can't find a way to recognize myself, I have begun to muddle into the landscape of her mind.

No other writer I know, while using a totally simple and accessible vocabulary, has coordinated so many of the terms of the writing to her own unique sensibilities. She is completely willful in this regard, requiring at times complete surrender, not of the reader's will, but of her/his identity and preconceptions, and not only of how a piece of literature goes, but even that it needs to go anywhere at all.

We are veiled from her whenever we have perceptions of philosophy as dense, of great writers as condescending, biting, derisive; consequently we also believe ourselves too "dense" to understand philosophy, and hence inferior to "greatness." Stein, however, operated from the premise of our intelligence and our worth. We often cannot believe the open-heartedness that is in her writing.

Because we are veiled we misinterpret. Large numbers of the reading public know that Stein said, "a rose is a rose is a rose is a rose," and believe she meant that roses are tedious, tiresomely all alike, when she meant the opposite, that every time you see a rose it is a different experience because it is located at a different place in the "sentence" of your life; and moreover that a rose "is," has existence beyond our clichés about it.

Many people in Oakland, California and the heavily populated surrounding area know that she said of Oakland, where she grew up, that "there is no there there," and believe she meant that Oakland is dull and shabby, lacking in culture. They believe this because San Francisco, across the Bay from Oakland, is considered classy and artful by contrast to the industrialized, heavily working class Oakland. A San Francisco joke is that Oakland exists because "they had to put the other end of the Bay Bridge down somewhere."

But Stein's comment was made after she returned home from her long self-exile in France, looking for the house that she grew up in, and finding it torn down, and the ten acres of fruit trees turned into avenues: "there is no there there," meaning she went looking for the old home and couldn't find it—a pensive and even sad statement, not a class judgement of Oakland.

Stein is a writer in ideas, not judgments; and she writes in ideas, they are thread and fabric of her works. To help us unveil ourselves to her, let me unravel my way into the fabric of her unique mind by introducing some terms for her ideas: equality, commonality, essence, value, continual present, play, and transformation.

Equality, or Commonality

Although her name is associated with French, especially cubist painters and other modern painters because she, and more especially her brothers Leo and Michael collected paintings, the painter who actually influenced her own work was Cezanne. Of an older generation and already becoming established when she became enthralled with his particular vision, this painter broke with nineteenth century classicism to produce paintings in which every square inch of picture mattered as much as any other. The whole field of the canvas is important, rather than the older vision in which central characters dominate, with a sky above and ground below.

Stein in her work with words used the entire text as a field in which every element mattered as much as any other, every part of speech, every word and, good poet that she was, every space and punctuation mark.

Equality is the term she used for this, though I prefer to suggest another, commonality, an idea I have been developing since the act of writing the Common Woman Poems in 1969. Using the idea of commonality means standing exactly where you and/or your group (of whatever current definition) are, and noticing what part of you overlaps with others who are standing exactly where they are.

Commonality differs from "universality" by having infinite numbers of changeable centers, where "universal" by definition and by usage, has only one—"uni," one. When universality is the principle, we search in another's work for that portion we can identify with—and dismiss the remainder as not relevant (because not "ours"). When commonality is the principle, we search for what overlaps with ourselves, then learn what we can from the remainder and leave it alone with respect as a whole that belongs to, that is, is centered in, someone else, not "us."

Commonality is more complex than equality because it has a subjective and a collective meaning in addition to the leveling action of equality. Equality of the whole field says that each element equally matters and is centered in itself. Commonality says that each element in the field equally matters and is centered in itself and in addition is in continual overlapping relation to every other element.

"What do we have in common" means how are we related subjectively and objectively, whereas "how are we equal" means how are we seen as similar by outside eyes. In Stein, shortly the outside eye of observation begins dancing in relation to an inside eye centering within the elements of the sentences.

Stein said of herself that she was not an efficient person but that she was good-humored and that she was democratic. "If you are like that anybody will do anything for you. The important thing is that you must have deep down as the deepest thing in you a sense of equality." Having a deep down sense of equality, she liked to talk to all kinds of people, she learned some things about her art from watching animals, and she believed children should have the right to vote.

She began developing her literary ideas of equality in her first novel, *Q.E.D.*, with three female characters, using a perspective she called "fairness" to describe an intense love triangle that included herself as one character. Soon after in *Three Lives* she extended equality of perspective to include the class and age of the characters, two of them being portraits of servants, one an old woman; while in the third and best known, Melanctha, she extended somewhat shakily across the great chasm in American life—race—by centering in the life of a working class "Negro" woman of Baltimore, MD.

Equality in writing characters in a whole field means being able to locate a centrality of worth in another person outside the sociological categories of religion, race and class, of women and men, of people and dogs, of dogs and trees, of stones and chairs and even or especially of paragraph and word, and word and letter.

In college Stein's most influential teacher, William James, had said that the moment one excludes anything from consciousness is the moment when one begins to cease being an intellectual. Stein expanded her sense of inclusiveness, and her fascination with "everyone" by including characters and subjects situated in daily life, the most mundane and ordinary everyday events becoming for her the stuff of philosophy and meaningful being:

A Box

> A large box is handily made of what is necessary to replace any substance. Suppose an example is necessary, the plainer it is made the more reason there is for some outward recognition that there is a result. *(Tender Buttons)*

She included the participation of the reader as part of "the whole field." She wanted us to work our minds, so much so that she discarded use of the comma in much of her work because, she said, a comma is like a servant, always holding your coat and opening the door for you. She thought this was condescending to and undermining of the independence of mind of the reader.

As she worked out her ideas of equality, she applied them to the nature of writing and thinking, and increasingly explored grammatical structures, allowing parts of speech usually relegated to "inferior" or dependent status to have equality in sentences, and to speak from their own centers in sentences based entirely in them and their relationships to other words.

The usually overlooked articles, for instance: "When is and thank and is and and and is when is when is and when thank when is and when and thank." ("Patriarchal Poetry")

And the usually overlooked prepositions: "Put it with it with it and it and it in it in it add it add it at it at it with it with it put it put it to this to understand." ("Patriarchal Poetry")

And the usually overlooked adverbs: "Able able nearly nearly nearly nearly able able finally nearly able nearly not now finally finally nearly able." ("Patriarchal Poetry")

It is no wonder we are taking our time understanding her, given that she is challenging our very basic patterns of relationship, at the level of linguistic relationship, for how we speak is how we think, and how we think is how we are.

In Stein's work the linear plot inherent in English language sentences falls away. The noun is no longer the all-important main character surrounded by subservient modifiers and dependent articles and clauses, the verb is no longer a mounted hero riding into the sentence doing all the action, while the happy or tragic ending of objective clause waits in the wings with appropriate punctuation to lead us through the well-known plot to the inevitable end period.

She let the characters (which in some of her writing are parts of speech or numbers, not people or other creatures) spin out from their own internal natures as she let them happen from within themselves rather than placing them in an externally directed context. She discovered them as she uncovered them layer by layer through the rhythms of their speech or parts of speech, and the patterns of their daily lives, she listened to them as her eyes listened to Cezanne's intensity of color, carrying this idea of equality further to when everything in a given field is seen as equally vital, life is perceived as a dance in which every element contributes to every other. In a painting of a woman sitting by a bush in a chair the sky is alive the bush is alive the woman is alive the tips of her hair are alive the dress is alive the shoe is alive the ground is alive the chair is alive, and when this is done in a paragraph rather than a painting the word chair is alive the word the is alive the word is is alive and the word alive is alive and they are all dancing with each other in common. They are not telling a story that we already know or can already know and certainly not in a progressive linear manner.

Essence

In addition to equality Stein used what she called essence. Searching for the "bottom nature" or essence of a character, and then later of an object or archetype, or part of speech, she found the repeated themes of characters being revealed in repeated ordinary phrases they use in speaking, and in the themes of their behavior and apparent inner motivation. After much close listening, Stein selected these repetitions as the essential rhythms of meaning that underlie all life/thought forms.

I once lived with a parakeet who "named" humans using a similar method as Gertrude Stein. At the time I lived not only with the appealing parakeet but also with a woman whose constant smoking had given her a severe chronic cough, while my nose ran continually as I was allergic to her smoke.

The parakeet was very responsive to and imitative of our language, entertaining us often with lengthy mumbled versions of human speech. He also identified us with special noises. Every time the parakeet saw the smoking woman he made this noise: cough-cough, cough-cough. Whenever he saw me he made this noise: sniff-sniff, sniff-sniff. He used these sounds to greet us in his bright-eyed and friendly fashion, exactly as we greeted him with his name, Gloriana.

I was only amused and a little embarrassed by this until I listened carefully and realized that cough-cough and sniff-sniff were in fact the sounds we made most often. He had called us by the noises we made the most consistently and repetitively in our everyday lives, revealing in both of us, very tellingly, our essence during that period of time.

Stein, believing that everything has its own "bottom nature," set out to write the biographical history of her family and all their neighbors by revealing the essences of all the characters, an effort that turned into *The Making of Americans:*

> As I was saying mostly all children have in them loving repeating being as important in them to them and to every one around them. Mostly growing young men and growing young women have to themselves very little loving repeating being, they do not have it to each other then most of them, they have it to older ones then as older ones have it to them loving repeating being, not loving repeating being but repeating as the way of being in them, repeating of the whole of them as coming every minute from them. *(The Making of Americans).*

Though the lengthy book has many psychological insights, her explorations of essence in *The Making of Americans* led her to much generalized and almost sociological cataloguing of kinds of people: "Independent dependent men and women have attacking as a natural way of fighting in them." She included the narrator in the whole field by repeating clauses characteristic of the role of storyteller: "As I was saying," and "There will be now a history of her."

Using the idea of everything belonging to a whole field and mattering equally, as well as each being having an essence of its own, she inevitably wrote patterns rather than linear sequences. This centers her squarely in a "feminine," that is to say, not in a traditional patriarchal construction, for she is a cosmic quiltmaker of essential relationships rather than a chronicler of linear heroic adventures.

Value

Plot and imagery are the elements that very often give a piece of writing cohesion, enabling the individual sentences to hold together and to hold our interest. In the absence of both plot and comparative imagery, what gives the work integrity within itself?

Stein answered this question for herself by borrowing a technique from painters known as value. The intensity of color after it is applied to a canvas is called tone; and there is great variety in the tone of pigments as they are made of such diverse substances in nature as metals and plants and petroleums. To coordinate this wild variety painters add a single color to each of the others, an undertone they all have in common, just as jellies all have added sugar in common. This added color is usually zinc white; painters use a scale known as a grey scale to decide how much white to add to each color on their palette, in order for all the colors to have value, or harmony with each other, once they are applied to the canvas.

Words get their "color intensity" by the emotion and circumstance of their social usage. Stein worked out her idea of value as she wrote *Tender Buttons* in a series of still life portraits based in everyday life with titles such as "Roast Beef" and "Milk":

> *A Method of a Cloak*
> A single climb to a line, a straight exchange to a cane, a desperate adventure and courage and a clock, all this which is a system, which has feeling, which has resignation and success, all makes an attractive black silver. *(Tender Buttons)*

To acquire *value,* Stein carefully chose a particularly physical vocabulary, not in the sense of gross physical imagery (blood dripping guts), but in the sense of not so many Latin-based words, and many more Anglo-Saxon. Because Latin is no longer a living language we memorize its syllables without knowledge of their original physical basis, and thus Latin-based words have little physical associative *value.* So: "sanguine" is the Latin for "blood"; blood is the more physically immediate Anglo-Saxon. The use of more immediately experienced (in the synaptic connections of the brain) Anglo-Saxon words gives her work a physical basis that lives in the vocabulary itself, and is not dependent on dramatic body imagery for its physical grounding.

On the other hand she decided that words with "too much association" did not work to establish the overall *value* she was after, either. Socially prohibited or violently loaded words such as "stench" and "nigger," and pathological physical images such as "yellow pus," she decided no longer to use—they did not harmonize with her overall intent.

One consequence of developing *value* and *essence* as the basis of her work, rather than social themes, dramatic imagery or linear plots, is that she developed a remarkable objective voice. To an uncanny degree at times, social judgment is absent in her author's voice, as the reader is left the power to decide how to think and feel about the writing.

Her paragraphs appeal to an esthetic of the mind that is harmonic, almost pastoral, and deeply meditative. Anxiety, fear and anger are not played upon, and this alone sets her apart from most modern authors. Her work is harmonic and integrative, not alienated; at the same time it is grounded and useful, not wistful or fantastic.

Grounding and the Continuous Present

Her use of time in grammatical structures that center in "ing" words, participles of current happening rather than past or future verbal constructs, results in what she called the use of the *continuous present.* This spinning of time within the text itself and on a word by word basis grew very naturally out of her understanding of her other principles: that everything matters equally, that everything has an essential nature; the establishment of a harmonic coordination of vocabulary, and the decision not to pursue linear plot. She used these tools plus current observation to ground her work in the physical present.

Concentration on such matters automatically places us in the present and grounds us directly wherever we are.

When someone is distracted from his immediate environment it is because he has something "more important" on his mind, some other story going on in his head that is not connected to where he is. Stein did not have any "more important story" going on; she centered her writing on everything that was happening within it at the time, so the words are in the time appropriate to their current relationship to each other, rather than being pushed around in accordance to a previously known "story."

To the extent that we do not feel familiarity in being so immediately grounded in any writing we get impatient in reading her because the details and the essences do not seem "as important" as some other idea of story, or fantasy that we have in our minds to take us away from our current state. And to the extent that we don't recognize her patterns, we try to stay connected to the "content" of information, to some objective state, and wander off from her subjectivity and patterned connectedness to find a "more important story."

Stein was not "experimental" in her work, she was very deliberate and had a solidly scientific methodology of observation and theory each time over the years as she developed new aspects of her art. She set out in college in a science field, medicine, and when she gave that up for writing she retained her scientific methods and her interest in subjects such as the human mind, geography, being, time, and the nature of language.

She criticized her younger self once when she said of a few of the still-life verbal portraits written in 1912-1914 and collected as *Tender Buttons* that they are "too much fantasy," they were not successful to her intent. She succeeded in her own view when she was grounded with an objective eye, looking at real beings in real life, as the basis for her portraits, however far-reaching the effects of her verbal patterning.

To create portraits of words based in observed reality, she and her lifelong companion, Alice B. Toklas, drove a cow around a field so she could observe it and construct a verbal portrait. Accounts vary as to which of the pair actually drove the cow.

Because she was rooted thoroughly in a scientific method of observing and listening, everyone who attempts to imitate her style sounds thin and artificial; they are fantasizing, making up what she was doing. She wasn't "making up" anything; she was using theories and observations of real life and real relationships in grammatical structures.

Stein's friend Pablo Picasso said that the artist is never experimental, experimentation is for those who don't know what they are doing. Gertrude Stein always knew what she was doing as can be seen from her essays and lectures which so precisely describe her theories and intentions.

Stein grew continuously and exponentially in her artistic life along the dimensions she laid down early on. The plots of stories, she believed, had already been told by the literature of the last century so why tell them again? Having rejected the Western literary plot mechanisms of conflict and resolution, hero-victim-rescue, and linear cause and effect progressions, she exchanged plot in the sense of linear progression of events for a more intriguing and difficult sense of it as place, context, field, entirety. Everything that is present in this place, matters. Without a linear plot, past and future merge and time spins in an endless present. What happens is happening at the time of the reading, the *continuous present,* the only time that exists in Stein's writing. As you read it is when it is happening, it is happening in its entirety, and it is happening right here at this moment inside you.

Play

A primary characteristic of Stein's work is that she does not emotionally manipulate. We are as readers very dependent on emotional manipulation giving us the clues to appropriate inner response, laid down by most authors, especially those least influenced by Stein.

Stein does not instruct how to feel about her subjects, often we cannot tell if "tragedy" or "comedy" is the appropriate emotional mask for us to wear while reading. As no guiding plot directs us through familiar action so we can feel joy when the hero succeeds and despair when he fails, no judging or tension-dripping dramatic voice of value shines through the vocabulary to tell us what the social, moral and emotional implications are.

What I have noticed in doing oral presentations of Stein's work is the individuality of audience response to her. Some people will look baffled, some serious, some whimsical and some will be in hysterics with laughter during the exact same passage; two minutes later, similar responses but not from the same people. Everyone is responding to her from inside the self, rather than the entire group laughing and saddening at points of narrative so predictable actors and speakers can mark them as places to go slow so as to allow for the response.

Rather than the emotional manipulation that is a characteristic of linear writing, Stein uses *play.*

This use of *play* operates with spontaneity and openness, and in addition with much space for movement. There is such leeway of interpretation in her work, such layering of relationship, such room to feel a variety of feelings and incongruities, to have insights and bursts of expression that seem to be a release as though energy collects, spirals and then spurts out in fresh insight or a catching of oneself in an old absurd thought. These outbursts are responses to what could be called doorway humor, that is, the humor spins on incongruities and contradictions of thought that accumulate in her repeating, finally acting to open a doorway in the mind through which a new idea can bubble or an old idea exit in a wheeze of delight. Just as the cervix also opens, on its own time schedule, for the releasing of a new thought (a baby), or the release, in bubbles and dribbles, of old thoughts in the built-up lining of the uterus.

Of the very particularly Steinian humor, "It isn't wit," Alice said, "the English have wit." Stein humor is not used to dissect, mellow, or disarm a situation. Rather it is used to further the described situation, and reveal the multiplicity of its nature.

Her humor is that of the essential geni, the "idiot" or king's fool who sees the emperor naked and finds this nakedness wonderfully interesting, or who finds something else entirely about the situation wonderfully interesting. Honesty, being the ability to admit—to let in some intelligence—honesty and humor are related. Being open to information means not placing moral straitjackets on it or processing it. Taking in new information completely honestly means believing it *and* not believing it at the same time, taking it for accurate and not accurate at the same time. Information being something new, the gathering of intelligence is related to humor. It is a state of being "in formation," in the act of being, of admitting. This is a transformational state, a state of possibly changing one's mind.

The continual play of Stein's language shakes our everyday belief that reality is hard-edged and fixed, and at the same time so fragile that we feel our version of reality must be taken seriously lest it crumble and our relationship to it and to our own personalities also crumble into madness. Allowing new dimensions of thought through, however, does not result in madness, but in an endless spiral of creative, motion-filled worlds—worlds of overlapping events.

Reality in Stein's work is never fixed, it is by definition and usage always in motion, taking its meanings from evershifting relationships which the humor aids by sparking our courage—through the shifts of ever moving text.

Transformation

I realize that one reason I have taken so many years to read her work, besides the sheer volume of it, is also the intensity of its effect on me. As a writer, I am sensitive to my own originality and embarrassed if I think I am imitating others. Especially when I was younger, in my twenties and thirties, I could not go near Stein without turning into her. Although I went to her as a starting point for two major projects, *She Who* and *Mundane's World,* I entered her work and then quickly pulled away as soon as I was able to make use of her forms and theories, lest my own work sound hopelessly imitative of her powerful style.

The time is long past for trying to consider her "experimental" or out at some fringe of literature. *Three Lives,* her first published work, was written in 1903, her last work was written in 1946, at the end of her life. Now as I write late in the century she helped form, she is central not only to American literature, but she continues deeply to influence American thought, and to further the development, begun by Walt Whitman, of a unique American literary language. And as a woman-centered language philosopher, she gives us the foundation of a new theosophy. Decade by decade her readership deepens and comprehends her more fully, as though we change along a continuum of her own thought.

She is not marginal, not experimental, not randomly selective, not just letting her mind wander, not nonsensical and not making fun of us. Most importantly she is not alienated. She is integrative and by being centrally located rather than linear her work is central to itself and to its own principles; it is referential to itself and to the ideas that she used to form it; as such it is philosophical, and it is what it is.

Her use of commonality leads to each element being seen from its own perspective. Meanings are drawn from the interaction of overlapping commonalities, and the refractive humor. Her use of essence coordinates with scientific ideas of energy, of waves. And her use of value leads to harmony and integration.

The question of how to "understand" her now clarifies itself, as the wrong question. To *under*stand, to get to the basis, the root or hidden meaning, is the wrong tool to bring to Stein as she so rarely uses symbolic imagery that has meaning beyond what happens between reader and the immediate language on the page. Perhaps *inter*stand is what we do, to engage with the work, to mix with it in an active engagement, rather than "figuring it out." Figure it in.

Now perhaps we have some answers to the puzzle of our difficulty in reading such intense simplicity. She is transformational—extremely so, entering as she does so freely the brain of language at the level of the synaptic connections establishing syntax, and hence, the essential meanings we each interpret as "my life." Stein is subversive at this level, given the extreme linearity of the plots of our society, so subversive that too much absorption of her thought-forms would render the reader dysfunctional, especially if we try instantly to implement them. Our own safety mechanisms cut us off from her before this happens, with the defense, "boredom, confusion."

Secondly, the work is subversive at the level of fundamental social relationships, postulating a field in which everything is equal. While this field description is as perfectly true a description as any other, it also flies in the face of every functional social moment we experience outside the experience of reading Stein. The moment we put "Patriarchal Poetry" or "Advertisements" down the cup does not equal the wall which does not equal the human sitting on the couch which does not equal the one shuffling down the street which does not equal the which or the not or the does or the sitting or the the or the or.

Not yet, anyhow.

Essential Clues for Really Reading Her:

1. *Play with her.*

Let her happen in you. One of the best approaches to Gertrude Stein is to play with her, and to allow her to play inside your mind without trying to guide her into any preconceived notion of sense. I think it is when she is approached with too much seriousness of intent, that her seriousness most eludes. When you get tired of playing, stop.

2. *When she gets tedious, skip around.*

Get over the embarrassment of not being able to read her easily, if, as it is with me, this is true. One reason for her tediousness is that she did not edit herself for length, and we often read as if we don't know when to stop until we feel we have eaten some candy. As philosophers often do, she left her work intact for the most part, in the bright little notebooks she used, thus leaving us with her complete, unaltered writing mind. Just as it is up to us to feel our own feelings as we read her, so we must also take some responsibility for editing her, reading what connects at the moment and leaving the rest for later, and without feeling either stupid in ourselves or resentful of the fact that she thought of every word she wrote as a gift of equal merit.

3. *Read aloud with a friend or two.*

I have found that reading her aloud deepens my interaction with the words, allows me to keep a watchful eye floating on top of her words while the rest of me waits to see what happens inside myself. And it is wonderful to see how someone else reacts differently, surfaces with an entirely different set of impressions and insights.

4. *Pick a sentence as a mantra or daily meditation.*

"How easily we ask for what we are going to have." This is a pleasing and provocative sentence to me, one of zillions of hers, and zillions are overwhelming. By concentrating for days on just one, I can make a practical use of her.

5. *Sing the lines.*

Reading with a group of friends increases enjoyment, but singing her lines is the most enjoyment of all, requiring as it does complete entry into her sense of expressive play and delight in life. You do not need melodic sense to do this, chanting and rhythmic howling of the words do just as well.

Ceremony: Let's Cook!*

During my mother's menopause—beginning when she is fifty-two and I am fifteen—my mother becomes "ill." Her illness is characterized by extreme anxiety and mental anguish, and by social withdrawal. For one frightening year, the worst of the two or three years of her crisis, she stays home in as complete a seclusion as she can manage. She sits in the dim living room in a rocking chair or paces the floor. She stops talking or at times combing her hair, sitting for hours with staring eyes that seem not to recognize me or my father. She emerges from her haze long enough to state her food desires so we can shop for her, but she not only has stopped cooking, she has stopped eating any meat, changing from our meat, potatoes, and gravy diet to one featuring a little hot tea, dry toast, and canned red kidney beans, which she eats unheated, a few raw vegetables, primarily carrots, and some fruits. She is on no medication and is not seen by a doctor. My father mentions that the nearest psychiatrist is forty miles away and that he does not want her committed, he is afraid they will harm her, and he just trusts she will sit there until she recovers—a man with great intuition, in an era that used lobotomy and shock treatment for depression.

Isolated from other women and with less than ten years of schooling in the rural Midwest, my mother believed that menopause could ruin a woman's life. Indeed, when a neighbor gradually sickened and died, my mother attributed her death to the fact that the woman "just never recovered from her change of life."

All by herself (and I was no help since her illness terrified me as well as my father, both of us believing she had lost her mind), my mother sat in her rocking chair and gathered herself unto herself, recovered her strength, returned to work for another decade. As I write, in her eighty-ninth year, she still eats toast, kidney beans, and raw carrots and still keeps house in her own apartment.

How Cooking Took a Long Time to Learn

Especially in Europe, there has been even recently an association between menstruating women and food preservation—vinegar sauces, brines, wine making, and the like. The connection is expressed in a variety of taboos that have continued through folk traditions into modern times: "The disabilities of women in a menstrual state as regards culinary operations are a matter of common knowledge in every country of Europe, not only among the peasants, but also in the higher classes. No French woman would attempt to make a mayonnaise sauce while in that state. In England it is well known that bacon cannot be cured by a menstruating woman."[1] Rural people in Italy, Spain, Germany, and Holland believe that flowers and fruit trees wither when touched by a menstruating woman; this is a Jewish belief as well as Christian. A Jewish American woman told me, "Menstruation in my culture is not kosher, and the word for the state you are in is *traif,* meaning unclean. You cannot go in the cemetery because it is hallowed ground and you would pollute it; you can't touch plants, or they will die."

*[*Editor's Note*] In the first chapter of *Blood, Bread, and Roses,* Grahn defines some terms that appear in this chapter: *Tapua* is a Polynesian word, the origin of *taboo,* meaning both "sacred" and "menstruation." *R'tu* is Sanskrit, the origin of *ritual.* A *metaform* is Grahn's own term for a physically embodied metaphor, an everyday object, artifact, creature, or human cultural habit traceable, through mythology and anthropology, to menstruation. It is both an idea translated into physical form and the physical form that embodies the idea (*Blood, Bread, and Roses* 20).

In Briffault's accounts, such beliefs could be found even in the early twentieth century: In the wine districts of Bordeaux and the Rhine, and the Chianti district as well, "women, when menstruating, [were] strictly forbidden to approach the vats and cellars, lest the wine should turn to vinegar." In France "they [were] excluded from sugar refineries" lest they turn the boiling sugar black, and in Holstein menstruating women did not make butter lest they ruin it. As late as 1878 the *British Medical Journal* reiterated that menstruating women should not rub pork with pickle-brine, "a cloud of medical witnesses" testifying to the accuracy of the belief.[2] What these avoidances mean, according to my theory of the creative principle of metaform, is that menstrual consciousness—as controlled by *tapua*—created processes of fermentation, preservation, and refining, as extensions of *r'tu*. In short, menstruation created cooking, and the substances we cherish as food were brought into human culture as metaforms.

If *r'tu* is based in blood, then ceremony, with its roots in *ceres*, cereal, and *mony*—one of those "moon" words—is based in bread. Bread is moon-cereal. Ritual takes place in seclusion and is the creative/decreative act. Ceremony takes place in public and is a display of the effects of ritual. Ceremony is the feast of what ritual provides, the display of what it has taught us. Ritual is the dark moon; ceremony is the full moon. In the ritual, the initiates are raw, naked, and bent low; at the ceremony, they are adorned, finished, and standing.[3] The menstruants emerge, are washed, combed, dressed, and set to cooking. The village arrives, the men in their spirit masks, the women with their overflowing bowls and baskets, the musicians with their flutes, rattles, and drums—and everybody celebrates. Bad spirits fade into the background. Good spirits dance.

To answer the question of why humans turned from simple gathering to farming I want to broaden the definition of cooking to include the cultivation of plants as well as the heating, mixing, and shaping of edible substances into dishes, recipes, potions, and the like. Women's root- and grub-gathering attention was drawn to certain plants for reasons of that distinctly human characteristic, *r'tu*. In considering the human mind as a menstrual mind, cooking is the preparation and provision of food as metaform. To simplify a complex subject, I have described aspects of "cooking" as follows: (1) cooking by establishing taboos regarding what can be eaten and when; (2) cooking by gathering or cultivating edible metaforms; (3) cooking to alter states of mind and body; (4) cooking by washing food clean of menstrual dangers and, conversely by adding menstrual dyes; (5) cooking to "purify" with fire and salt; and (6) cooking by combining sacred metaforms.

Cooking Through Establishing Taboos

Any definition of cooking surely begins with the tabooing of certain foods, since this is what brought eating under conscious external control. We cook by saying what is and what is not appropriate to eat. In menstrual seclusion, food taboos were prominent and many were consistent across a variety of cultures. The menstruant could not eat red meat or fresh fish. In North America, she could not eat salmon. She must not eat salt, fat, or grease. In India, she should not eat hot spicy foods, as they would increase her "dragon power," her menstrual influence.

At times, no one in a village could eat certain things. In particular, people often made taboo those animals who had helped create their consciousness: snakes, coyotes, lizards, jaguars, bears, wolves, eagles, oppossums.

My Judeo-Christian culture does not eat insects, and while I thought this was a matter of "taste," it is explicitly stated in Leviticus 11:41 that the children of Abraham will not eat creatures that crawl on the ground; they are "abominations." Food taboos sharply distinguish culture from culture, tribe from tribe, even in close proximity. In the Philippines, I am told, one's family either eats shark or absolutely does not. Food taboos divide cultures sharply when some people keep as pets (dogs, fish, birds, pigs) what others love to eat. Some Arab peoples hate dogs, considering them dirty, and won't eat pigs; Americans won't eat dogs, considering them "family," but do eat pigs; while some Southeast Asians adopt pigs into the family as venerated ancestors and eat dogs.

Salmon was so taboo to some tribal peoples on the northwest coast of the United States that a man could not bring the fish home to his family even if they were starving. Sockeye salmon was particularly forbidden. It has the reddest flesh of any and is red on the outside as well. A school of sockeye looks like blood streaming in the river. Salmon was also a sacred fish in parts of Europe, along with the speckled trout, which also has red flesh.

A myth of how one people went about reversing the taboo on salmon is contained in the story "The Origin of Salmon," related by Mamie Offield of the Karok people, who lived in the Klamath River region in northwestern California: Once two sisters declared that no one could eat salmon, but Coyote decided to change that, so he cut some red bark from an alder tree and ate it in front of them, declaring that the red bark was salmon. When they saw this, one sister said to the other, "Let's cook," and they made an opening through a wall in the stream where they had hidden the salmon, and released them.[4]

Two sisters, we know from the myth of the Wawilak Sisters, embody "synchronous menstrual flow," and therefore these figures may reflect ancient ancestors of origination. They make the red-fleshed fish taboo until the male shaman (Coyote) introduces a metaformic substitute, the red flesh of the alder tree. The story is about a change of rite, and of world-change, when a new kind of people come into being. At the end of the story, the two sisters (along with their dog) are turned into quartz, while across the river, flowing with salmon, the new kind of people are performing the Jump Dance of world renewal.

In Western mythology, the forbidden apple of conscious knowledge is a central feature of the creation story of Genesis. Fruits are particularly associated with goddess mythology; the fig and date are womb-shaped and stuffed with seeds. The pulp of the pomegranate strikingly resembles menstrual blood. The little round "Lady's apple" with its blood-red skin and moon-white flesh has a particularly evocative quality, and like the fig and date, it is connected to sexuality and pregnancy. I was taught not to eat these little "crab apples." Into recent times, barren Kara-Kirghiz women of Central Asia rolled on the ground under a solitary apple tree to gain fertility.[5]

In the Sumerian mythic drama "Inanna Meets the God of Wisdom," the vulva of the goddess is directly connected to the apple tree:

> She went to the sheepfold, to the shepherd.
> She leaned back against the apple tree.
> When she leaned against the apple tree, her vulva was wondrous
> to behold.[6]

The apple tree was associated both with the star goddess Inanna and her lover/husband Dumuzi, Adamuzi, Adam—the "red clay man," who was both shepherd and bull god in the area spilling out from the Tigris-Euphrates valleys and encompassing the region of the Garden of Eden as described in Genesis. The apple Inanna/Eve offers the man is a metaform for the knowledge of differentiation (and consequent shame) accumulated through millennia of menstrual rites. The forbidding of the fruit is an act of taboo, one that trickster Snake persuades the woman to break.

We cook by specifying not only what to eat but also when it is appropriate to eat, and when not. When menarche or menstruation is over, that is the time to eat foods tabooed during seclusion. After her emergence from seclusion, the menstruant's entire community, or at least her extended family, often participated in a feast.

In my family, we eat very little on Sunday until late afternoon, when we have the largest meal of the week, always based on a celebrated roasted meat that has to be discussed and admired in detail before, during, and after cooking. My father cooks or supervises the ceremonial meals. My mother cooks the everyday food and does the shopping and meal planning. The kitchen and most of its contents are "hers." Her recipes are simple. She specializes in five or six meals handed down to her: white boiled beans served with ketchup; bacon, and eggs; liver and onions; pork chops and brown beans with mustard and molasses; deviled eggs sprinkled with paprika; creamed tuna on toast; and the world's absolutely best, most beautiful, and most irresistible cherry pie. One way my mother's food metaforms differ from my father's is in the amount of actual blood present. While my father likes his meat rare, my mother overcooks everything and then often "dresses" it in red or orange sauces.

If it was natural for the protohuman remote ancestors to eat raw vegetables, nuts and fruits, insects, eggs, and occasional rats and birds, then where did our elaborate system of food production and presentation—my mother's fancy cherry pies—come from? From the menstrual mind.

Cooking by Gathering and Growing Metaforms

Many researchers, for example, Evelyn Reed, believe that women began agriculture by expanding plant- and insect-gathering techniques through use of the digging stick.[7] The ancient females began transferring the roots they dug to other terrain, carrying them to their favored dwelling areas, and thus beginning a process of selective planting. The plants they chose for close attention were, as we shall see, those with ritual significance.

The heavy burden of farming and intensive gardening carried by women around the world reflects its origins as women's invention, with work traditions held in place through religious ideology centered in female history. In some cultures still, only women do the planting, tilling, and harvesting. It is not that men created farming and then somehow enslaved women to do most of the work for them, but rather that many women have not found methods (ideology) for shifting some of the burden to men, and men take advantage of women's self-containment. The rationale for continuing the imbalance of work often lies in a mutual belief that men won't "do it right" and the risk of crop failure isn't worth the experiment. Religious ideas separating "women's power" from "men's power" are at the root of this.

Early farming was not yet by seed; it was not heterosexual reproduction but parthenogenesis. Daughter plants grew from mothers through the splitting off and replanting of one root from the clump, the whole new plant then growing up genetically identical to the original—creation through separation. In keeping with the menstrual mind, women gathered plants that resembled their ideas of *r'tu,* and they were attracted to red and white plants in particular. Red yams, whose flesh resembles blood, for instance, or roots such as sago or potato that are more or less white when peeled, and round, the general shape of the full moon/sun. Even bananas (plantains), which in Western markets are generally long and yellow, are most frequently found in reddish colors and in short stubby curled bunches resembling a vulva or a bloody hand (though individually, the penis).

The moon has been so important to the development of agriculture that the *Farmer's Almanac* still uses it as the primary guide for deciding when to plant. At one time all planting was done in accordance with the lunar calendar. Onions are so closely related to the moon that they are the only crop that is planted (in the old tradition) at the dark of the moon rather than one of its fuller phases. Not only do onions have the perfect round shape and luminous color of the moon, they also put up a flower that is globular and stark white—a moon above and below the earth.

Garlic subdivides its white lunar body into distinct crescents, or cloves. Both garlic and onions were considered sacred in ancient Egypt, portrayed in murals in the hands of goddesses, and used medicinally in the female wicca tradition into recent times in Europe. Midwives in villages spewed a mouthful of onion juice over the newborn to ward off disease; medieval Europeans wore and sucked garlic cloves as a defense against the bubonic plague; and in World War Two, when penicillin was in short supply, garlic was used by the ton as a "blood purifier" to protect wounded soldiers from infection.[8]

We eat what we eat based on what the cooks have found ritually appropriate to feed us. One of the primary uses of early cultigens was for red, purple, and orange dyes—menstrual colors. Potatoes, like many other crops we think of as food, were used for purple and red dyes as well as for eating, and perhaps before they were used for eating.[9] The metaformic appeal of such crops led to fabulous variety: more than eighty kinds of potatoes grow on the mountain sides of Peru; selected by precolumbian women for millennia, yams and sweet potatoes range from huge to tiny, sweet to dry, purple and red to white.

The brilliantly colored foods of South Asia and South America represent the ancient selection of plants—cinnamon, turmeric, curry, chile, saffron, paprika, nutmeg, cloves, ginger, even potatoes—that impart a desirable red, orange, or yellow dye as well as strong sensual flavors and smells. Many of the old, traditional cooking liquids of the world are red—toasted sesame oil, soy sauce, Caribbean cooking oils. The deeper red and orange curries of food in India and Southeast Asia are colored vividly as offerings to the deities—food *cosmetikos*. In Southeast Asia, as in Japan and other places, the presentation of the food is equally important to its nutritive qualities. Its visual effect is considered part of its life-giving nourishment—because the deities are pleased by its esthetic presentation, an esthetic based in *r'tu*.

Hot peppers, ginger, and other stinging spices were used as medicinal purifiers to chase evil spirits away, and women used tingling plant substances as purifying agents at menarche and childbirth. Gums and saps were associated with menstruation not only because of their stickiness but because they were seen specifically as "the blood" of the tree or plant: "Acacia gum, which is gathered from the African desert acacia, is also known as 'clots of menstrual blood.' It has important functions in healing and magic. Acacia itself stands for woman."[10] In America women, in particular, chew gum, and the gum is often mixed with cinnamon, peppermint or other "cleanser."

When I am eleven I do what all the girls do, I consume an amazing number of red objects: cinnamon-flavored chewing gum, strawberry ice cream and sodas, raspberry popsicles and uncooked jello, red wax that oozes sugary liquid down the chin, "red hots"—little spicy candies that dye tongue, hands, and clothing bright red—and pomegranates, whose seeds drip from little girls' hands from one end of the southwestern town to which we have moved to the other. Perhaps in keeping with girls all over the world, we sought to drip <u>redness</u> with zestful appetites passed along the unspoken premenarchal tradition.

The association of red-fleshed foods and menstruation is articulated again and again in ritual traditions. Anthropologist Jane Goodale describes a Tiwi rite, performed by men but supervised by women, in which the men gather a small, poisonous red yam from a marsh near a sacred tree. The men coat themselves with the red flesh, and they sing songs about how "they have now been changed into women."[11]

Carrots, my mother's favored vegetable, and one she never served without praising it—"I just love carrots, don't you?"—were cultivated by her Celtic ancestresses. The word "carrot" is from the Celtic, meaning "red of color." The wild plant is distinguished from all similar varieties by having a striking red flower. The roots of wild carrots are woody and inedible, so the question arises of why the ancient women (it is a very ancient cultigen) would have brought the plant home and paid so much attention to it, eventually developing the red and orange flesh that makes the carrot such an important vegetable and livestock food today. Part of the answer is in the seeds, which were used as an *emmenogogue,* a term meaning a substance capable of bringing on menstrual bleeding. Celtic women could coordinate their collective menstruation with the seeds of plants that resembled menstrual blood enough to be named simply "reds." Parts of the plant were also useful as both orange and blue (woadlike) dyes, so carrots were used for several different aspects of *cosmetikos.*[12]

In the Scottish Highlands, women invoked fertility in special chants as they gathered carrots on Carrot Sunday, the week before Saint Michael's day (September 29). This high-spirited, sexual festival for the saint who was most closely identified with the pagan god of light, Lugh, featured the baking of a special all-grain cake (a bannock, or *struan*, used for divination), horse stealing, bareback horseraces by both sexes, and the exchange of gifts, especially between the sexes. Women gave gifts of carrots in special linen sacks. They dug their carrots with special, three-pronged forks, and tied the bunches with red thread. The association with races, sacred light, and a cake makes this festival, discontinued in the early 1800s, a kind of yearly menarche, with carrots as the "earth's blood."[13]

The carrot plants, inedible in our terms when first cultivated, provided dye and an agent of menstrual synchrony and then were selected, watered, and encouraged to produce the big edible red roots horses love, and the varied tender sweet orange roots humans love. Carrot varieties now come in shapes from globular to penile, making them a metaform with some of the properties of Snake, and thoroughly suitable for a yearly festival of exchanges between the genders. That the red roots were equated with menstrual blood of the earth seems logical and congruent with other peoples who saw the red flesh of the yam as woman's blood.

How could I possibly not believe that when my mother went through her menopausal "mental breakdown," she returned along an ancestral line to the red kidney beans and carrots of her maternal heritage, stabilizing herself culturally as well as physically. By going deep within herself she found, even in her isolation in a male-centered world, a way back to the central feminine that worked for her.

Cooking by Altering States of Mind and Body

Cooking and herbology overlapped for much of human history; old grannies might serve spring greens or brandy as a "tonic" and put as much hot mustard on the outside of the body as in foods to be eaten. An astonishing number of plants have been used in the past to regulate menstruation, especially as emmenogogues. For example, in the ancient Greek rite of Thesmophoria, the women used the lygos vine to bring on menstruation.[14] Plants used as emmenogogues included carrot seed, as we have seen, but also sage, myrrh, rue, saffron, mugwort, pennyroyal, myrtle flower, bayberry, tansy, motherwort, snakeroot, blessed thistle, parsley, and also ergot, which is a mold on corn or rye. Some plants, such as the berries of the laurel or cottonroot, were so cathartic as to be used for abortions as well as emmenogogues. Obviously, some of the plants that would bring about a menstrual flow would also serve as contraceptives. Many herbs, such as the madonna lily, were used for "general female conditions," which included such symptoms as swollen or clogged breasts, excessive bleeding at childbirth, and the like. But the synchronous timing of menstrual bleeding seems to have been a foremost purpose in the ritual use of herbs.

If menstrual ritual first directed women to cultivate or otherwise single out certain plants, by metaphoric extension they (and male shamans) found other conditions to heal with plants. For example, carrot seed was also used to treat jaundice, a condition characterized by a carrotlike complexion. By using such metaphoric affinities, herbal medicine developed, more or less effective at extending human life, and couched in terms of the metaforms of *cosmetikos*. Thus herbs gathered during a certain period of the moon were believed to hold a certain power of the moon. Witches of medieval Europe gathered herbs naked, as though to return to a primal state of ancestral power when the herbs were originally used.

Hemp, marijuana, poppy, peyote, coca leaves, chocolate, coffee, honey, datura, and tobacco are just a few of the plant products used from extremely ancient times to induce, ceremonially, altered states of mind.

Tobacco, often said to be the most sacred plant of all among Native Americans, was used primarily as a drink, then as snuff or for chewing, and finally for smoking.[15] In addition to its narcotic effects, the dark blood color must have enhanced its metaformic qualities, and the lush red-brown juice dripping down at the corners of the mouth would have been a desirable or warning look for some peoples. By using such substances metaphorically as well as physically, humans associated them with the rites of creation. The plants, like Eve's apple of knowledge, assisted in teaching.

Artists and others whose occupations require us to remain psychically "centered," tell me that it is true for them as it is for me that menstruation is accompanied by altered states of consciousness. Women used drugs for thousands of years to heighten the psychic effects of menstruation, and mind-altering substances were everywhere associated with menstrual rites, being given to girls at menarche and even more often to boys at puberty, in order to enhance their ability to have visions.[16] Dreams were believed to be given by the moon, and evidently also by menstruation. In many menarchal seclusion taboos, the menstruant was forbidden to sleep because she must not dream during this numinous time. In other menarchal seclusions, she was expected to tell her dreams. Dream interpretation became a primary office of lunar priestesses and shamans around the world, and remains a primary feature of divination and other forms of healing—including modern psychological treatments. (The visionary priestesses of ancient Greece were also associated with Snake—hence the title Pythia, "pythoness," for the divining priestess.)

Worldwide, women are recognized as the original brewers of fermented drinks from fruits, roots, leaves, bark, and grains. The brewster, or alewife, was a central figure from Africa to China, South America to northern Europe. The alewife made beer out of beer bread; she made pulque, rice wine, honey-wine, and fermented fruits of all kinds. Pineapple and many other cultigens are believed to have been used for alcoholic purposes before they were cultivated for food, and the primary use of grapes remains winemaking. Even grain may have first been cultivated for beer rather than bread. There is evidence that the fermented uses of grain preceded any other, and that beermaking preceded winemaking.[17]

Mead, an early beer, was red, as were other beers and ales, and they were used ceremonially. "Celtic kings became gods by drinking the 'red mead' dispensed by the Fairy Queen, Mab, whose name was formerly Medhbh or 'mead.' A Celtic name of this fluid was *dergflaith,* meaning either 'red ale' or 'red sovereignty.'"[18] In a Sumerian creation story, the goddess Inanna visits the god Enki, who instructs his serving man to give her beer, not just any beer, but *emmer* beer, "for my lady." Emmer wheat, an early cultigen, is red. The earliest recipes and depictions of beermaking are Sumerian and are under the auspices of a beer goddess,

Ninkasi. Barley bread, probably baked twice to make it storable, may have been used primarily to ferment beer used in Sumerian taverns. Metaformic elements surface continually in the process of beermaking: the barley sprouting was guarded by dogs, and the recipe of bread, wine, and honey (possibly date honey) was a warm red color. When the beer-bread dough was mixed, aromatics were added, as though to add a "good smell" to the dense menstrual "flesh" of the barley meal. References to beer in other Sumerian texts relate it to medicine, ritual, and myth. Alewives served the beer in special public houses, and men dressed formally in long skirts drank the red liquid through long straws, perhaps a continuation of the rites of separating waters that began in the menstrual huts.[19]

In ancient Greece, grapes were so closely related to menstrual blood that they were not hung overhead, lest they drip on a person's head and cause harm; and in Europe their juice was called "blood of the grape." Claret was the traditional drink of kings and also a synonym for blood; it meant, literally, "enlightenment." The saying "The man in the moon drinks claret" connects with the idea that the wine represented lunar blood.[20]

"Lunar blood" was thus a fruit transformed by cosmetic *r'tu* into a metaform for sacred menstrual blood, available to anyone who qualified to participate in or officiate at, ceremonial rites. In mythology, alcohol became a magical drink, the elixir of immorality, the drink of prophecy and divination, the aphrodisiac of all wisdom—like the Soma drink that Laksmi gave Indra, which enabled him to set the stars in the heavens.[21] The Moon Hare of China grinds the "elixir of immortality" on a mortar and pestle, and the Scots still call whiskey the "water of life."

In culinary practice, wine is treated like a menstruant; it is kept cool and in the dark. Wine is wrapped in a towel when presented in formal dining and is served in special glasses, which, like the menstruant's utensils in the "shade," are used for nothing else and are often broken after use.

Cooking by Washing Grains: Getting the Red Out

As our ancestors gathered around them foods with the shapes and colors that embodied and extended their rituals, they took another step and began processing them. Surely one of the earliest processes was washing, begun in order to collect dyes for menstrual signaling or, conversely, to get the red out of a substance tainted by its association with menstrual blood.

Cooking by washing the red out, I would like to suggest, may be an explanation for the incorporation of grains and beans into the human diet. Cereals and legumes, now considered staples, are inedible unless soaked and heated—complex processes impossible without utensils. And as we know, the menstruants had to develop utensils because they couldn't touch anything. What motive would lead early humans to soak their food in water? Menstrual colors would provide motive, and menstrual utensils would provide method.

In a very limited experiment, I filled my kitchen with cups of reddish foods from my cupboards: red and pink beans, kidney beans, black beans, coffee, hot red peppers, dark wild rices, cloves, nutmeg, ground chili peppers, and red popcorn. (The popcorn is called "Indian Red"; it is only in modern farming that so much corn is yellow in color.) I covered them all with cold water. After a few hours, the liquid in every cup except the popcorn showed a red, purple, or yellowish red-brown color. After I boiled the popcorn for half an hour, its water turned a satisfying blood red. But I had been attempting to see if *cold*-water washing would render a red color from foods that were fundamental to the tribal societies that first cultivated foodstuffs. If women were irresistibly drawn to red, and were trying to obtain a dye, they might wash the cereals and legumes that were too hard to be eaten, or were poisonous in their original form.

The washing of certain grains and legumes would have led to their softening into edibility—the wild rice and the corn were both nicely chewy after an all-night cold water soak. They were edible with cold washing alone, before the application of heat. Thus women may have "cooked" wild grains long before fire was used in human culture. Of course, sunlight would add warmth to water in the outdoors, especially if they used the bowls and cups developed in seclusion rites.

Grain is mythically and ritually associated with menstruation. In one region of Africa, where millet was first cultivated, the grain was dedicated to Muso Koroni, earth goddess of the old religion of the Bambara people. The goddess, who we have met in her leopard form, causes women to menstruate by slashing them with her claws.[22] Threshing of grain in ancient Egypt was always a sacred rite. In old Europe, the threshing sickle was frequently horn or antler, with the inside curve of the crescent lined with chipped red, black, or blue stones. The farmers in this way cut the grain dead with the crescent moon.

The connection between grain and menstrual blood comes through explicitly in a custom of the Dogon people.[23] The Dogon cultivate eight different grains. The eighth grain, the *fonio,* is threshed with elaborate ceremony. Yet only select persons are willing to eat it, for it is considered identical to menstruation (the two words have the same root). The grain is treated with the same disgust as menstrual blood, so only "impure" men, a special class of persons who handle the dead, will eat it. Some women refuse even to thresh it. The holy priest, or Hogon, cannot be touched, because persons touching him might accidentally have under their nails some dust of the *fonio* grain and thus contaminate him.

This not very nutritional grain is grown in specially designated plots. Although in Dogon society almost any sound is forbidden at night, the cutting and threshing of *fonio* can be done only at night. The young people of the tribe are called out to do the threshing by the sounding of a cow horn or antelope horns. They are fined if they do not attend the *fonio* rite.

The young men and a few strong women stand in a circle to beat the grain stalks stacked on the ground. They do the flailing in a rhythm based in the number three: the flails fall in groups of three beats, with one third of the threshers coming down on each beat. The women carry the *fonio* grain away in goatskins. Sexual songs between the men and women mark the event. For the Dogon, the threshing of *fonio* is a kind of blood sacrifice, the grain falling as blood drops on the earth in payment for the blood debt acquired by the knowledge of incest (imaged in metaform as the jackal having sexual intercourse with his mother the ant mound vulva) and the whole rite enhances wellbeing of the human womb.

English folk customs recorded in the nineteenth century seem to have residues of ancient menstrual customs and their relation to breads. A number of games centered on a substance called "cocklebread," or "barley bread." In addition to its use in beermaking, perhaps at one time barley was a grain treated in a similar manner to the Dogon's *fonio* or was made into a special menarchal cake:

> Young wenches have a wanton sport, which they call moulding of Cocklebread; viz. they gett upon a Table-board, and then gather-up their knees and their coates with their hands as high as they can, and then they wabble to and fro with their Buttocks as if they were kneading of Dowgh, and say these words, viz.:—
>
> My Dame is sick and gonne to bed,
> And I'le go mowld my cockle-bread.
>
> In Oxfordshire the maids, when they have put themselves into the fit posture, say thus:—
>
> My granny is sick, and now is dead,
> And wee'l goe mould some cockle-bread.
> Up with my heels and down with my head,
> And this is the way to mould cocklebread.[24]

In West Cornwall, it was mother who called her to make "barley bread" up with her heels, and so on. Barley bread is "Cockley bread" in other districts. The terms "Dame," from "dam," and "granny is sick" refer directly to menstruation in folk language. *Dam* means "blood" in Hebrew and "mother" in other Indo-European languages.[25] "Cockles," a name for the bivalve mollusc, have vulval lips. According to *Mrs. Grieves' Herbal,* cockle is also the name for a wild plant with poisonous seeds. Perhaps in small amounts it induced menstruation and an altered state of mind, and was mixed with the barley flour.

From such examples, we can see that bread is more than "moon-cereal." Bread is "blood-cereal," and its inclusion as a cake at menarche was the weaving (or cooking) together of complex metaforms that connected the menstrual center of humanity with the plant world, seasons, light, the color red, and menstrual synchroneity.

Cooking by Purifying Meats: Getting the Blood Out

Chris Knight has suggested that using fire to dry meat and get the blood from it was part of the configuration connecting hunting with menstrual rite. Extending this idea, fire cooking thus derived from ritual "purification" of the "menstrual" meat that men brought back to the base camp. In many tribes, cooking was never done at the dark of the moon. Knight postulates a round in which half the month was "dark," with no cooking and with heavy emphasis on kinship, or blood ties; and the other half "light," centered on the full moon and on hunting, cooking, feasting, and heterosexual relations.[26]

The practice of steaming or "roasting" both menstruants and women in childbirth make it clear that fire is deeply connected to the fundamental blood metaform. Women aided the synchronization of their periods with steam baths, dancing, and massage.[27] In some South American tribes, the menstruant was wrapped in a hammock and hung over a fire to steam for long periods of time, or she might be hung near the fire hole to "fumigate." She fasted during this ordeal as well, emerging in an emaciated state, and sometimes dying of it.[28] Cooking fires were treated carefully during menstruation; in many tribes the menstruant had her own fire, which was extinguished after seclusion. In other tribes, she was not allowed to light a fire, as though its "purifying" nature would interfere with her natural flow, her power. Possibly, she was herself a threat to the vital element of fire.

Other substances, such as salt and vinegars, were also used to remove blood from food. Many delicious recipes in the Philippines and other parts of Asia use lime juice to "cook" seafood and other meats. The European folk beliefs prohibiting menstruating cooks from making mayonnaise, sugar, wine, bacon, and other processed foods testify to how women went about creating these recipes to begin with—as methods of "purifying" metaformic (and therefore, in menstrual logic, dangerous) substances brought into the ancestral kitchen. Because the power of menstruation is "raw" it could not be mixed with "cooked."

The making of pork sausage in rural Portugal is one such process. According to anthropologist Denise L. Lawrence, menstruating women still retain some of the older customs: they stay out of the sun, drink nothing cold, and do not eat ice cream.[29] They do not bathe or wash their hair during menses. A major event of the year is the preserving of a pig in the form of sausage, an event surrounded with taboo. A menstruating woman cannot enter the house during the procedure, lest a glance, however inadvertent, spoil the meat. Her menstrual gaze "is the means by which contamination is communicated from her body to the meat. But it is not her casual glance that is feared. Rather, it is the fixed gaze *(otho fixo),* or stare, that is believed to cause the pork to spoil."[30] Since this gaze can be accidental, her menses exerting inexorable control over her, and since no one can know when during her period this power is upon her, it is safer if all menstruating women are banned from the house during the time of sausage making.

The pork itself is treated as if it were a secluded menstruant, being covered and kept in a darkened room with the windows tightly sealed against "lunar contamination," as moonlight that fell upon the meat while it is marinating would spoil it: "Residents argue that a pig should not be killed, the meat seasoned, or sausages stuffed when the moon is changing phase lest the meat spoil."[31]

Salt was a purifying agent in the old wicca religion of Europe, and of course it is also a primary agent of food preservation, since it dries meat by drawing the blood out of the flesh. Salt was a sacred substance in many cultures and was sometimes used as money. In healing, salt was used to "draw" out illness— "purifying" living flesh of "evil"—and the mustard poultice enacted the same idea. My mother put a paste of salt on my mosquito bites to "draw out" the poison. Eating of salt was a common taboo in menstrual seclusion rites, for it, like fire, could interfere with the woman's natural flow.

Purifying techniques eliminated the volatility of the meat, which is in the blood's irresistible attraction to bacteria, mold, and insects. The ritualized practices of separating blood from meat, of separating red meat from menstruation and its parallel rites, and of using salt, spices, and fire to "purify" enabled high protein products to be kept for long periods of time. The elaborate preparation of ritual foods thus almost completely differentiated the human diet from that of the apes and the distant ancestors.

Cooking by Combining Metaforms: Bread Shaped Like the Moon

The circle is so common in our cultures, we cannot imagine not "seeing it." Nothing in nature emphasizes it—except the full moon and the sun at sunset, when its shape can be seen. As I argued earlier, ancestral people at first could not see the moon as an integrated object. They had to learn its shapes one at a time, through studying round, crescent, and half-moon metaforms, repeated through millions of lifetimes. Shaping the meal of grains and seeds into a full moon or sun shape would have been a logical ceremonial practice. Then everyone would eat the metaform together, studying the shape of wholeness.

A few breads are shaped like the crescent moon: the croissant, fortune cookies, and turnovers. Round breads appear everywhere: dark European loaves, fruit, meat, and nut pies, tarts, pizza, Navajo corn cakes, tortillas, Scandinavian and Native American pancakes, fry bread, johnnycakes, waffles, Middle Eastern pita bread, Scots scones, African millet bread, Norwegian and Iraqi flat breads, East Indian chapatis, Chinese moon cakes, rice cakes, bean cakes, cookies, corn bread, rolls, biscuits, hamburger buns, sweet buns, hot-cross buns, Italian sweet buns—and my mother's cherry pie, which was red as well as round.

The rhyme that accompanied my mother's presentation of the pie, sung in her quavery, off-key voice, was "Can she bake a cherry pie, Billie Boy, Billie Boy, can she bake a cherry pie, charmin' Billie?" This courtship song implies that what makes a woman marriageable, in menarchal terms, is her ability to present an appropriate metaform of her initiation into adulthood. Apple pie, cherry pie, strawberry rhubarb pie—round shapes with metaformic red interiors, served on special occasions—a gift women present to the family, a sacred pie. (That isn't how I approached my mother's pie, however; I greedily sneaked in when no one was looking and stole cherries from under the beautifully latticed crust. And I was always caught, and chastised in such a manner as to tell me she was pleased I loved her pie so much.)

Western mythology and customs give clues that the making of round bread was at first highly ceremonial, and that it became especially vested with the royal classes and court priestesses. The word "lady" is associated with aristocracy and with disciplined, studied manners; its original meaning was "loafmaker," from Anglosaxon *laef-dig*. A Sumerian creation story begins, "In the first days, in the very first days...when bread was baked in the shrines..."[32] In the theocratic city-states of antiquity, grain was stored for redistribution in the temples. Archaeology has unearthed large ovens in early temple compounds dedicated to the goddess of the moon. Perhaps round bread, at first, was primarily eaten at ceremonies honoring the tradition of the lunar "Mother."[33]

Round cakes were also made by people who did not necessarily cultivate grain. Acorn gatherers on the California coast and other places made circular cakes of acorn meal. The women mounded sea- or riverside sand into a round well with steep walls to hold the meal inside. Once the white meal was spread in this form, it exactly resembled the full moon or the setting sun. The meal was then often mixed with clay, dyeing it red. Menstrual customs among many acorn-gathering tribes forbade the menstruant to pound acorn meal.[34]

Making a cake that everyone shares is part of Kinaaldá, the Navajo menstrual ceremony. In this central ritual of Navajo life, a major part of Blessingway, the menstruant's whole family, men as well as women, participate in the making of a round corn cake, several feet in diameter, that is cooked in the ground. They use a string-and-stake compass to make the circle exact, and the men dig the hole with careful attention to symmetry. The ingredients are cornmeal, egg, oil, sweetener.[35] When finished, the cake resembles the sun, come down to earth. Like the Kinaaldá cake, the European ceremonial cake is a compilation of metaforms developed over the ages. The flour or meal is ground very finely, and only the best (freshest and most valued) ingredients are used. The European cake is often built into a mountain shape by stacking succeedingly smaller rounds upon each other; four layers are typical, though many more are not unusual. Typically the wedding cake is iced with white frosting into which are embedded metaformic emblems: pearls like the moon, roses the color of blood, and white doves.

Surely we eat our histories, our mythologies, and our moral values; we eat our security and our desires; we eat our metaformic minds and our divinities. In these traditions we maintain a slender thread of connection to our ancestral mothers, and we continue the cultural world they, and women everywhere, created.

Notes

[1] Briffault, *The Mothers,* vol. 2, p. 389.

[2] Ibid.

[3] See Knight, *Blood Relations,* and Lévi-Strauss, *The Raw and the Cooked.*

[4] Guss, ed., *The Language of the Birds,* pp. 5-9.

[5] Frazer, *New Golden Bough,* p. 115.

[6] Wolkstein and Kramer, *Inanna, Queen of Heaven and Earth,* p. 12.

[7] See Evelyn Reed, *Woman's Evolution,* p. 116. Indigenous peoples, in Australia, for example, say that digging sticks "belong" to women. "Anthropologists also point to the fact that in the primarily horticultural economies of 'developing' tribes and nations, contrary to Western assumptions, the cultivation of the soil is to this day primarily in the hands of women" (Eisler, *The Chalice and the Blade,* p. 69). United Nations reports on women farmers and the world economy, and mythology with its many associations of the female with plants and agricultural rites, all confirm the probable female origins of cultivation.

[8] Grieve, *A Modern Herbal,* s.v. "Garlic."

[9] On potatoes used as dyes, see Sauer, *Seeds, Spades, Hearths, and Herds,* p. 129. Sauser's general theory is that ceremonial purpose was at least as great a motive as desire for foodstuffs in the development of cultivation by women: In South America, "they colored food and painted themselves with the fruit of the Bixa, whence, perhaps, the origin of the name red Indians" (p. 42). "Southeast Asia included the spice lands of early commerce—and the emphasis on the coloring of food, person, and clothing, especially yellow or red (as by turmeric), with ceremonial significance attached thereto as life-giving, from birth through marriage to funerary offering" (p. 27).

[10] Francia, *Dragontime,* p. 36.

[11] Goodale, *Tiwi Wives,* p. 195.

[12] Grieve, *A Modern Herbal,* pp. 161-66.

[13] Ross, *Folklore of the Scottish Highlands,* pp. 147-50.

[14] Meador, *Uncursing the Dark,* pp. 92-103.

[15] Sauer, *Seeds, Spades, Hearths, and Herbs,* pp. 48, 128-29.

[16] Among some peoples, the idea of giving boys a menstrual, or visionary, state of mind was extended to include males at any time of life. A particular drug is planted, tended, harvested, and prepared exclusively by women among the Kogi people, said to be the last intact precolumbian agricultural tribe. But the drug, in white powder form, is eaten only by the men, who keep the powder with them at all times, in gourd containers they describe as "wombs." The powder induces a meditative state, teaching the men to concentrate on the religious principles of their people,

to remind them to keep the old taboos and to remember the old ways in the face of encroaching modern society (see Ereira, *The Elder Brothers,* pp. 88, 92).

[17] See Sauer, *Seeds, Spades, Hearths, and Herbs,* p. 142. Also Katz and Maytag, "Brewing an Ancient Beer," p. 24.

[18] Walker, *The Woman's Encyclopedia of Myths and Secrets,* p. 637.

[19] Thanks to Anchor Steam Brewing company for sending this information, and the instructive poem, which they got from archeologists when they decided to repeat the recipe of Ninkasi in a beer of their own: Ninkasi beer. See Katz and Maytag, "Brewing an Ancient Beer."

[20] "Medieval churchmen insisted that the communion wine drunk by witches was menstrual blood, and they may have been right. The famous wizard Thomas Rhymer joined a witch cult under the tutelage of the Fairy Queen, who told him she had 'a bottle of claret wine...here in my lap,' and invited him to lay his head in her lap" (Walker, *The Woman's Encyclopedia of Myths and Secrets,* p. 637). But the claret would have been drunk as a metafrom for menstrual blood, just as Christian communion wine is a metaform for the blood of Jesus.

[21] In a compound matrix of menstrual logic, "the same elixir of immortality received the name of *amrita* in Persia. Sometimes it was called the milk of a mother Goddess, sometimes fermented drink, sometimes sacred blood. Always it was associated with the moon. 'Dew and rain becoming vegetable sap, sap becoming the milk of the cow, and the milk then/becoming converted into blood:—Amrita, water, sap, milk, and blood represent but different states of the one elixir. The vessel or cup of this immortal fluid is the moon'" (Walker, *The Woman's Encyclopedia of Myths and Secrets,* p. 637).

[22] Knappert, *The Acquarian Guide to African Mythology,* pp. 168-69.

[23] This account is from Griaule, *Conversations with Ogotemmêle,* p. 150.

[24] Gomme, *The Traditional Games of England, Scotland, and Ireland,* pp. 74-76. Also Jayakar, *The Earth Mother,* p. 60, explicitly states the rural Indian belief that an "essence" of sacrificial power passes from human sacrificial blood to blood of horses, goats, oxen, and sheep and is then found by digging in the earth, in rice and barley. Also, corn-grinding is part of menarchal seclusion rites among the Hopi (Ortiz, *Handbook of North American Indians,* vol. 9, p. 599). Thus at least the following grains have been related to menstrual *r'tu* or mythology as the "earth's blood": rice, barley, millet, emmer wheat, corn, and *fonio.*

[25] Walker, *The Woman's Encyclopedia of Myths and Secrets,* p. 638.

[26] Knight, *Blood Relations,* p. 414.

[27] Ibid., p. 255. Along the southern California coast, Ipai and Tipai people "roasted" girls at menarche on beds of steaming leaves for a week. See Heizer, *Handbook of Northern American Indians,* vol. 8, p. 603.

[28] Frazer, *The Golden Bough* (1930), vol. 1, p. 57.

[29] Denise L. Lawrence, "Menstrual Politics: Women and Pigs in Rural Portugal," in Buckley and Gottlieb, *Blood Magic.*

[30] Ibid., p. 124.

[31] Ibid., p. 125.

[32] Wolkstein and Kramer, *Inanna, Queen of Heaven and Earth,* p. 4.

[33] Wooley, *Ur of the Chaldees,* p. 116.

[34] Heizer, *Handbook of North American Indians,* vol. 8. Acorn cakes were often dyed red; the Miwok mixed red clay with acorn meal (p. 416); the name of the Pomo means "at red earth hole" and includes the name for a hematite used to stain acorn meal red (p. 277).

[35] Begay, *Kinaaldá,* p. 99ff.

Ground Zero: The Rise of Lesbian Feminism

Adapted from a version published in *The Whole World's Watching*

Maybe twenty people had gathered outside the office on that chilly late afternoon in 1969, shivering in light jackets from more than the late afternoon fog that cloaks San Francisco on a nearly daily basis. We were posted there as a human shield against police bullets. Behind our backs the office looked benign, blinds pulled flat like a dry cleaners that had decided to close during business hours. Now and then the shadow of a person moved about inside. Nothing would tell you this was a Black Panther Party (BPP) office in a state of siege.

As we tried to look casual, our lips were pulled tight; joking remarks to ease the tension were one-liners and didn't get a response. I suppose everyone was as scared as I was, though at the time I thought they were brave and I was the only one who was shaking there on the sidewalk with my radical girlfriend, the artist Wendy Cadden. The call had come hours earlier that the BPP in San Francisco expected to be raided by FBI and police officers. At that time, before the People's Park demonstrations proved otherwise, it was common wisdom in the Sixties Movement that the authorities wouldn't fire on white people.

For weeks police across the country had systematically attacked BPP offices and homes, shooting up the walls, ravaging furniture, and destroying food earmarked for Panther programs to feed the hungry. The FBI had infiltrated the highly visible organization, and in Los Angeles a shoot-out had left two Panthers dead. Tipped off about the raid, the San Francisco Party had sent out a radio SOS, asking for a buffer of white radicals to stand outside their office as a living wall of defense. Evidently the tactic worked, as someone in the crowd spotted a group of heavily armed police, but no shots were fired—at least not that day. I mention this event to point out how thoroughly immersed in radical movements on various fronts the germinal founders of Lesbian Feminism were, and also to point out how influenced we were by the Black Power movement.

Of that small buffer band, three of us would go on to found lesbian-feminism within the year, joined immediately by a fourth, Pat Parker, a BPP member at the time. In November 1969, seven lesbians who felt unheard and unseen at a West Coast gay men's conference got together in the hallway and agreed to meet. Our earliest weekly gatherings varied in location from the apartment I shared with Wendy in San Francisco to a house rented by Carol Wilson and Alice Molloy in Berkeley. From here we founded a women-only movement that would live separated from men and develop woman-centered consciousness. All had been activists for years in the general countercultural anti-war movement that was by now at near civil war pitch. We had also participated in various other movements. One young woman was active in union organizing, another was a child of the Old Left and had been radicalized through growing up in South America; still another was part of the Black Power movement. Most of us were grassroots, improvising strategy as we went along rather than taking direction from a national organization. I had picketed the White House for gay rights with the Mattachine Society in May of 1965; Carol Wilson and Natalie Landau had helped found Daughters of Bilitis with Del Martin and Phyllis Lyon, and all of us had participated in the April-May 1969

People's Park uprising and the building of "instant parks" to force attention onto ecology and the need for a movement protective of the earth.

Such experiences had honed each of us, and we were wound tight. From being helpers and supporters, foot soldiers, and cadre members in earlier movements, we now became—to our astonishment—the central movers in our own. The hideous destruction of the Black Panthers, in addition to our own experiences as exiled lesbians, female, and working class persons, taught us the dangers of high-profile leadership, paramilitary public stances, and hierarchical structure. We became cautious enough to form a "leaderless" movement, and fearless enough to try to make it exactly the movement we needed it to be. To protect ourselves we passed certain kinds of information on a "need-to-know basis" and took action in small groups.

When someone came to our meetings and asked who the leaders were, we responded, "You are. What do you think needs to happen?" We used my radical writings to focus attention, and other voices joined in. By the time we started Gay Women's Liberation, as we called ourselves, in late 1969, a new gay militancy had emerged following the New York Stonewall Riot in June of that year, and six months later in January of 1970 a group of radical New York women seized control of *RAT,* a movement newspaper advocating revolution, giving a national voice to a few emerging radical lesbian voices. This happened just in time for me to distribute copies of Rita Mae Brown's and Martha Shelley's articles, as well as my own, at our West Coast meetings, where sixty to eighty women were now gathering every week. We established our own independent press immediately.

I had published my first pro-lesbian article in *Sexology Magazine* some five years earlier, but couldn't find a publisher for most of my poetry, or a satirical piece, "The Psychoanalysis of Edward the Dyke." Now, the writing seemed to catch fire. The set of seven "Common Woman Poems"—quoted orally with their message of a commonality of women who wanted to change their lives, including women with lesbian lives—that I wrote in frustration in October 1969, were suddenly plastered on refrigerators all over town and I couldn't keep up with the demand for copies. Using a mimeograph machine brought by members of Gay Women's Liberation, I turned my writings into a book designed to bring the word "lesbian" into less rarefied and more ordinary use by making the word "dyke" part of the name of a book "everybody" wanted. There was no distribution for it, and no women's bookstores yet. But I was working with a group of gay men poets, who had a friend named Henry Noyes, a gentle, silver-haired man who owned a radical San Francisco bookstore that mostly sold literature imported from China. He loved my book, so there in the display window of China Books sat my little blue square of Lesbian Feminism named *Edward the Dyke and Other Poems,* in a sea of blood-red volumes about Communism and Mao.

With the mimeograph machine set up in our kitchen, Wendy and I had the beginnings of a press, which would evolve into the Women's Press Collective, supported primarily by lesbian feminists but also including heterosexual feminists. Our plan was to put lesbians at the center of a woman-led world.

Our next move was the formation of all-lesbian or all-women, lesbian-centered, households. The households were the basis for economic resource sharing, through barter and distribution of goods, such as boots (we dressed like the soldiers we considered ourselves), that enabled full input from working-class women, which most of us were. For the first time in our lives, economically poor women like me could devote real time to writing, thinking, and acting, entirely in behalf of women. Needless to say, we were ecstatic.

Terrace Street House, the one I lived in, came about because two avidly enthusiastic Gay Women's Liberators stripped to the waist in celebration of our new-found lesbian sexual liberation and sat on the front steps of Carol's rented Berkeley brown shingle house, where we held our largest meetings. An eviction notice arrived by the end of the week—evidently the landlord didn't distinguish between celebrating sexual liberation and sexual advertising.

But the women continued to form community. Down payment, and thus lesbian ownership of the new house, Terrace Street House in Oakland, was financed by an ex-lover of one of the occupants. This set the precedent for local lesbians supporting, economically and otherwise, projects that increasingly became part of collective endeavors. These projects were the direct result of lesbian households and the solidarity made possible by our joint living arrangements. However, the projects were dedicated to our feminist—as well as our lesbian-feminist—movement. So, while the Women's Press Collective, and A Woman's Place Bookstore—founded a year later and also located in Oakland—were heavily supported in every way by a small number of lesbian-feminist households, members of the collectives that ran them included nonlesbian feminists who lived with husbands or boyfriends, or alone. We considered our institutions to be for the benefit of "all" women. Our lesbian households were the solid center that held the projects together.

Each household revolved around a project, usually more than one, such as the publication of a radical newspaper, a meeting place for socialist unions, or direct engagement with issues of mothering and co-mothering. Terrace Street House supported the Women's Press Collective and its various publications, as well as A Woman's Place Bookstore collective, and volatile community meetings of up to sixty women in the oversized living room, discussing—not always successfully—lesbian issues as well as sexism, racism, classism, and what to do about them. The walls were pinned with Wendy's collection of artwork in progress, the dining-room table permanently displayed Alice's newspaper and my book layouts for publication, and the kitchen table featured a smorgasbord of Carol's electric saws and greasy carburetors along with sprawled books, last night's spaghetti sauce plates, coffee cups, jelly, sometimes a lid of marijuana, and always the blue packets of "roll-yer-own" tobacco that Alice and I both smoked to keep expenses at a minimum.

Laura K. Brown's household not only supported the Oakland Feminist Women's Health Center, the house itself was the clinic. During the day collective members rose early and hid their bedding, dishes, pots, and clothing in the cupboards. Then they set up a clinical environment with a waiting room and self-help exam tables. At night when the last client had left, they reversed everything. They also harbored a woman who was underground. "We just pretended she didn't live with us," Laura told me. Health clinic women were very militant, performing abortions in the years before the U.S. Supreme Court's *Roe* v. *Wade* made the procedure legal.

From our formation as a movement we became the active principle on behalf of other women. Shorthand for this was the quotation, "Feminism is the theory, lesbianism is the practice." While small consciousness-raising groups flourished in living rooms among heterosexual women, lesbians wanted to act, and many already had a critical and even revolutionary analysis of "the man's world" that had disaffected most of us. Some women had been cast out of their families, had left a battering or otherwise disabling marriage, or had been classified as criminal or mentally ill because of sexual orientation. Some couples were raising children of ship-wrecked heterosexual marriages, their own and others'. Many of us had been gathering and talking in living rooms and gay bars for years and already had a desire for a much more public presence for powerful women.

As our movement developed, grassroots and "leaderless," poets stepped forward with the explosive lines and phrases addressing sexism, racism, and classism that would inspire the movement for years: "the common woman is as common/ as the best of bread/ and will rise" and "women-loving-women," I wrote, and "death/ *you* shall be poor," and "the subject of lesbianism/ is very ordinary/ it's the question of male domination/ that makes everybody/ angry," and "when She-Who turns over/ the world will turn over." Pat Parker wrote, "brother, that system/ you hit me with/ is called/ a fist," and about racism she said, "sister, your foot's smaller/ but it's still on my neck," and "I, Woman/ shall be the child/ of myself" and "I am a child of America/ a step child." We described lesbian life as overtly as we could. My metaphor of my lover's teeth being like "white geese flying above me," was from research indicating same-sex bonding among geese; Willyce Kim went more sensuously for the cunnilingual savoring of "eating artichokes"; while Lynda Koolish audaciously wrote, "I fuck women." East Coast poets also led the first articulations of lesbian presence with Rita Mae Brown's "an army of lovers cannot fail," and Fran Winant's "eat rice believe in women." To bring lesbian sexuality to the forefront, I repeatedly read a 1967 poem about a tongue at the edge of a vulva in a scene of cunnilingus, ending, "swim, she told me, and I did", and Pat brassily read, "a woman's flesh must be sucked and eaten." Of even more importance we combined sexuality with warrior-dyke stances and poems protective of "all" women, poems with social critique of the treatment of women, of classism and racism, of the military-industrial complex. Pat and I teamed up in a biracial performance, joined frequently by our friend Kim, a Korean-American, in a fortuitous public effect of dyke multiculturalism. While these tactics may seem tame now after the opening blossom of their effects, at the time we performed, lines like ours had never been uttered in such a politicized and public context.

Our readings drew large, loud, engaged audiences, all women, who went wild—sometimes screaming and standing on chairs—six hundred, twelve hundred at a time. These gatherings helped tell us all that we had a movement, and that it had collective power. We were ecstatic at finding each other, exploding in every direction. Our bookstores and presses, music festivals and self-help clinics proliferated and became the college we had always wanted, the college that would let us center on ourselves as subject, the expressed concerns of women, fully worthy of research and contemplation, of public policy and political power. We became women-centered, seeing a vision of the hugeness of this enterprise, and its capacity as an agent of change for the whole society.

We considered ourselves a guerilla army and dressed that way, finding each other sexy in fatigues, boots, and colored, tight-fitting undershirts with no bras. We loved our hair long but cut it to keep it out of our press machinery, especially after that terrifying day when Janet's hair got caught between ink rollers and slammed her head against the machine before we could jump to the off button in response to her scream.

We had to be very grounded and awake not to get hurt, and then we got hurt anyway. Wendy nearly lost a finger to septicemia (ten days in the hospital) when her hand slid into the rollers on a late-night print run of our anthology *Lesbians Speak Out*. I came perilously close to losing an eye when a fast-moving small bar on the press crushed some bone of my left eye socket in a late-night run of Alice Molloy's book *In Other Words*. I think we experienced the entire industrial revolution in a few years, as we experimented and taught each other how to buy, fix, use, and move heavy machinery.

Lesbians made feminism manifest on the face of the earth, and more. The combination, in Lesbian Feminism, produced cultural feminism, which created not a revolution, but communities supportive of women-centered endeavors. By 1970 lesbians from New England to California were trying to acquire land to establish women-only communities, and successfully establishing women and lesbian-only households. Eventually the warrior aspects of our movement clashed with government forces and our ties to underground activists drew repressive attention. Some grassroots projects began to implode or became targets of various forces, interior and exterior, after 1975, and particularly when we began pushing for economic power. A couple of institutions, including the Women's Press Collective, went down violently—from midnight vandals, and in the midst of controversy and dissension. But though this was devastating to us, and destructive especially to working-class women's voices, much of what we had managed to accomplish continued out into the world, and other presses arose after ours died.

By 1978 the political and revolutionary messages embedded in our artful words and songs, our theories and emerging philosophies, our woman-centered practices and images, including spiritual practices, were spreading all over the world, giving courage and impetus to lesbian activists in Argentina, Cuba, Canada, Denmark, the Netherlands, Australia, India, Japan, England, Spain, and Germany. The bottle of long pent-up lesbian desire—for existence, for self-knowledge, for historic presence, for visibility, for sexual acceptance, for respect, for credit, for female autonomy and solidarity—could no longer contain its passions, and exploded out in every direction. We were changing the world. What we set off has not yet reached its full flower.

We were so successful at establishing lesbian feminism and women's studies that younger women had some breathing room to more thoroughly explore sexuality, issues of power and oppression, and to parse out our "commonality" and our essentializing of "woman" into a thousand streams of specificity and diversity. I recall the time of my personal day-to-day engagement with lesbian feminism, 1969-1978, as a great outpouring of female energy—sexual, artful, revolutionary, contentious, joyful, incomplete, frightening, enraging, disturbing, connective—and dangerous.

Some of the best spokeswomen, artists, thinkers, and project organizers from those early years have died or stopped forward motion, but most have continued to evolve. Until we have acted out and said everything we learned from those blazing brilliant household collectives, this movement isn't over.

JUDY GRAHN is a lifetime artist, teacher, and activist, whose writing has been foundational to several social movements in the United States and internationally, including L/G/B/T/Q and Women's Spirituality. As a poet and social theorist, her work has been widely published, distributed, anthologized, and translated. Her work has been staged, choreographed, and set to music.

Grahn teaches writing, as well as aesthetics, cultural theory, and women's literature. She is co-director of the Women's Spirituality Master's Program at the Institute of Transpersonal Psychology in Palo Alto, California; and serves as adjunct professor of the Writing, Consciousness, and Creative Inquiry Interdisciplinary MFA Program at the California Institute of Integral Studies, in San Francisco. She co-edits and publishes *Metaformia: A Journal of Menstruation and Culture*. Her new collection of short lyrical poems is *love belongs to those who do the feeling* (Red Hen Press); she is working on a memoir and a third book-length poem, "The Queen of Cups."

Aunt Lute Books is a multicultural women's press that has been committed to publishing high quality, culturally diverse literature since 1982. In 1990, the Aunt Lute Foundation was formed as a nonprofit corporation to publish and distribute books that reflect the complex truths of women's lives and to present voices that are underrepresented in mainstream publishing. We seek work that explores the specificities of the very different histories from which we come, and the possibilities for personal and social change. Please contact us if you would like a free catalog of our books or if you wish to be on our mailing list for news of future titles. You may buy books from our website, by phoning in a credit card order, or by mailing a check with the catalog order form.

Aunt Lute Books
P.O. Box 410687
San Francisco, CA 94141
415.826.1300
www.auntlute.com
books@auntlute.com

This book would not have been possible without the kind contributions of the Aunt Lute Founding Friends:

Anonymous Donor
Anonymous Donor
Rusty Barcelo
Marian Bremer
Marta Drury
Diane Goldstein
Diana Harris
Phoebe Robins Hunter
James Lee
Diane Mosbacher, M.D., Ph.D.
Sara Paretsky
William Preston, Jr.
Elise Rymer Turner